## An Astute Reader's Comments:

*Bugging Out* is a gripping story of a young married man who volunteered to be drafted for the Army to reach a higher goal of being an educated father and professional. Tom O'Connell bares his memoir . . . warts and all.

Tom O'Connell's years as an arrested free spirit in Mrs. White's group foster home was the best preparation possible for a determined 'volunteer draftee' in the U.S. Army. Tom survived both periods of emotional torture to write another fascinating and gripping memoir.

For someone like myself who avoided being in the military, reading Tom's *Bugging Out* gave me insights, feelings and fears as if I were a fellow draftee with Tom.

—Dr. Finbarr M. Corr, Therapist, Professor, Writer
Author, *"A Kid From Legaginney"*

**TOM O'CONNELL, B.A., M.A.**
Irish Storyteller
tomoconnellbooks.com
P.O. Box 25
Dennisport, MA 02639

# From the pages of
## *Bugging Out: An Army Memoir (1954)*
## *by Tom O'Connell*

As the sergeant herded us toward the Greyhound bus, he told us to "move your asses fast," so that's what we did because fear was setting in now, and fear, I was to learn, is the Army's favorite tool to gain obedience. (Chapter 1)

Then a moment later, the first major twinge came. The first big tug. The inner pain. The awareness. The harsh reality. The loneliness. It came when I turned over on my side sleepily and reached out for her . . . and I found myself clutching at nothing but air. (Chapter 1)

**Letter (to Mary), Tuesday, March 30, 1954**

*Today we were busy as usual. We applied for our ID card, then did all kinds of basic march steps. We had a class in military courtesy and a couple of hours of PT-physical training, in which I did exercises that I never even knew about before . . . We're all tired and we all have colds. We all hate the food, as well as the Army itself.* (Chapter 3)

"The M-1 is a gas-operated, air-cooled, clip-fed, semi-automatic rifle." The pot-bellied training sergeant paced back and forth, addressing his captive audience of tired recruits. "It weighs nine-and-one-half pounds, it's forty-three inches long, and with a bayonet it's fifty-four inches. You men better damn well know this stuff I'm telling you or your asses are gonna be reamed." (Chapter 4)

My infected toes were bleeding, weeping, swollen, and stuck together. The wool socks felt like sandpaper as they fused with the raw flesh inside my combat boots . . . I could hardly pull the boots on or off anymore. (Chapter 6)

**Individual Sick Slip** 13 May 54 O'Connell, Thomas F Co.
I *No marching over one mile for three days.* (Chapter 6)

My lungs are not tropical lungs. I think I was given a Temperate Zone body, and the tropical June heat at Camp Gordon was oppressive . . . If Fort Dix had been a kind of Purgatory, then for me Camp Gordon was a descent into the hot center of hell. (Chapter 8)

Am I getting adjusted to this torture? Let's face it. There's no such thing as adjusting to the Army. Tolerating it, or suffering it out, maybe. But adjusting to it? Shit! (Chapter 8)

I don't have to fake being a nervous wreck. I am one . . . Maybe I should help things along and go on a quiet hunger strike and lose a lot more weight and let my nerves go to pot instead of trying to pretend I'm adjusting to this insanity. (Chapter 9)

I shrugged. "You're the great mind reader, Doc. Heal my mind. Tell me I'm screwy to think everything's shitty down here in Georgia. Tell me I'm really in paradise and not roasting in hell. Straighten me out, Doc. Change my world view." (Chapter 10)

Diamond Jim leaned back in his oak swivel chair, ran his fingers through his sandy crew cut hair, and darted his eyes from my face to a folder marked O'Connell on his desk. "You're another one of them fucked up college boys, aren't ya?" (Chapter 12)

"Tell me your plan, Tom" "It's top secret, Norm." "You won't confide in me?" "A good bug-out confides in nobody. Sorry." (Chapter 13)

I felt my feet touch solid ground again but the hand was still clenched hard at my collar. Pearse growled, "You're a wise bastard, O'Connell." Looking like a crazed beast, he drew his right hand back for what I knew would be a very damaging punch in the mouth. (Chapter 14)

Diamond Jim narrowed his light blue eyes and scowled. "No comment? Are you fucking with me, O'Connell? It don't pay to fuck with old Dad, you know. No comment? Well, I'll be dipped in shit." (Chapter 15)

"Well, there are two things I don't quite believe, but they're also true."

"What are the two things?"

I sent a wad of spit flying at a nearby tree and hit it. "Bull's eye!" Then I said, "The two things I don't quite believe are Diamond Jim and the U.S. Army. They are both very unreal to me." (Chapter 16)

# Bugging Out

## An Army Memoir (1954)

## Tom O'Connell

**Sanctuary Unlimited**

Published in the United States by
Sanctuary Unlimited
P.O. Box 25, Dennisport, MA 02639
Library of Congress Control Number: 2002096027

Library of Congress Cataloging in Publication Data
O'Connell, Tom   Bugging Out: An Army Memoir (1954)

1. O'Connell, Tom 1932   2. Journalists-United States-Biography.
3. Personal History. 4. Volunteering for the Draft.
5. "Peacetime Army" Life as a Married Draftee.
6. Eisenhower Era. I. Title.

This book was printed in the United States of America.

To order additional copies of this book, contact:
Xlibris Corporation
1-888-795-4274
www.Xlibris.com
Orders@Xlibris.com

28628

To lovers of personal freedom and autonomy
who have difficulty with arbitrary authority
and find it painful to adapt
to systems that attempt
to dehumanize
participants.

———

*"In the centre of the castle of Brahman, our own body, there
is a small shrine in the form of a lotus flower,
and within can be found a small space.
We should find who dwells there,
and we should want to know him."*
—Chandogya Upanishad 8:1

———

*Thanks*
To all those who have helped me
to find my way through various life passages,
challenging transitions, endurance tests,
and intriguing mazes
during this adventurous journey
that we call life.

# Synopsis

**Bugging Out: An Army Memoir (1954)**
*Locations: Fort Dix, New Jersey and Camp Gordon, Georgia*
**Tom O'Connell,** *Author-Educator-Lecturer-Journalist*
**Publisher, "Lifestyle Journal" at sanctuary777.com**

When the fighting of the so-called "Korean Conflict" was over, and the Vietnam era was only an embryo, there was a time of relative peace that was called "The Eisenhower Years." But the draft was still a fact of life for young men like me.

This didn't bother me because I saw compulsory military service as an opportunity, not a problem. I was financially strapped at the time after working my way through three years of college, and the idea came to me that it might be good to drop out after my junior year, get married to Mary, and then offer myself up to the draft process.

This plan would make me eligible for the GI Bill of Rights after completing my two years in the Army. Then I would go back to Boston College for my senior year with Uncle Sam paying my tuition plus some money for basic living expenses. Mary and I agreed on the plan, and it sounded very logical to us.

As this memoir opens, I was about to become a draftee and there was a slight complication. Not only was I married, but Mary was already expecting our first child and I was just starting to adjust to the idea of being a father so soon after being married.

Also, I was completely oblivious about how Army life might affect me. My thinking was that since countless thousands of guys had served in the military, why couldn't I? The problem was that I was not other guys; I was a character whose name should have been Thomas Freedom O'Connell instead of Thomas Frederick.

How could I remain free in the regimentation of Army life? I had no idea. After all, I lived in a world of fantasy in those days. Dreams of glory! So the reality of Army life completely escaped me until I was on my way to becoming a citizen soldier.

If some expert had done a personality profile on me to see if I was cut out for Army life I would have been disqualified after answering the first few questions. But how was I to know this about myself? After all, I had been raised on John Wayne movies and immersed in patriotic themes during all of my early years. How could I think otherwise?

I was in for a very rude awakening. Almost instantly I realized that just about every aspect of the military training was an assault on my independent personality, not to mention my sensitive body. And this posed a serious conflict between the need to do my duty and the necessity of trying to avoid losing my sense of self.

"Bugging out" soon became an option for me, yet I had never even heard the phrase as a civilian. I knew what "goofing off" was but not "bugging out."

This is the story of what I learned about "bugging out" soon after being inducted into the Army, and how I became a confirmed "bug-out" without ever planning to do so.

# Foreword

This page is about the words I used in this memoir and how they came to me. Initially, I took a close look at the word "memoir" which derives from the French word for "memory." Our English word "memory" is defined as the "process of recalling to mind facts previously learned or past experiences." Using my memory to produce this book, I also triggered "impressions" that can be described as "notions, feelings, or recollections." Therefore, what we have here is a blend of distinct memories and strong impressions.

Half a century after my U.S. Army experience, I have written a memoir based on my ability to recall many people, past events, and impressions. However, I was not able to do this through memory alone. Actually, while in the Army I knew even then that I would write about my military experiences some day, so I often scribbled observations and saved them. Also, I wrote a daily letter to my spouse during the months we were apart, and they are still in my files. They have been very useful in this work.

Apparently, I was operating like an archivist gathering data to be filed away for future reference. In addition, the Army, which was fueled by paper, provided an ongoing record in the form of military orders and other information.

As for the dialogue I have used here, obviously I could not possibly have remembered each word spoken. But I could vividly recall the reality of the experiences, the people, and my own emotional responses. Because of the powerful impact my Army experience had on me, I have been able to clearly remember situations that carried strong meaning. Those memorable impressions helped me to put together this memoir.

To sum up, what I am presenting here is a very personal collection of memories, observations, and impressions. Have I exaggerated? I don't believe so. If anything, while aiming for objectivity, I may have understated some of what happened during my first year of Army service.

At any rate, my experiences from March until November 1954 were intense in their own right and needed no exaggeration. Therefore, be assured that this memoir is a reasonably accurate account of one "voluntary" draftee's experiences in the "peacetime Army" of 1954 during the period when the active fighting during the Korean conflict was over and the Vietnam era was in the earliest embryonic stage of its birth process.

Sincerely,
Tom O'Connell
Yarmouth, Massachusetts, USA
December 7, 2005

# PART I

## (March to June 1954)

# 1

At one extreme there are patriots, and at another there are "draft dodgers," but I was in a different category that you don't hear much about. I was a "bug-out." And if you looked into a dictionary back in the fifties you wouldn't be apt to find the word. More recently, dictionaries have defined what bugging out is. To "bug out" means "to leave or quit, usually in a hurry" or "to avoid a responsibility or duty." When I entered the Army those definitions certainly didn't apply to me. After all, I was a very responsible person, planned to do my patriotic duty, and had never even heard the word "bug-out."

Have you heard of Murphy's Laws? Here's one for you: "If everything seems to be going well you have obviously overlooked something." Although nobody seems to know who Murphy was, or what happened to him, his laws seem to hang around the same way those irritating truths in old proverbs linger.

The older I get the more sense Murphy's laws make to me, like the one about the bread tending to fall so the buttered side slaps against the brand new rug. But back in 1954, if you had quoted Murphy to me to get me to be less cocksure about my plans for the future, I would have told you exactly where you could shove Murphy's laws, and Murphy, too, if you could lay your hands on him. I was an optimist!

You see, back in 1954 when I made a plan, by God, that plan was bound to work out. Nobody could tell me otherwise because

I had great confidence in my rational mind then. And I thought my rational mind was telling me the exact route to follow.

Here's what I believed was the right logical course of action. I would drop out of Boston College after my junior year. Then I would work for a while full-time. Then I'd notify the Dedham Draft Board voluntarily that I wasn't going back to college that fall. Mary and I would marry. Eventually, the draft board would take away my college deferment, make me 1-A, and I'd become draft bait.

Then the letter from Uncle Sam would come. I'd put in my two years in the Army, get discharged, and go back to BC on the GI Bill of Rights for my senior year. After graduation, as my rational plan moved toward completion, I would go off into the sunset to a successful career with Mary as my spouse. And we would live happily ever after.

Well, what could be more logical than that? This was what my allegedly rational mind told me, and in those days I believed that so-called rational mind of mine. Nowadays, of course, I'm not sure on some days that I have any mind at all, not to mention a rational one. And there are times when I think that my irrational mind knows more about what's good for me than the "rational" mind does. Also, in those days I was not aware of the expression, "Life is what happens while you're making other plans."

In any case, back in 1954 when I was in the top ten percent of my class at BC, I was sure I had one of the most finely tuned rational minds in the history of the human race. So I followed its dictates the way a political flunky follows the party line, with no questions asked. Some people look back on the fifties with nostalgia. I look back on them with a pit in my stomach. Actually, with the exception of my daughter Peggy's birthday, I usually try not to remember the year 1954 at all.

However, I was scanning my backlog of unread magazines a while ago, and an illustration caught my eye. It was a collage of old newspaper clippings on assorted subjects, and one of them brought that ancient pit back to my stomach. It was a historical retrospective on the Selective Service System and the draft registration requirement that had begun in 1948 for my

"Depression baby" generation. The article reminded me that over the years the word "draftee" had become more and more archaic as a volunteer Army of professionals had become the order of the day. Peace on earth, good will toward men, and God bless our professional Army.

The last thing in the world I felt like thinking about this year was my Army time in the fifties. But as I read the article, it all came back to me against my will. "The peacetime Army" is what they called it when they took me in March of '54. The Eisenhower years were considered "peacetime years" because they were seen as times of stability, trivial cares, and minor worries. They were the good old days, some people say now. Oh boy, what a time we had, they say. After all, the fighting of the Korean "conflict" was over and the carnage in Vietnam hadn't begun. At least not the United States portion of it.

The first step toward entering the U.S. Army had been my Army physical examination.

**Selective Service System**
**Local Board No. 26**
**Norfolk County**
**Memorial Hall**
**Dedham, Massachusetts**

**Order to Report for Armed Forces Physical Examination**
**Nov. 24, 1953**
**To Thomas F. O'Connell, Jr. #192632368**

*You are hereby directed to report for armed forces physical examination at Local Board 26, Town Hall, Dedham, Mass. at 7:00 a.m. on the 9th of December 1953. Katherine C. Jones,* **Clerk of Local Board**

On that expedition, starting at Dedham's Local Draft Board No. 26, I had been appointed group leader of the draftees from my town and neighboring communities. Since I was age 21 and married, they must have assumed I was mature, and of course I also operated under that delusion myself.

**Dec. 9, 1953**
**Office of the Director of Selective Service, Washington**
**To Whom It May Concern:**

*Special confidence being placed in the integrity and ability of Thomas F. O'Connell, Jr., he is hereby appointed leader of a contingent of selected men from Local Board No. 26, State of Mass., Address: Memorial Hall, Dedham, Mass.*

*He is, therefore, charged with the enforcement of the Selective Service Regulations governing selected men en route to Joint Examining and Induction Station during the journey from Dedham, Mass. to Boston and return and all men included within the contingent are directed to obey his lawful orders during the journey.*

**By Order of the Director of Selective Service,**
**Katherine C. Jones, Local Board, Clerk,**
**Date Dec. 9, 1953**

Due to my great leadership skills we arrived safely at the Boston Army Base and I carried off my assigned responsibility very well. Naturally, this prompted a vision of myself as a born leader of military men. Yes, during my two years as a draftee I was bound to rise rapidly through the ranks. I could clearly visualize that.

The physical exam at the Army base near Boston's waterfront was held in a hall that seemed as large as an airplane hangar, and the exam itself was a source of amazement, embarrassment, and amusement. As I stood with the other draftees and volunteers during the mass physical exam, I knew that I was becoming part of a strange drama.

Here I was, a very private person, standing nude with a batch of other potential soldiers, being reduced to one of many nudists soon to become one of many privates. But at that moment, before I actually entered the Army, I only knew I didn't enjoy being bare-assed in that huge room full of bare asses. Also, I didn't have high respect for those alleged doctors who looked like refugees from some medical school that had trouble getting its accreditation.

"Spread your cheeks," ordered the doctor with the thick glasses and the down-turned mouth. He wasn't talking about the cheeks on either side of my face.

I reached back and took one buttock in each hand and spread them as the doctor inspected my anus, and I wished I had a nice burst of gas in my bowels at that moment to let go in his face, but no such luck.

"You're okay," he said to me and I thought, Of course I'm okay, doc. Other than my anxiety complex, my high blood pressure, my allergies, my skin sensitivities, and my sleepwalking, I'm in terrific shape to become a citizen soldier.

When the physical was over and the pseudo-doctors had finished prying into my body and had proved to themselves that I was in fit condition to become an integral part of our war machine during this time of relative peace, we were told to get our clothes back on. We took our sweet time doing it because at that moment we were still civilians. And what was the big rush to do anything? We weren't under orders yet because the oath wouldn't be taken until "induction" day.

So that was it at the Army Base. Line up. Drop your pants. Bend over. Spread your cheeks. Questions. Forms to fill out. Questions, questions, questions. Forms, forms, forms. An endless supply of them.

**Certificate of Acceptability**
**O'Connell, Thomas Frederick, Jr., 56 Belknap St., Dedham, Mass. Selective Service Number 192632368 LB# 26, Memorial Hall, Dedham, Mass.**

*I certify that the qualifications of the above named registrant have been considered in accordance with the current regulations governing acceptance of Selective Service Registrants and that he was this date:*

    1.  *"Found fully acceptable for induction into the armed services."*

**9 Dec. 53, Army Base, Boston 10, Mass.**
**Name and grade of Joint Examining and Induction Station commander:**

*Thomas F. Burke*, **1st Lt Inf**

So it was back home again, and it was a while before I got the piece of paper that would change my life: On the day after my 22nd birthday, during my third month of marriage, the memo from "The President of the United States" had been sent to me.

**Selective Service System**
**Order to Report for Induction**
**Feb. 12. 1954**

**The President of the United States**
**To Thomas F. O'Connell, Jr., Selective Service Number 192632368**
**56 Belknap St., Dedham, Mass.**

**GREETING:**

*Having submitted yourself to a Local Board composed of your neighbors for the purpose of determining your eligibility for service in the armed forces of the United States, you are hereby ordered to report to the Local Board named above at Memorial Hall, 2nd floor, Dedham, Mass. at 7:00 a.m., on the 16th of March, 1954, for forwarding to an induction station.*

**John T. Kiely, Member of Local Board.**

On the day I was inducted, I didn't realize that I was one of the last married draftees, and may well have been the very last married draftee with a pregnant wife. Nature had acted very promptly after Mary and I had become husband and wife. And the draft board had also acted promptly. But, as I've already said, it was all part of the very logical master plan I had devised, and which Mary had agreed to.

Look, the idea of avoiding the draft was completely foreign to me. Also, I wasn't your traditional draftee. I was one of an unusual breed, a "volunteer for the draft." Before I actually entered the Army, you might have even called me an enthusiastic patriot.

In those days the draft was as American as your grandmother's apple pie, or maybe the too thick oatmeal she mixed for you in the morning for breakfast. If you were a male, and you hadn't put in your time in the Army or another military outfit, you might as well have considered yourself a eunuch. A neuter gender. A misfit in masculine society.

Thinking back on "induction day," the phrase sounds innocent enough. According to Webster's, "induction" means "the formality by which a civilian is inducted into military service under the provisions of a draft law."

However innocuous the word "induction" might be, I was unable to envision at that time the period of chaos, uncertainty, and mental torture I was choosing to pursue as an enlisted man in the U.S. Army. The only thing I was certain about was that I had pals in the military, and they seemed to be doing okay with it, and induction day was coming. So what was the big deal? That was that.

Where would I go for basic training? I didn't know. Where would I go after basic? There was no way of knowing. I was moving away from a life of making free choices and pretty much knowing what each day would hold. And I was entering a life of never knowing what was coming next. But hadn't legions of other guys gone through the process without any major problems? If they could, why couldn't I?

Hey, we had our plan worked out, and it was a very logical plan. Also, the first stages of the plan were working exactly as I had plotted them out several months before. So what if the Army was a big mystery? I'd work things out, just as Mary would work out her nine months of pregnancy.

Look. You conceive. You wait out the nine months. You deliver. What could be more simple? As for my two years in the Army, wasn't that similar? You volunteer instead of waiting and wondering. You get inducted. You serve the two years and get discharged. You get the GI Bill and go back to college and finish. What could be more simple?

On the morning of induction day, I was bleary-eyed from getting up while it was still dark out, and I sat there in the back seat of the Killorens' old Studebaker, holding Mary's hand, trying to minimize the impact of our impending separation.

In those days, what an amazing faculty I had for blocking unwelcome reality from my mind. As we rode toward the draft board's office we were both very quiet. Since I couldn't picture what the Army would be like, I kept telling myself I'd have to go sooner or later anyhow, and why not get it over with once and for all.

In addition, I truly had some very patriotic sentiments. I loved our country and I was proud to be entering the Army that helped preserve our country's freedom. Hey, I had always treasured freedom! Especially after spending nine years in a group foster home which had seemed to me to be like a prison sentence. In 1946 I had been released from that home at age 14 so I could live with my grandmother, and since that day I had been a deeply committed believer in both personal and national freedom. "Don't tread on me!"

When her father parked the old Studebaker in front of Dedham's Memorial Hall, I saw the mist in Mary's eyes and then my own eyes started to fill up, but I caught myself, pretty much the same way actor Van Johnson had done in a World War Two movie. Like him, I went into my brave mode and said, "Keep your chin up, honey. Everything's gonna be okay." Then I had kissed her with a latent military hero's kiss, told her heroically that I'd write her a letter every day, and I promised heroically to get home as soon as I could, depending on where they shipped yours truly, the American hero, for basic training.

I took my small brown canvas bag full of toilet articles and underwear and things, and I thanked Bill Killoren for the ride, said goodbye to him and Mary's mother, and after another soft kiss from Mary, I got out of the car and started walking toward the draft board with a sort of numb feeling in my legs and a light feeling in my head. I pictured myself as a participant in a romantic military drama like Tolstoy's *War and Peace*.

A good slogan for me in those days would have been, "Reality is a nice place to visit, but you wouldn't want to live there." So, despite my belief that I had a logical mind, I really didn't spend much time in reality. Instead, I chose to focus on my own illusions.

My Army illusion made sense to me. I was about to serve my country, doing my duty as a citizen of a great republic. I would soon put on the uniform of a soldier in the greatest Army in the world. And I would carry out this illusion with minimum difficulty.

However, my fantasy image of myself was suddenly shattered. As I turned to give another wave to Mary and the Killorens, I walked right into a parking meter. God, what a burst of pain in my chest! I grunted "Ugh." Then I muttered "Shit" and tried to catch my breath, heroically acting as if nothing had happened at all. Isn't that what John Wayne would have done?

As I looked at the Killorens' car, my eyes caught Mary's misty eyes, I shrugged my shoulders in resignation, waved again, and this time as I headed toward the door to the draft board I avoided painful obstacles such as parking meters.

While I climbed the steps of the old Town Hall, I tried to keep up my spirits. But as I attempted to rub away the pain in my chest, I began to have un-heroic thoughts about leaving Mary after four months of wedded bliss. Did we do the right thing, agreeing that I would drop out of college the way I did, setting me up as draft bait? Well, it was our plan wasn't it? Of course it was the right thing.

"Tuck in your shirts, you men!" shouted a voice to my rear. I turned, and seeing the two bars on his shoulders, I realized he was a captain. But my reaction to his order was negative. Mind your own business, you jerk.

There I was, during the earliest moments of my military service, already resisting authority even though I had volunteered for this adventure and knew I'd have to submit to superiors.

Look at the power crazy expression on this guy's face, I thought. They haven't even sworn us in yet, and already he's giving us orders. I don't think this guy's looking at himself objectively in the overall perspective of things. In the big picture, this captain's nothing. Well, almost nothing. Actually, I'm the one who's about to be nothing. A lowly private, that's what I am becoming, and a private is very inferior compared to a captain.

"All right, you men." It was the captain's voice again. "You're about to be sworn into the Army of the United States." My immediate reaction to his comment was one of slight anxiety because I suddenly realized that a point of no return was about to be reached. In the course of a few spoken words, I was going to leap from citizen O'Connell to Private O'Connell. And there was no going back. Not for two years.

We raised our right hands for him. We repeated the oath to serve our country. We gazed at the flag. A slight mist covered my eyes. And for a brief moment I felt an emotion I still believe was a powerful burst of patriotism. Although I knew there would be many things about the Army that irritated me, I minimized them because I was confident that I'd do my best to carry out my duties. I was determined to serve my country well. "God Bless America." The patriotism was sincere because I had been raised on patriotism as a kid during World War II. "God and country." That was that. What other option was there?

"Okay, you soldiers!" shouted a fat sergeant. "Line up your asses over here. We got some forms for you to fill out." The captain had been polite to our group of citizens, but now we were soldiers. Line up our asses, huh? So that was the way it would be?

We filled out the questionnaires, and we were told that we'd be sent to Fort Dix, New Jersey, for processing. Some would stay there for eight weeks of basic training and others would be shipped elsewhere.

As the sergeant herded us toward the Greyhound bus, he told us to "move your asses fast," so that's what we did because fear was setting in now, and fear, I was to learn, is the Army's favorite tool to gain obedience.

When we got to the bus we found the door closed, so we stood outside shivering in the mid-March rawness near Boston Harbor. I turned up my jacket collar, plunged my hands into my pockets, and hunched up my shoulders to brace myself against the frigid wind. Then an elbow nudged my ribs. "Hey, pal, how's it going?" There was a short dark body next to me, with two charcoal eyes peering up, a broad smile flashing, and a hand extended for a shake.

Taking the extended hand with its strong grip, I shook it. "Hi. How's it going?" I returned his greeting without answering his own question about how it was going.

"No sweat! I'm Charlie Olivera."

"I don't have a name now. It's gone. I've become a number. U.S. five one three . . ."

"Aw, come on, knock off the shit. What's your handle?"

"Tom O'Connell."

"I wonder if we'll end up in the same outfit at Dix. Ya know anything about the Army?" "Absolutely nothing." "Well, guess what they call this rushing shit and then standing around out in the cold freezing our nuts off? 'Hurry-and-wait.' It's the Army motto. Where you from?" "Dedham." "I'm from the North Shore. Just turned twenty-two." "Me too." "We're older than these kids. Do ya think maybe we're past our prime?"

"I don't think there's such a thing as a prime, Charlie. Like I don't think there's such a thing as normal or average or sane."

He laughed. "You're a hot shit, Tom. Hey, look, they're opening the door. Somebody must have said the magic word."

"The magic word?"

"Yup, the word is chicken shit. We'll be up to our ears in it in this man's Army."

The sergeant ordered us into the bus, and Charlie waved me toward the back, where he let me take the seat near the window. I tried to arrange my long bony legs so they'd be comfortable, but there was no way to do it. Little Charlie, who was about five foot two compared to my six feet, had no trouble with his legs.

I reflected on why they designed busses for short people. I decided it was to save space, jam in more seats, and make more money. But even if they had designed the seats for people like me, I'm sure I wouldn't have felt comfortable anyhow. Actually, I came into the world as a restless, extremely sensitive type. Yet I keep trying to be comfortable, even though I know it's almost impossible for me. Call me restless and obsessive. That's how I can still get, and that's how I was much of the time back there in 1954.

"We're in the Army now," said Charlie as he put his ten fingers together and gave his knuckles a loud crack. "I had it made at Cushing Academy for a year. Class president there. In high school I was All-Scholastic in football. Senior year, Schoolboy All-American team. Directed stage productions. Acted too. Then I had my own jazz combo and played at spots around Boston like the Hi-Hat. But finally the draft caught up with me, so here I am. How'd you hold out so long from the draft? Were you in college?"

"Yup. BC." I told him how I'd dropped out after my junior year and got a job as a construction timekeeper at the new College Town Sportswear building going up on Morrissey Boulevard in Dorchester. "Then Mary and I got married, and I let Uncle Sam know I was available."

"You've gotta be shitting me, Tom. A married draftee? And a volunteer?"

I showed him my wedding ring. "I'm married. I've been drafted. I'm a volunteer. Therefore, I'm a married volunteer draftee. Good logic, huh? I got a hundred percent in my logic final at BC, Charlie. Give me a little time and I'll work up a perfect syllogism for you. I don't want to let my Jesuit training get rusty."

"Hey, what was your major? Religion?"

"Sort of. But just call me a liberal artist, Charlie." I grinned over at him, knowing I was feeding him the retort.

"Yuh, I know. A liberal bullshit artist." We both laughed.

I told him of my year of "working like a dog" at the Boston Envelope Company after high school to save up my first year's tuition. Then he started telling me about his family. Soon it was my turn to give my usual short version of my early life, how I had "lost" my mother when I was little, and had lived in a group foster home for nine years before settling in with my grandmother and father at the age of 14.

Then I gave him the quick version of how my father, while I was still in high school, had gone to Maine with his girl friend Hazel and the money Granny had earmarked for my first year of college, and proceeded to set up a motor court near the ocean in Wells while I was left to handle my own life at Granny's house. "So I went to work in a factory for a year after high school to save up my BC tuition. I managed to complete three years before deciding to get married and then complete my Army time."

"You didn't have much of a family life, huh?"

"Hey, I kicked around in temporary foster homes even when I was very little, Charlie, but once I got myself sprung loose from the group home and went to live with Granny, things weren't so bad for me. I was pretty much on my own."

"But you had a tough deal growing up, pal."

"Look, Charlie, why complain? Anyhow, I don't have my crying towel with me today. The way I see it, the past is the past. It's over and done with. I believe in living in the present with an eye on the future. But even though I asked for this Army routine, it looks like it's gonna be rough for a free spirit like me who likes to make his own decisions."

"You don't know the half of it, pal." He shook his head. "I know 'cause I put in some time in the National Guard. The Army's shit for the birds."

"I think of it as a necessary evil, and plenty of other guys have put in their time, so I don't figure it'll be too much sweat."

He laughed. "Oh boy, you got a lot to learn, pal. Wait till you're down there at Fort Dix thinking about your bride, and they've gotcha doing KP and digging ditches. You'll probably snap your cap."

I shrugged. "I've had hard times before and I've always survived."

"Good luck to ya, Tom. I hope you survive this time, too. No shit, I really do. But not being married myself I dunno how this life's gonna grab you."

"I'm not only married, Charlie. Mary's expecting."

"You're gonna have a kid? And you've been drafted? I don't get it."

I told him about our plan based on the reality that I'd have to put in my Army time sooner or later anyhow. I told him I'd be using the GI Bill to do my Senior Year at BC when I got discharged in two years. Then I said, "Look, as shitty as the Army may be, it's my ticket to finishing college when I get out."

"Bullshit! The Army's your ticket to misery with a capital M." He shook his head. "I thought married guys were out like Strout as far as the draft is concerned, and especially married guys with pregnant wives."

"If I wanted to avoid the draft I could have, but instead I chose it!"

"That's what's so crazy," said Charlie. "Where's your bride staying now?"

I told him. Although ordinarily I resisted most direct questions about my life, this disarming little character had the ability to open me up. There was something very likable about his combination of charcoal eyes, bushy eyebrows, big nose, low forehead, and quick smile. He was a down-to-earth guy. A rugged street fighter type with a good heart. In five minutes it was like you had known him all your life.

During my first few minutes with Charlie, the bus had pulled out, and we were on the road to New Jersey. It wasn't exactly *The Road to Mandalay*, but there was a spirit of adventure in me, and it was the first time I would be going south of New York. That would be interesting, wouldn't it?

However, as the bus left Boston I felt an abrupt jolt of loneliness. Deep loneliness. It was masked a little bit by Charlie whose questions helped to keep my mind occupied. I told him how Mary would be staying with the Killorens in Franklin now, since we had given up our apartment in East Dedham, sold the old Dodge, and left the few furniture items we owned either at my grandmother's place or with the Killorens.

"She'll be staying with her folks at least till next September when the baby comes. I'm not exactly thrilled with the idea of her staying with them, but what can we do? Her folks aren't exactly what you'd call easy to get along with. They gave us a really hard time when we decided to get married. You know how some people get married on a shoestring? Well, we didn't even own a shoestring. We had to put off getting married a month to pay off some of her charge accounts and get started on the right foot."

"You got no help, huh?"

I replied that we had gotten less than no help, but that was okay because I was used to "foraging for myself," an expression I told him was directly from Granny O'Connell's lips, and I explained that "foraging for myself" seemed to be the story of my life, at least up to the present moment.

Now I was foraging for me and Mary, and in September I'd be foraging for a little newcomer as well. I made light of it with Charlie, but I was scared. Yes, scared. How could I have predicted that we'd be expecting just one month after we were married? We had done nothing to prevent it, but we had assumed there'd be a little delay. But no lead time for us. Marriage. Honeymoon. Pregnancy. Morning sickness.

Although it was a thrill to think I'd be a father, it was also a worry. Could I handle caring for a family? Coming from a non-family, I didn't have any idea what a real family was. How did you take care of one? How did you act as part of one? But I was always a good learner of new things, so I figured I'd learn this new thing, too.

Charlie asked me how married life agreed with me, and I told him that it agreed with me to the extent of raising my weight in just a few months from a skinny 145 pounds to a more substantial 172. He chuckled and told me the Army would have me down to 145 again in a couple of months, and I felt like telling him to shut his pessimistic mouth, but I knew he was probably telling the truth.

God, how I loved that extra 27 pounds I had put on. Yes, marriage had agreed with me, and from skin-and-bones I had been transformed into the size person I had always dreamed of being. And now the Army was going to take it away? Damn the Army!

"Army cooking's shit for the birds," said Charlie. He explained that he had tasted more than enough of it in the National Guard, which had better food than the Army's. "What I mean, Tom, is it's sort of like the local greasy spoon being better than Joe and Nemo's hot dog joint in Scollay Square."

I told him I wasn't a fussy eater, and that nothing could have been worse than my grandmother's cooking anyhow, even the Army food. Then he asked me about Mary's cooking, and I told him it must be good if it had put 27 pounds on me in four months. "Yup, Mary's really coming along in the cooking department." I grinned. "There are still a couple of burnt pans out in the back yard behind where we used to live, filled with snow and ice, but when the spring thaw comes pretty soon they'll be nice and clean and somebody will find them and use them again."

"So she burns stuff, huh?"

"Doesn't every new bride?"

"How would I know? I'm not married, and I'm in no hurry for it either, pal."

"To each his own." That was my basic philosophy of life then, and I guess when you get right down to it, it's still a strong aspect of my philosophy. Do what you want to do as long as you don't screw someone else up when you're doing it, and as long as you don't expect me to do exactly the same thing you do, and as long as you don't expect me to praise you for doing something I think is pretty ridiculous or immoral.

However, as life has unfolded, I have periodically swerved away from my basic detachment and moved into another more active mindset. Every so often I've been apt to go on a crusade for one idea or another that I was totally certain about.

Well, the Greyhound bus bounced along, and the talk got back to school, and Charlie asked me how come if I was so hard up I managed to go to such a highly rated school as BC. I told him I was willing to make sacrifices for things that meant a lot to me, and that I'd always had an obsession in my brain about going to BC. "After all, Charlie, I only applied for admission there and no place else. I think I'm subject to obsessions." I chuckled. "When I get my mind on a thing it's awful hard for me to get off it."

He said he knew what I meant because he was a little that way himself about sports, music, and women. To make him feel that I didn't think I was a big shot, I told him, "BC's not as highfalutin as you think. A lot of regular guys go there. Most of us commute every day and hardly anyone lives in the dorms. Actually, we used to call it the poor man's Harvard, but I don't think over at Harvard they call themselves the rich man's BC, right?"

"Right . . . with a pencil. The way you been talking, sounds like you always do exactly what ya want to do, Tom."

"Why not? It's still a free country, right? I think if a guy puts his mind to something, he can do just about anything."

Somehow this trend of conversation got me talking about the decisions Mary and I had made together, and how we were going through with them no matter what anybody said or thought. I told him how we agreed on just about everything, seldom argued, and never even swore when we were together.

"What the hell ya trying to do? Get yourselves canonized as living saints?"

"Nope. We just have a good effect on each other, that's all. Once we got together I put a lot of my wise-guy language and habits behind me."

"I suppose you go to church every Sunday too."

"That's my business."

"Well, I'm one of those Christmas and Easter Catholics."

"To each his own, Charlie. *Chacun a son gout.* Every man to his own taste. I don't care if you never go to church. It's your problem, not mine. You know what my grandmother would call you? A lukewarm Catholic."

"She sounds like a real hot shit."

"She's in a class by herself. If she isn't nagging or complaining, she's praying. But where I was raised in Norwood, and even in some parts of Dedham too, there weren't many Protestants, and we were told there were only two kinds of people in the world, Irish Catholics and those who wished they were."

He laughed. "Where does that leave us Portuguese?"

"About halfway up Shit Creek with half a paddle, I guess. If my grandmother met you, she'd probably say he's all right, the little Olivera fella, for a Portuguese."

"Big deal." He told me about his family, and their prejudices, and that when he had started getting serious with his steady girl, they had a fit because of her Scandinavian background. This led to an exchange of photos, and we complimented each other on our taste in women. Then he asked if Mary would be coming down to Fort Dix on the coming Sunday for visiting hours.

I told him I didn't know about the visiting hours, or anything else about the Army, for that matter. He pledged to be my personal tour guide, and said he had visited Dix to see some pals the year before, and he knew the place pretty well. He also said he knew all about "bugging out."

"What the hell is that?"

"That's when you screw out of something the Army expects you to do."

"And if you get caught?"

"You get shafted, what else?"

I told him I planned to do what I was told to do, and he could spare me the lessons in bugging out. "Look, I just want to put in my time, stay out of trouble, get out with the GI Bill of Rights in two years, go back to BC and finish college, and that's that. The last thing I want to do is shaft myself trying to buck the system."

"You're gonna go gung-ho all the way, huh? Well, you'll change your tune pretty fast after we hit Fort Dix. When you do, just stick with Charlie, and we'll make the Army work for us instead of us working for the Army."

I got a kick out of his attitude, and figuring there was no point in arguing with him, I just said, "Right, Charlie." At Mrs. White's group foster home I had learned how to get along with strong minded, opinionated people. One of the best methods was silence.

I turned my attention to the passing landscape, but Charlie continued to talk until he finally got my hint, and we went into a period of silence and rest. The alternating periods of silence and conversation filled the nine hours it took the Greyhound to carry us the 350 miles or so to our destination near Newark, New Jersey.

During the rest periods, thoughts of my life with Mary kept popping into my mind. Lounging around after supper at night. Listening to music together. Reading. Talking. Going to bed together. Creating our own private world. Wedded bliss. Nice conversation. Good food. Peace of mind. God, what a couple we made. And we were sure that nobody else in the world could possibly be in love as much as we were.

Love? I had never really known what it could be until Mary. Then it had been all-consuming. Yet as we bounced along the highway en route to Fort Dix, it was too soon for me to get the full impact of separation from my wife. After all, I had been with her that very morning. So I hadn't spent a full day away from her, and couldn't imagine how twenty-four hours of separation would be. Well, I was soon to find out.

It was after midnight when the bus passed through the Main Gate of Fort Dix, and my eyes were about halfway open. When we entered the Reception Center, the driver braked to a stop, and my eyes opened wider, although I was still groggy. Charlie was in a similar twilight state of mind.

A husky sergeant politely invited us to leave the bus. "Get your fucked-up asses in line, and shag ass out of this here bus, and follow me."

So this was the Reception Center. Like many Army phrases and names, "Reception Center" had a nice ring to it. You could almost picture yourself being welcomed with open arms, like someone coming home from a long trip. But the name and the reality were two different things, like many other experiences in life that seem one way at first and then turn out to be quite another.

We were herded by the sergeant into a large bare hall, with hard oak folding chairs to sit on. There must have been nearly a thousand new soldiers there in that drafty hall and as the sergeant verbally pushed us along toward some seats in the rear, he did his best to explain to us what our status was. "There ain't nothing lower on the face of this mother-fucking earth than a private E-one in this man's Army. In other words, you guys ain't nothing but shit, and don't none of yez forget it."

The same sergeant then went to the front of the room, stood behind a large oak table, and announced to the whole group, "Now we're gonna give you cruddy fucking private E-one's an orientating so's you'll know where your asses are at in this here Army. During the next few days youse guys are gonna get processed, and this here is the official welcome from the Commanding Officer." He picked up a sheaf of papers attached to a clipboard, and began to read a canned lecture to us.

Meanwhile, the word "processed" had triggered Charlie's imagination. "Hey, they're gonna process us, for Christ's sake, just like sardines."

I nodded my sleepy head. "Yuh, I'm beginning to feel like a canned fish."

The sergeant's voice boomed out. "Knock off the fucking talking down back, or your asses are gonna be mine!"

We knocked off the talk, and the sergeant went on with his canned lecture, aimed at those of us who were about to be processed like sardines. The message he read to us was also given to us in print, along with the time of religious services, office hours of the chaplains, and information about the Sunday visiting hours.

### HEADQUARTERS RECEPTION STATION
### 1299th ASU
#### *Fort Dix, New Jersey*

*I wish to express my sincere welcome to the new life upon which you are about to embark. You have come from all walks of life, and it is through the training and conditioning that you are about to receive that you will emerge a man among men, a man of whom your family and dear ones will be justly proud. You are now serving the greatest nation in history, and that nation is proud to receive you as a soldier in the Army of the United States.—H.R. Moore, Colonel, Commanding*

When the sergeant gave us the Commanding Officer's greetings, his enunciation was very effective, and I remember that as I listened to the words and tried to believe in them, I got a little mist in my eyes as I put myself into the context of a citizen patriot who had volunteered for the draft and was about to serve his country well. To this day, I tend to do the same thing at flag raising ceremonies. One minute I can be cursing what's going on in this country, and then they start the "I Pledge Allegiance . . . ." and I relate to it, and it's like I'm a kid again, a true believer in this nation and all the good things it stands for.

So I listened to the husky sergeant, and I absorbed the words, while in my mind I think I pictured a benevolent Commanding Officer who would offset the crassness of the sergeant who was his representative and canned speech reader.

The sergeant continued: "Now we're gonna explain to you mother-fucking private E-one's this here Personal Conduct Manual and Soldier's Guide." He held up one in each hand. Then we all got the books and were told how to use them, receiving guidance page by page until it was after midnight. Afterward our tired bodies were lined up for a "partial issue" of Army clothing, and finally we were marched to our barracks in B Company by a tall, lean, colored [as we said in those days] sergeant whose neatly pressed and starched fatigue uniform was topped off with a well-buffed glossy helmet liner. The name "CAREW" was stenciled in white on the shiny olive drab surface of the liner.

The "fatigue" uniform was very aptly named, as I soon learned. When you were wearing it you tended to be overworked. You didn't see many dress uniforms around the Reception Center, but you did see neatly pressed and starched work uniforms on non-commissioned officers, and you noticed that they were faded. I assume that all new recruits were aptly called "green recruits" because they had the darkest green uniforms.

On the other hand, maybe we were like green apples who were not ripe yet. At any rate, the more faded your uniform was, the longer you had been in the Army, and that was a status symbol of sorts, like the faded blue jeans of recent generations. However, in the Army nobody ever thought of purposely fading a fabric. It just happened in the natural course of events.

Sergeant Carew feigned politeness as he ushered us into the barracks. "Be it ever so humble, gentlemens, there just ain't never no place like home." He was referring to the long since condemned wooden structures of the Reception Center which had been set up as temporary buildings before the second World War, and somehow had never been torn down and replaced. Inside they had open studding, no plaster, and no insulation.

I guess Charlie thought Carew was trying to be friendly, and he slapped the sergeant on the back. "You said it, Sarge. This is one helluva home, right?" Charlie laughed. But Sergeant Carew was not amused. Not by a long shot. His dark face seemed to gain a tinge of red, and his eyes widened and whitened as he glared at Charlie and growled, "Your ass is mine, little soldier!"

"Huh?" Charlie was taken off-guard.

"Your ass is mine, man. You don't call your sergeant Sarge and you don't slap your sergeant on his back no time, and sure as the good Lord above made hairy asses, you is gonna learn to call me Sergeant, little soldier."

Charlie nodded. "Yes, Sergeant."

The sudden formality on Charlie's part didn't change anything. Carew pointed to the floor. "Drop down and give me a quick twenty-five, little soldier." I rapidly realized that meant 25 push-ups without stopping for a breath. Charlie, who was in excellent physical shape, did them easily. When he was up to about twenty, and not even panting, a loud voice rang out from my right. "Hey, ain't that something? Look at the little guy knock off them push-ups. Hey, go man, go!" In a moment that outspoken recruit found himself on the floor next to my buddy, doing ten more push-ups than Charlie. I was quickly getting a few clear messages about the ways of the Army.

When Charlie was done he came over to me and whispered, "Didn't I tell ya the damn Army was chicken shit?"

I nodded, but didn't answer him. I was not about to become Sergeant Carew's next victim. Not if I could help it. And I wasn't the only recruit who had absorbed the sergeant's clear message. The assembly of new soldiers became very quiet while Carew instructed us on the fine art of bunk making, and the delicate procedure of spit-shining our combat boots.

By the time we were able to get ready for bed, it was around 1 a.m. Because our last names both began with "O" the two of us were destined to be located next to each other in most of our activities, unless another recruit with an "O" came in between us. It was an alphabetized Army.

Tired? I think numb is a better word. I took the lower bunk, and Charlie took the upper. I explained that I was a sleepwalker from time to time, and to avoid my stepping on his face in the middle of the night he would be wise to take the upper.

He accepted my logic, but not without telling me I probably could have avoided the draft if I had told them I sleepwalked. I reminded him that the draft was a necessary evil for me and that I had no interest in avoiding it. ". . . and besides, I'll need the GI Bill to finish BC when I get out."

"Fuck the GI Bill."

I had a retort, but I kept it to myself. My off-color days had stopped when I had become engaged to Mary. Well, for the most part they had. The off-color thoughts still arrived uninvited, but I tried not to act on them.

I didn't appreciate Charlie's remark, and I also didn't appreciate the way he had lowered his vocabulary to include the Army's favorite all-purpose word. I noticed that he hadn't used it on the bus, but now things were different apparently. He was opting for the lowest common denominator. Well, damned if I'd let the Army corrupt me and my language. The construction timekeeper's job hadn't done it, and the U.S. Army wasn't going to do it either. I might say "hell" and "damn" and "shit", but not "fuck."

As I lay there on my back on the bunk, my eyes closed without any help from my conscious mind, and I was about to sink into oblivion when a raucous voice echoed from the other end of the barracks. "Hey, how'd that Personal Conduct Manual grab you, huh? Like the part about us respecting the men under us? Shit, we're down so low there's nothing but dirt under us, for shit's sake." The barracks filled with laughter. "And did you get that part about most great leaders being courteous and kind? Ho-ho-ho. Like the sarge saying our asses were gonna be his." More laughter. "The part I liked best was when they gave the instructions about how you're supposed to hold a spoon. Hold it just like you'd hold a pen or a pencil, it said. Remember?" The laughter continued.

The sarcastic recruit had zeroed in on the realities of the Army right away, and my pal Charlie was not about to go silent at such a time. "If ya don't know how to hold onto a damn pen, I guess you're shit out of luck when it comes to holding a spoon!" Everyone laughed, and the banter went on for a while, getting more and more ridiculous, and finally the exhaustion caught up with us. As the noisy coal-fed, hot air heating system belched its uneven warmth into the drafty, un-insulated barracks, our bodies began to seek sleep, and the noise and talk came to a halt.

Then a moment later, the first major twinge came. The first big tug. The inner pain. The awareness. The harsh reality. The loneliness. It came when I turned over on my side sleepily and reached out for her. Yes, I reached out for Mary. Do you think that's strange? After all, I'd been reaching out for her in that double bed of ours for four months, night after night. Do you think my psyche was supposed to suddenly forget to trigger a habitual action that had risen to the level of sacred ritual?

So I reached out for her, and I found myself clutching at nothing but air. Then I opened my sleepy eyes and I became all too aware that the spirit of Mary was there with me, but her physical form was at the Killorens' house in Franklin, Massachusetts. God, did I feel alone there in my army bunk with its hard mattress and flat springs. I felt more alone than I could have imagined. Why hadn't I anticipated it? Because we avoid unpleasant personal forecasts, and even the most pessimistic of us try to shield ourselves from harsh truths. Hell, we can cope with each situation as it comes along, right? Wrong! Mary, I don't know how I'm gonna handle this without you. I don't know how I can . . . .

I suddenly remembered the letter I had promised to write every day to her, and I tried to get up to a sitting position, but my body was interested only in the prone posture. So I slumped back again and saw her face there in my closed eyes, and I said to her, Mary, I'm so bushed I don't think I could even hold a pen in my hand, never mind press it against a piece of paper. Forgive me for not writing tonight, but tomorrow's my first full day in the Army anyhow, so I'll write tomorrow, and every day after that.

I love you, Mary. What a girl you are. Even with all the morning sickness you never moan and groan, and now that your blood pressure's up you don't let it dampen your spirits. I wish you were with me so the Army wouldn't get on my nerves so much. But I'm getting a loud, clear message already. Without you, this Army's gonna be hell. I need you, Mary. I feel so incredibly alone!

### Letter. Wed., March 17, 1954

*We got to sleep about 1:00 a.m. because of the noise made by various loudmouths. At 3:15, 2-1/4 hours later, they woke up the bunch of us who were dead tired after the long bus trip, and since 3 a.m. till now we've been moving around in a 'scurry and wait' manner. We got all our uniforms, etc. today—perfect fits! I am very fatigued, mostly from the long periods of standing around. Actually, it was one long day since yesterday when I left at 5:30 a.m. from your house . . . . I have missed you unbearably.*

*Any minute they are going to drag us out of the barracks and God knows what time we will get to bed tonight. If I get the sleep I'll be okay, but it was a hell of a first day. The food is awful, compared to your cooking, and it will take me a while to get used to it . . . . Everybody here is in the same boat. Nobody likes the Army. I won't go into too much detail because I am so prejudiced after my first taste of the Army. Actually, basic has the same effect on everybody. And this processing period is a frustrating thing. Nobody knows anything about the future during this period of a week or so . . . I'm just living on rumors.*

*Don't be demoralized by this letter. I'm adjusting myself slowly. All I want in life is to be close to you and to have a nice home for our children. Nothing else matters, darling . . . . Now, just the thought of you makes me happy. I pray fervently that you will be able to come with me after basic. I can't live without you near me, even now. I only pray for the strength to endure your absence. Nobody in the world can possibly know how much I miss you and how much I love you.*

# 2

The week of processing at the Reception Center was coming to a close, and we were in formation on the hard cold ground, standing at attention, waiting for our early morning roll call. As I stood there I tried to figure out what day it was, but my mind couldn't focus clearly on the concept of time.

Since that first night at the Reception Center, the time had not arranged itself in neat segments the way it had in civilian life. Actually, that first week had been one long day interrupted at random by two, three, and four-hour bursts of sleep. There had been no consistency to either the waking or sleeping hours. You went to sleep when they let you. You got up when they ordered you to. And they made it very clear to you that your time was not your own. None of it.

"Hurry and wait" and "Scurry and wait" were certainly the slogans that fit just about everything we did. Stand in line. Wait. Get your Army uniforms. Wait. Get your Instructions for **"Marking of Clothing and Equipment as prescribed in AR 850-5."** Wait. Some of the stuff was issued right away. The rest would be issued when we got to our assigned training organization. Surprisingly, we were told we had to pay for our own stencil. It would be our own private property, a small symbol of individualism.

Here are some samples of the clothes marking instructions.

- *Article: "Helmets and liners." Location of Marking: "Inside visor (use black stencil paint)."*
- *Article: "Belts." Location of Marking: "Inside, 6 inches from buckle."*
- *Article: "Carrier, ax, intrenching." Location of Marking: "Inside flap, near front."*
- *Article: "Carrier, gas mask." Location of marking: "Inside cover flap near top seam, to right of left eyelet reinforcing seam."*

Also, one very important form was issued for the monthly income my dependent Mary would receive starting in April. It was a form that meant basic economic survival to us. We would be on one of the lowest rungs of the economic ladder, but at least we were on a rung.

## Allotment Authorization

*O'Connell, Thomas F., Jr. Pvt. E-1 US51305178 Effective Date of Allotment Apr 54. Amount: $91.30. Allottee's Name and Address: Mary L. O'Connell, 11 Sherman Avenue, Franklin, Massachusetts. Certifying Officer: D. F. Schwarzkopf, Captain, Inf Date: 19 Mar 54.*

During my waking hours, which amounted to about twenty per day, the full reality of the Army dominated my consciousness. The more I began to understand the Army and its power over me, the more I realized that it was alien to every fiber of my being. Just about everything the Army did to us, for its own obvious and possibly necessary reasons, I found negative. One example was the shearing of my curly brown hair right down to my scalp. The point was to produce uniform looking heads for all privates. Also, the constant verbal harassment inflicted on us was designed to wipe out all forms of individuality, and if there was anything in life that I did not want to part with it was my individuality.

The physical exhaustion made it clear that we were not taking part in a picnic or the Boy Scouts of America. On reflection, at a very young age I had found the Boy Scouts intolerable too, and didn't stay in it long. I had difficulty with the authority of so-called superiors, the Eagle Scouts. So here I was now, facing the irrational demands of non-commissioned officers whose abusive manners helped us to understand that no matter what the order was, we must obey, and that we had no rights, especially the right to be treated with respect.

To say that all this went against my grain would be the understatement of the century. Even the "alien-to-every-fiber-of-my-being" concept doesn't make the grade. How about every sub-atomic particle of my nature? That comes closer to what I want to say. In other words, the Army really rubbed the wrong way against all of me!

Yes, in one week my attitude had changed dramatically. Just about overnight I had been transformed from a staunch citizen patriot to an inwardly reluctant and balky soldier. Instead of just simply accepting the Army and its ways, as I had planned to do, and putting in my time like everyone else, and going along with the idea of it being a necessary evil, I had already begun to buy into Charlie Olivera's idea that the system was insane but you could beat it if you played your cards right.

The philosophy known as "bugging out" simply meant shirk instead of work, avoid instead of accept. Although I wasn't totally converted to Charlie's ideas that first week, I was getting very close. I think what had helped me more than anything else to shift my view was the all-out effort to wipe out my individuality. I knew that in combat conditions there was little room for independent thinkers, but I just couldn't adjust my own thinking to total acceptance of the inhuman treatment inflicted on us at the Reception Center.

It wasn't just the endless waiting in lines, the exhausting work demands, the torturous tours of duty in the mammoth kitchen on KP, the diet of creamed chipped beef on toast that was called "shit on a shingle," the rumor that there was saltpeter added to our food to retard our sex drives, the rotten Army language rotating around the word "fuck," and the total chaos and inconsistency of our existence.

No, it wasn't just those things. It was what the Army was so rapidly doing in its attempt to reduce the pride I had been trying to develop during the previous years of my life. After all, in my early twenties I had begun to feel as if I had moved beyond the stigma of having an insane mother, the shame of early abandonment by a father who had left me in a Catholic Charities group foster home for nine years, and the embarrassment of having Mrs. White as my legal "guardian."

Hadn't I experienced my share of humiliation already? Now, at this stage of my life when I had learned to be proud of my intelligence and my resilience despite adversity, was I supposed to let the Army rob me of my self-esteem? No, dammit, the Army had no right to do that to me, and the Army was not going to get away with it!

As I stood there at attention waiting for my name to be called, I thought about the bad dreams I had experienced quite often during my earlier years, and I knew that now I was living through a situation that was in some ways worse for me than a bad dream. The problem now was that the bad dream was really happening, and to make any sense of it I knew I would have to dream the bad dream for two years, as planned. But I couldn't tolerate the thought of two years in the Army. Even the idea of two months or two weeks was repulsive to me.

Standing there with exhausted legs that felt like buckling, I was indulging myself in self-pity as I kept thinking of the colonel's welcoming message that had been read to us on our arrival. The thought of it almost prompted me to laugh out loud in derision. "I wish to express my sincere welcome to the new life upon which you are about to embark."

This is a life? What a gross exaggeration! This is no life. This is some kind of Purgatory right here on earth, and the more I experience it the more I realize that basic training's gonna be my own private hell.

Yuh, this is a new life okay. A life of horseshit and bullshit and goat shit and chicken shit. God, what a week. I started out with a positive attitude and now I'm changing from a patriot to a pacifist. Maybe I'll consider giving up the Catholic Church and join the Quakers and become a conscientious objector if I have to put up with much more of this. They say war is hell, but as far as I'm concerned, the so-called peacetime Army is as close to hell as I ever want to . . .

"O'Connell, Thomas F., Jr."

"Uh . . . here!"

I could hear Charlie chuckling next to me. He knew I was apt to mentally depart from this planet in brief spurts. It was one way I had of trying to maintain my sanity. The roll call continued with shouts of "Ho," "Yo," "Hee-yup," and every once in a while a straightforward "Here." Maybe the little variations in their responses was what some soldiers did to make themselves think they still had some choices. But those kinds of choices were meaningless to me. Give me back my life! Give me back my freedom! Give me back my Mary!

"All right, you mens." It was Sergeant Carew's voice, forcing its way into my brain. If you didn't hear Carew and do what he said, you would soon live to regret it, and my brain knew this even when I was distracted with other thoughts. "You is gonna beautify the area, gentlemens. It's time for a little po-lice call." Early in the game we had learned that policing the area meant picking up cigarette butts, bits of paper, and any other debris that might be lying around on the hard ground near the barracks. Nobody knew where the term had originated. My conjecture was that it derived from the routine the police went through when you called them about trouble in your neighborhood. They would search for a prowler, a vandal, or a robber by examining the ground for clues. So we went into our search, not for clues, but for debris. Detectives in search of litter.

"In this man's Army if something don't move, we pick it up," said Carew as he fanned us out in long lines and led us back and forth across the sparse, trampled brown grass near the barracks.

In the half-light of dawn, I tried to focus my heavy-lidded eyes on the ground in front of me.

Shuffling along, I considered how inappropriate it was for me to pick up other guys' cigarette butts. Hey, I gave up smoking years ago. Why should I have to pick up what's left of other guys' weeds? Let the smokers pick up the butts. Damned if I'll do it. Up Carew's ass if he . . . uh-oh, there I go again swearing to myself. Car trouble makes me swear, and the stupid Army does too. But I should try to contain it. I shouldn't let the Army dominate my life. And I should watch my language. It's my only link around here to the concept of civilization.

I leaned over, laid my palm out flat about an inch above a butt, clenched my fist so it would appear that I was picking up something, straightened up again, and grinned. Yes, O'Connell one, Army nothing.

Well, that was how my mind was working after only a few days in the Army, and my body was following the dictates of my mind. In my own little way, I was beginning to bug out of even the smallest requirements like "beautifying the area." To hell with the area. Let it beautify itself!

Sergeant Carew shouted, "If it don't move, gentlemens, pick it up!"

A familiar voice retorted, "And if you can't pick it up, what are ya s'posed to do, Sarge? Paint it?" The rest of us laughed. But not Sergeant Carew. Mario, an Italian from New York, had stuck his neck out again, and Carew was only too happy to serve as the undisciplined recruit's guillotine.

First Carew used an identification routine, making the offender spell his name and give his serial number, place of birth, and rank. When the sergeant had the information he had asked for, he said, "Well, mother fucker from Brooklyn, you is gonna learn yourself to keep your mouth shut, and you is gonna learn yourself that you don't call your sergeant sarge. You know what I means, Private?"

The Italian shrugged his brawny shoulders. "Yuh, sure, Sarge." Again he had unwittingly committed the unforgivable sin. Carew's glistening dark brown eyes narrowed as he glared at his victim. "Your ass is mine, you shit kicking horse's ass private! You is going down on your knees and you is crawling the rest of this here po-lice call. Drop your ass down, man. And I ain't your Sarge. I'm your Sergeant!"

Mario shrugged, lowered himself to his knees, and crawled the rest of police call on the hard cold ground. Whether this particular recruit was capable of receiving a clear message was questionable, but everyone else in our group received it loudly and clearly. Yes, we had been the receivers of countless similar messages during that first few days in the Army, and those who had forgotten those messages were rapidly reminded, and weren't apt to forget again if we knew what was good for us.

After we had policed the area to Carew's satisfaction, we were led to an open plot of ground behind the barracks area where there sat a large pile of frozen sods. He ordered us to take the shovels that were standing in a rack near the pile, and then to pry the sods apart, and carry them on the shovels to the rear of a barracks half a block away.

We proceeded to carry out our task, and in each load I carried a bare minimum of sod. O'Connell two, Army nothing. O'Connell three, Army nothing. The rugged Italian, obviously undaunted after crawling around the area on his knees, shouted, "Hey, youse guys, how's about this for carrying sod, huh?" His shovel was high above his head, and balanced on the tip of it was a very large piece of sod. Everyone laughed because it seemed that anything the Italian did had a funny twist to it. I conjectured that if he lay dying, somehow he would make the scene seem amusing.

As for me, because of my exhausted mental state I was surprised that I was still able to laugh. But maybe when things are at their worst, that's when we're able to laugh the best. At least, that's how it has been with me much of the time. At my lowest I may cry and groan and moan, but then I'll make a switch and get angry or sarcastic or even laugh. Maybe it's my way of saying, "What the hell, somehow I'll survive."

Sergeant Carew went over to the Italian, put his black face about a half-inch from the recruit's olive face, and in a carefully modulated tone he said, "Looks like we is gonna have to straighten your ass, man, but good." As Carew talked, the Italian gave him a gray-toothed grin. "Yes, you is gonna dig one deep hole, you fuck-up from Brooklyn."

As the Italian began burrowing his hole, Carew gave him a succession of tongue lashings to help motivate him. When the soldier was done and panting for breath, the sergeant smiled his broadest smile and said, "Well, that there is one excellent hole, man. Now get your Brooklyn ass on up out of there." The Italian smiled, thinking he was finished his work. But the smile faded when Carew ordered, "Now you is gonna take all that there dirt from where it's at and you is gonna put it back in that there hole, man."

The rest of us continued to lug sods while the Italian filled in the deep hole he had dug, and as I shuffled along I thought about the night before when I had figured I was done for the day, and was lying on my bunk, and then found myself on a surprise work detail. Another colored sergeant with about a 38-tooth smile had volunteered me and ten others for what he had described as "a task."

The task was to scrape up inlaid linoleum that had been fused to the floor by thousands of boots over a period of about 14 years. It had been installed in these "temporary barracks" at the outset of World War II. Our tools were blunt screwdrivers, which made it an almost impossible job, causing very painful and bloody blisters. But I was learning that there were no impossible jobs in the Army. No matter what the order was, questions were unauthorized and the comment "impossible" was not allowed.

On that occasion, however, my friend Charlie had very neatly avoided the work project by disappearing about ten seconds before the sergeant had given me his pointed finger. Later in the evening, when I had come back to the barracks more exhausted than I can possibly describe, Charlie was still among the missing, so he had also avoided the surprise KP that I soon found myself on until it was just about dawn.

KP. That's short for kitchen police. There's that word "police" again. This time it meant the dirty work in the kitchen, which in the Army is called the Mess Hall, a place where food is prepared and eaten. The person who came up with the word "Mess" was very astute. Yet after living with Granny for so many years before marriage on a malnutrition diet, I didn't find the Army food that objectionable most of the time.

The way the Army does things is pretty much exemplified by that particular day in my life. As I looked for debris to pick up from the grassy plot near the barracks I was just about numb and my mind was certainly elsewhere, almost anywhere. Being up nearly all night working had left me with the feeling that I had no memory of ever sleeping, and since the day was just beginning, the possibility of future sleep seemed very distant. And guess what? This, I learned, was to be the day of our intelligence testing to determine our entire Army future.

Why should I be upset about last night? Do I have a right to be upset? After all, I'm just a warm body as far as the Army's concerned. I'm a number, not a person. I have no rights. "Okay, you gentlemens. You is going to do some more of this here processing now." I breathed a heavy sigh as I put down my shovel. I had never been much for physical exercise, and was far from what you'd call physically fit. So that first week had been an endurance test for just about every part of my body. Ache? You name it; it ached. Elbows. Ankles. Knees. Back. Eyes. Chest. Everything.

Carew, with no further explanation, ushered us to a large bare hall similar to many other large bare halls I had found myself in that week, and I received a battery of intelligence and aptitude tests. Staying awake was a problem. But the idea of going to an advanced school after basic instead of directly into the Infantry helped motivate me to keep awake, and when I was finished I knew I had done well. My instincts were confirmed a while later when some of us were told that our scores in the first series of tests put us into position to take the test for Officers' Candidate School.

Why bother with the OCS test? The last thing in the world I wanted to be was an officer in the Army, and I had no intention to go on to OCS if the test qualified me. But Charlie had told me it was shrewd to take the test regardless of our intentions so the Army would think we were potential officers. Also, Charlie had learned that every so often during basic training, they assembled OCS types for lectures and movies, and that was better than endless basic training, KP, and work details.

A "detail" in the Army, by the way, is a task usually handled by a group. The Army enjoyed having its own language in which meanings of many words were totally diverted from their civilian denotations. As Charlie often said, "There are two ways of doing something, the right way and the Army way." Charlie wasn't the only one who said that, and I soon learned that it was true.

I took the OCS test and later that afternoon a corporal in Personnel told me I had scored high. "Good." Then the corporal said, "You'll have a few weeks to make up your mind about whether you want to go to OCS or not." He said it would mean extra time in the Army, and even though I already knew this, I acted as if this were news. I told him I'd have to give it some serious thought, even though I knew I was about as likely to opt for OCS as I would for a voluntary tour of duty in the Far East.

When I asked the corporal if my college background would help me get into some advanced training after basic, other than OCS, he reviewed my file, muttering aloud as he went through it, and then he laughed. "With an excellent background like yours I'd say you've got a fine chance of becoming a mess cook or a Signal Corps pole climber. Yessiree, the Army will use you to the best of your ability. In other words, the Army will use you as it damn pleases. How does that grab ya?"

"Sounds like crabs and ice water to me."

He did a double-take and asked me to translate for him. I said it was an old expression my Uncle Bill had used quite a bit. "It means something like 'shit out o' luck' or 'on the outside looking in.'"

The corporal told me that in fourteen days he was going to be outside the Army looking in, and I said, "I wish I could say the same for myself."

He told me I'd survive the two years, and I shrugged and told him I hoped I would, and when he said it was time for me to move along to make way for others waiting behind me, I couldn't resist saying to him, "I really appreciated your comments about my future in the Army, and I want to wish you lots o' luck on the outside . . ."

"Why uh . . . thanks, Private." He had a perplexed look on his face, but that didn't surprise me. All my life I've left people with perplexed looks on their faces after outbursts that seemed to come out of my mouth without me having any forethought about their impact. Maybe it's the orphan thing. When you've been left without a mother and abandoned by your father, you've lost the most important things in life and then you tend to be pretty independent, so what have you got to lose from flinging a few loosely arranged words around now and then?

**Letter, Thurs., 18 Mar. 54 (date-military style)**

*Today we took a series of 10 examinations including aptitude and intelligence tests. This took from 7:00 a.m., when the captain gave an orientation speech in the theatre, until about 3 o'clock in the afternoon . . . . I was one of the many to take the OCS (Officers Candidate School) test . . . .*

*After taking the OCS test we marched across the camp to get our first pay which is called the 'flying 20.' 20 bucks. Before you get paid they tell you that a captain will be taking 'donations' for the Red Cross—one dollar is 'requested.' After that $1.00 for stencils for clothing. After that $.60 for a haircut—you should see it—a complete baldy, almost. After that a group picture* *which will cost $1.00—Great Army . . . just got word my group is getting up at 3:45 for KP . . . going to bed now. All my Love, honey. I'll write again tomorrow night and every night.*

One day blended with the next as I went on with my processing, and somehow I had lost track of Charlie in the pushing and shoving and waiting. Even though his name was close to mine in the alphabet, we had often found ourselves separated by other names that fit in between Olivera and O'Connell. Processing included many more long lines. I received shots in my arms to protect me from health menaces. I took additional Personnel interviews. I filled out more forms. Finally, I got my orders for basic training. I would be staying at Fort Dix, and would be assigned to I Company for Infantry basic.

Back in the barracks that evening after "chow," which was now our all-purpose word for every meal, Charlie told me about his orders for basic, and they were the same as mine. "I Company, here we come!" he shouted, snapping his fingers and going into an impromptu ethnic step dance. In a minute, with his slamming feet, he had the entire barracks clapping. When he was done everyone applauded, and Charlie grinned his crowded-toothed grin while bowing as if he were on stage.

When I said, "You ought to be in show biz," he laughed and reminded me that he was a professional musician as well as a singer and dancer, and he said, "Don't ask me which instrument I play most. I played a lot of the best rooms in Boston with my quartet." He said he hoped he could get into Army Special Services and play in the band after basic. I told him about the corporal's comments on my Army future. "If that's the way it is, with your instrumental background you'll probably qualify for a job as a three-hole punch operator in an office."

"Who cares, as long as it isn't the Infantry?" Then I noticed a strange look on his face. Suddenly he whispered, "Let's bug the hell out of here, Tom. Quick!"

I took my writing pad, and without a backward glance I promptly followed Charlie to the rear of the barracks, and then out the back door. Just as my feet touched the ground outside, I heard the voice of the sergeant with the 38-tooth smile, who had managed to put me through a night of scraping linoleum instead of getting some sleep on the night before our intelligence tests. "You mens, I'm gonna need ten o' you mother-fuckers for a little shit detail down at the supply depot. So get your asses out of them there soft bunks . . ."

"You're a life-saver," I said to Charlie as we slid into the darkness and left B Company. "You've got a highly developed bug-out instinct! Thanks for tipping me off."

"I owed you this one, after the other night."

"You didn't owe me. It's every man for himself, isn't it, when it comes to survival?"

"What about people helping each other?"

"That's fine, Charlie, but nobody has to. It's all voluntary. You don't have to do a damn thing you don't feel like doing. Like the night you saw that sadist coming after us for the shit detail, you didn't owe anybody anything so you took off like a big-assed bird."

"If I had time to warn you, I would have," pleaded Charlie. "No shit. But even so, weren't you the guy that said he wasn't gonna indulge in bugging out?"

"Time and tide and Army torture have shifted my attitude."

"Bet your ass. I always say give a guy a little time and he'll smarten up."

"No shit, Charlie, is that what you always say?" I laughed. "Hey, speaking of smartening up, how come you didn't bug out of KP last night?"

"I tried, but the supervision was too good. That fat-assed corporal didn't take his eyes off me for a second."

"Maybe he liked the way you wiggle it."

Charlie laughed. "Do you think he was a fruit?"

"Could be, but mostly I think he was just plain stupid. When I showed him the bloody blisters on my hands from the linoleum scraping he just grunted, 'Shit, that ain't nothing. You can still wash pots and pans, soldier.'"

Reflecting on his own night of KP, Charlie said, "I hope to hell I never see another chicken. I'm not cut out to be a damn butcher."

"Now I know why you didn't bug out of KP, Charlie."

"Why?"

"Because you were chicken. Get it?"

He groaned. "Don't tell me you're a punster."

"It's a high form of humor."

"Who said?"

"I said, I guess."

"I'm too beat to play with puns, Tom."

"Me, too. It seems like one long day since we've been here. Hey, where are we heading, Charlie? The Telephone Center?"

"Yuh, that's the best bug-out spot. We can get a coke there and I can grab a smoke and you can write one of your famous letters. Hey, you got any of your flying twenty left?"

"A couple of bucks. By the time we paid for our haircuts and our marking kits and sewing kits and group pictures and made our little so-called voluntary Red Cross donation, most of the dough flew away, that's for sure."

"The Army's got a great sense of humor," said Charlie. "They give you a chunk of your first month's pay with one hand and take it back with the other. Hey, look at the green recruits over there. I feel like a veteran already. You know what? It's a good deal staying at Dix for basic, but they say maybe we won't start training right away."

"Great! All I need is another week or two of this meaningless horseshit."

"Mm. Also, they don't give out passes till after the fourth week of basic. This week and next week won't count. It's gonna be at least six weeks before we get our asses out of here. Tom, another six weeks around here and I'll be walking around with my head looking out of the crack of my ass."

I laughed. "You've got a knack for clear descriptions, Charlie."

"I got a knack for something else too, brother, but I better not talk about it or I'll end up with lover's nuts."

I shivered in the frigid March air. "If it gets any colder we'll have frozen nuts."

"We've got it knocked," said Charlie in a burst of optimism. "The winter's almost over. Last winter was a bitch here, ya know. Half a dozen guys died from pneumonia."

"Pleasant thought. That's one helluva way to die for your country. Well, soon it'll be April and spring will be here and all is gonna be okay with the world, right? Do I have any complaints other than blisters all over my hands and aching ankles and shaky knees and a runny nose and a never-ending headache and an ass that's dragging on the ground behind me? Hey, I'm in good shape."

"You and me both. My hip's been acting up the past couple of days. I smashed it playing high school football. It only hurts when I'm sober. And if I can help it, I'm never gonna stay sober."

"You're quite a character, Charlie."

We arrived at the Telephone Center where I completed my letter to Mary while Charlie blew smoke rings and daydreamed. We each had a coke. Then, as I was sipping on mine, I heard another recruit talking to his girl. This triggered the impulse to call Mary collect and I didn't check the impulse. I was anxious to see if she could find a ride to New Jersey on Sunday for visiting hours. I hadn't heard from her by mail yet about that possibility. The brief call left me very dejected.

When I rejoined Charlie after making the call, he saw my somber expression and asked, "No deal?"

"No deal. Between Bill Killoren not wanting to take his old shit box on long rides, and the doctor telling Mary to avoid long car trips, I guess I've had it."

"Don't sweat it." Charlie slapped me on the back. "We'll find a way to bug out of this shit hole pretty soon."

"I'm not ready for AWOL, Charlie. It's self-defeating."

"That all depends on how you go about it."

On our way back to the barracks, I silently immersed myself in my own shell, and inwardly cursed the fact that I would not be seeing Mary on the coming weekend. However, as we neared the barracks I shook myself from negativity to present reality and said, "If the water's warm for a change, I'm gonna take a therapeutic shower for my nerves. Besides, I'm getting so I can't stand my own smell."

"I'm afraid to sniff under my own arms. I think I'm growing cheese there!"

We both laughed and I said, "The Army's just one big cruddy smell. Sometimes the stench is so bad I can't tell if it's me or the guy next to me."

"Just so long as there's no guy right behind you."

"Especially when you drop the soap in the shower."

When I took my shower that night I was all alone in the large open shower room where there was almost never any privacy except during those rare times when nobody else happened to show up. I was treated to lukewarm slow-moving water for about a minute, and then it turned ice cold, so I finished in a massive shiver while trying to wash off the remaining soap suds.

**Letter, Saturday, Mar. 20, '54**

*On Friday morning Company B went on KP at 3:45 a.m. I had about 3 hours sleep the night before, my average since I've been here . . . . I served on KP about 9 hours, then went through processing till 7 p.m. . . . . I was told that I received "a very high mark in the OCS test." Passing mark was about 115 and I received a mark of 143, which goes on my service record and may help me, if I'm lucky.*

*From 7 p.m. until after 10:00 p.m. I worked with a blunt screw driver scraping up inlaid linoleum that was laid in 1942, an almost impossible job since the linoleum was practically part of the floor. Oh well! After that I went to bed and was so tired I couldn't sleep until about midnight. We got up at 4:30 this morning and cleaned the barracks, then went to chow, and to processing. We had a couple of hours of marching, then the 3 shots, one for tetanus, one for cholera, and one for typhoid . . . I just missed having KP tonight and enjoyed my first two hours off by hearing your voice on the phone and by writing this letter, shining my combat boots, shaving, taking my first shower, etc.*

*A few of the boys and myself made a little pact on profanity. Some of these characters swear every other word, and if you don't watch out it can rub off on you. Every time any one of us hears the other using forbidden phrases he forks over a nickel to the winner. I made 5 cents tonight.*

When I got into my bunk a little later I found myself wide awake and frustrated. Mary was on my mind and I could not distract myself from thinking about her. I closed my eyes and in my imagination I saw her broad smile, her long auburn hair, and her soft warm skin. As her spirit filled my mind, my eyes became misty and I reflected, It's funny how I was never too lonesome before I met Mary. I guess I was used to being a lone wolf. But now, how I love and miss that girl. The aloneness is so painful.

It's hard to believe her name's Mary O'Connell now. We belong together. How many more nights do I have to spend like this? I want to love her and hold her and tell her everything will be just fine with her and the baby. I wonder how she's feeling right now. I hope her blood pressure levels off. It's like I left part of myself back home with her. The stupid Army only has my warm body. It doesn't have my soul. I'll never turn my soul over to the Army. In the Army you're only supposed to obey orders and not be concerned with your soul. To hell with the Army. Was it really just a few days ago when we said goodbye? My sense of time has completely left me.

### Letter, Sunday, March 21, '54, Fort Dix, NJ
*It was swell to talk to you on the phone today and to give you the good news that basic for me will be at Fort Dix . . . tomorrow we'll go to the place where our basic will be done.*

*We were lucky today since we had no KP and our time was our own.*

*I spent most of the time shining my boots. It takes about a half hour just to shine about 3 square inches. You use about four or five coats of polish and an equal amount of saliva which makes it shine. I have two toe sections done.*

# 3

With shaved heads, we moved from the Reception Center to Infantry basic training in I Company, but instead of starting basic we were put on hold in a mode described as "pre-basic." The rumor we had heard about not starting the eight-week basic training cycle for another two weeks proved to be true.

This meant that instead of actually taking classes that would train us for combat we were subjected to an endless succession of work details such as washing and waxing floors, extra hours on KP, "practice" marches of eight miles over hill and dale, organizing field packs, drilling in formation, standing at attention until you thought you were going to keel over, hauling laundry in trucks, working at the laundry, sanding desks, shellacking floors in Headquarters, digging ditches out on the range, and just about anything else our superiors, the "permanent cadre," could dream up for us to do.

In the midst of all this, a young recruit from Puerto Rico was discharged because of heart trouble, and I wondered if my own high blood pressure might turn into a problem for me, considering the lack of sleep and the constant exertion.

**Letter, Thursday, March 25, 1954**
*Today we ate K rations for supper. They were digestible, almost. Today I didn't have a chance to find out about visitors' day. I'm almost positive it's from one to six on Sunday . . . . I*

*was loading laundry bags, sorting clothing, and sandpapering desks all afternoon. Then I ate supper and was put on KP in the Company mess, an enormous mess hall, from 5 p.m. to midnight. I broke open exactly 1800 eggs into a massive vat for the next day's scrambled eggs. Then I peeled oranges and mopped floors—only an 18 hour work day—I'm still kicking, so don't worry.*

*They're trying to get us used to a rough life and they're sure doing a swell job of it. Today we got our rifles and bayonets. We still haven't received half of our equipment. Before supper each night we have to do chin-ups, you jump to an iron bar about 8 feet high and then pull your chin up to it. It's swell after you've been working all day. Oh well. I need those small bars of soap. We often shave with cold water here, and sometimes with no water at all.*

*I feel like crying every time I think of how much I wish I could hold your hand and look at your pretty face. When I get depressed I try to think of ways of getting out of the service and then I say to myself . . . that I must do what I think is right, and I will have to stick it out because I know I shouldn't do anything else.*

*I hate vulgar talk more than I ever did, even though I hear it more than ever. I don't swear at all except for a few mild things. I don't like this life at all, but I am in the U.S. Army and have to make the most of it and hope for the best. I think I will be a lot stronger and less nervous when I get through with this. Keep your chin up, honey. I know it's harder to smile than to cry at a time like this but we'll both try to smile and think of how much worse off we could be.*

## Letter, Friday, March 26, 1954

*Just finished having a GI party, cleaning the barracks. We dug a few trenches, etc. today. It looks like we're going to be here two more weeks before we even start basic and that isn't good. They give us crumby details all days long.*

*Please send me one pillow slip to replace one stolen from me, as well as some coat hangers . . . I never knew I could be so lonely for anyone. I live just for one sweet little girl that loves me and whom I love with all my heart. In about 9 weeks I can be with you for two whole weeks . . .*

When I reflect on the letters I wrote to Mary during my early months in the Army it is very obvious to me how conflicted I was. I would try to cheer her up with some of my comments, but my own deep feelings against the Army would gradually creep into my notes. Then I had to use self-restraint and try to make light of my frustration and exhaustion, for Mary's sake. After all, she was an expectant mother. So I would complain a little but try not to overdo it. Actually, my hate for the Army and its way of dehumanizing soldiers was so extreme there were no words to express it anyhow.

The first week of pre-basic, with our Platoon Sergeant Cummings always on our backs, was as exhausting as the Reception Center had been. During one long night on KP I peeled the skins off countless oranges, using a tablespoon as my tool. At the same time I came down with an internal problem aptly described by the Army term "GI shits." But something wonderful happened that week. In our outfit, Charlie bumped into a corporal he had known back home. And what a difference that made.

"They've got a pass racket going here," Charlie told me. "Even though we're not supposed to get a pass until after our fourth week of basic we can get out of here this weekend for twenty bucks each. This is the deal. On Friday night we get a round-trip ride to the Boston area with the corporal, and they throw in a pass and sign us out and back in again on Sunday. They make a few bucks on us and we get the hell out of here for the weekend. Are you in on it?"

"Is the Pope Catholic?"

On Friday night we surreptitiously left our barracks with small overnight bags, as inconspicuously as we could, and everybody else was so distracted there were no questions asked.

What a weekend that was. After two interminable weeks in the Army it was just like Heaven being in Franklin with Mary and her family. Simple things took on a whole new grandeur. Sleeping until you felt like getting up. No cadre on your back. No work details. Eating in a house with a family. Going to church. Loving each moment with Mary. But then all too soon, I was off to Framingham in Bill Killoren's old Studebaker to meet the corporal for the 350 mile ride back to Fort Dix. Back from civilian reality to Army unreality. Sleeping in the car as we flew down Connecticut's Merritt Turnpike at more than 100 miles per hour to "make time." Praying that the corporal wouldn't lose control of the car. Arriving safely. Sneaking into the barracks. Sinking into a deep sleep.

### Letter, Sunday Night, March 28, 1954, (Monday morning) 3 a.m.

*Arrived safely after a wonderful Heavenly weekend with my baby. I hate to leave you for a minute. I love you so. I will write tonight when I have more time. I slept a little in the car so don't worry, I won't be too tired today . . . . I pray that I will see you next weekend, my love.*

### Letter, Monday, March 29, 1954

*Boy it was like a second honeymoon to be home with you for the weekend. I can only write a few lines tonight because of the rough day I had today. I had KP from 3:30 in the morning to 7 pm this evening without a break.*

*Your cookies and fudge were delicious and the boys complimented you on your baking skill. I'm very tired at present and will hit the sack in a minute. Different fellows have told me that your expense will be taken care of if you go to a government hospital like Chelsea Naval or at Fort Devens. I will find out for sure this week.*

*I will see the chaplain and have him tell me all the information about us being together after basic, and so forth. I hope I have time tomorrow night. Olivera's house had a fire so he got an emergency leave and is now away from the barracks. I don't think I have much chance of being on leave this weekend.*

*P.S. Thanks for being so brave and strong when I leave. Your sweet smile makes it seem that you won't worry too much and that is what I'd like.*

Since there was so little freedom in basic training, and also a shortage of money, it was necessary to make checklists and set priorities. Here is an example from Tuesday, March 30:

- **See chaplain**
- **See personnel—licensed driver, stock clerk & shipping, carpenter, time clerk**
- **See eye doctor**
- **Get handkerchiefs**
- **Check on visitor's pass**
- **Toothpaste, shave cream**
- **Sewing Kit**
- **Patches**
- **Rawhide shoe laces**

**Letter, Wednesday, March 31, 1954**

*It was about 7 pm when I started this letter. It is now about 11:30. In the meantime I have been scraping paint. I wish I had a minute free. We are restricted every night. The times when I called you were mostly on the sly. Down here at I Company they don't believe in letting us get out to the PX or anything. Olivera isn't back yet, so the pass situation doesn't look too good.*

Now it was Friday morning of our second week of pre-basic in I Company, and we were standing in formation for roll call, waiting for the arrival of our top sergeant. He was built like a tank and his face had no smile lines on it. As I stood there waiting I dwelled on the miseries of that week, and agreed that our esteemed leaders were not exaggerating when they called us "the shit end of humanity" and treated us accordingly.

That's what I'm beginning to feel like, I thought. But thank God I bumped into Charlie at the Boston Army Base. Otherwise I wouldn't have bugged out of this hole last weekend. It's hard to believe I was actually home with her. It seems like so long ago. She had indigestion pretty badly, but she hardly said a word about it. Nice going. She just gets over the morning sickness and damned if something else doesn't crop up.

Charlie wins the prize as the master bug-out. Imagine him getting us out of here last weekend and then after he's back here a day he makes like his folks back home had a fire in their kitchen and now he's gone on emergency leave. I hope he's back in time to get us out of here again this weekend. He's my key to getting in on the pass racket.

"Atten-hut." Another sergeant alerted us to the arrival of the top sergeant, the leader of the I Company training cadre. Out of the corner of my eye I could now see our leader while I stood there at attention.

As the massive soldier swaggered into clear view, I took in the full picture. The chin blended in rolls of fat with the chest. The dark bushy eyebrows almost completely concealed the small eyes. The fat torso encased in a tailored dress uniform was bedecked with campaign ribbons and the prized Combat Infantryman's Badge.

"Youse men assigned to I Company is gonna be soldiers whether you like it or not. We need men and that's what we're gonna get. As for the weaklings we'll kick their damn asses out of the Army. One thing we don't need in combat is . . ."

My thoughts were interrupted by giggling to my rear. At first I thought the man behind me was making the unforgivable mistake of laughing at the top sergeant. Then I saw that even our serious leader was having a difficult time maintaining his own composure. I learned why when into my line of vision came the unclad running figure of the squat Italian from Brooklyn who had already become a legend in I Company because of his amazing attraction for punishment. He was running through the Company area totally in the nude except for one item of apparel, his helmet liner. As he trotted across the drill field his head was erect and his face betrayed no inner emotion.

It was early April and unseasonably cold, and as he came closer it was apparent that his whole body was covered with goose bumps. He trotted in an arc across the drill field with his hairy testicles swaying in the breeze and his longer than average penis bouncing from one raised leg to the other. Then the buttocks of the Italian, who had earned himself the title of Mario the Magnificent, disappeared past the Orderly Room and the recruits of I Company dissolved in laughter.

"He's hung like a buffalo!" shouted a soldier to my rear, and a roar of laughter followed. When the laughter died down, our leader announced, "This is what happens if . . . ."

He was cut off in mid-sentence when the hairy unclad form of Mario the Magnificent began his second pass through the Company area with his helmet liner bobbing as he ran along.

"The WACs in the next block must love this!" shouted a voice to my left. WAC stood for Women's Army Corps. The usual sense of discipline disappeared from I Company as cadre and recruits alike fell into a round of stomach-cramping laughter at the expense of the troublesome Italian.

When his buttocks had once again passed out of sight near the Orderly Room, our leader called the group to order and shouted, "This is what happens if a guy's taking his shower after Mess and he don't get his ass to the formation when the whistle blows."

Well, I guess they aren't kidding when they say our asses belong to the Army, I thought as I absorbed the scene. But I'll be damned if I'll ever let them make me prance around like that. I'll go to the Inspector General first. But Mario's a sucker for punishment. He attracts it like a magnet.

As he made his third pass through the Company area, accompanied by the renewed laughter of recruits and cadre, he trotted past the end of the formation, then made a change of route, and ran along the dirt drill field directly toward the spot where the first sergeant was standing. At that point, he stopped abruptly, did a right face, and stood naked at attention.

"What's the story, Private?" Our leader maintained a serious mien.

"I wanna go on sick call, Sarge," replied the Italian, just loud enough for the rest of I Company to hear. The top sergeant, looking as if he might be caught between the urge to laugh and the need to maintain order, asked, "What's your problem, Private?" The Italian was silent for one brief moment. Then his voice came through loud and clear. "I think I got frostbite in my pecker, Sergeant!"

The men of I Company could stand at attention no longer. Their laughter was too much for them as they rocked from side to side, slapped each other on their backs, held their sides, and even threw themselves onto the ground in comic hysteria. When the laughter diminished, our leader's face was extremely red. "Go to the barracks, soldier," he ordered, "and put your uniform on and report your ass to the Orderly Room."

"But Sarge . . ." The nude Mario placed his brawny hands on his hips and did not budge. "I'm not shitting ya. I really think my pecker's got frostbite." The next burst of laughter was deafening.

Our leader was not amused. He shouted, "Atten-hut!" Then he glared at Mario and pointed to the barracks. "Get your ass into the barracks, soldier!"

Mario shrugged his broad shoulders, turned, adjusted his helmet liner, gave his fellow recruits a confused look, and then trotted slowly toward the barracks. As his last nude appearance came to a close, an unchained barrage of laughter followed him to his destination.

"Atten-hut!" We responded to the sergeant's command, although many of us could hardly stop laughing. "That soldier," shouted the first sergeant, "He's what we call a fuck-up." Some of the recruits laughed. "It's no fucking joke being a fuck-up. What we do to fuck-ups in I Company is we fuck them up and put their asses in the grease trap."

At the very mention of the grease trap all discipline was restored. The cleaning of the pit that each Mess Hall used as the container for used cooking grease was a nausea-producing ordeal. But there was always an adequate supply of soldiers who got out of line and found themselves in that pit working and vomiting.

Our day of pre-basic drilling began. It was a moist day, and the New Jersey skies opened up as they had been opening up without cease day after day, and the spring rain found its way into our allegedly waterproof ponchos and supposedly water resistant combat boots. The men of I Company dug our ditches in the rain, received outdoor lectures in the rain, and marched back and forth on the drill field for hours in the rain. There were no rain checks, and my body reacted as I had feared it would. My ankles ached. A back tooth throbbed. My throat was raw. Sharp pains shot across my chest. My heart raced at top speed. My feet became white and clammy.

**Letter, Tuesday, March 30, 1954**

*Today we were busy as usual. We applied for our ID card, then did all kinds of basic march steps. We had a class in military courtesy and a couple of hours of PT—physical training, in which I did exercises that I never even knew about before. Don't worry, I feel no worse physically than most of the fellows down here. We're all tired and we all have colds. We all hate the food, as well as the Army itself.*

*Mentally, I don't think anyone has ever been so lonesome as I, but I try to be strong because I know you want me to. When I get discouraged I say, "Oh well, it can't last forever."*

There was an interruption of my letter when a little cleanup campaign was sprung on us. After cleaning up, I went back to the letter, and as I look back on the poem I included in my letter to Mary, I can see now how torn I was between hatred of Army ways and devotion to doing my patriotic duty.

*After cleaning up I received your wonderful letter about last weekend. It certainly was wonderful to be within hand-holding distance of the sweetest wife that ever lived. Don't worry, honey, I will try to get out of here every weekend, but don't plan, just pray. I live just to be with you. I'm positive that you and our little baby will be taken care of by Uncle Sam in an Army hospital.*

> *Tell me not sweet, I am unkind*
> *that from the nunnery of thy chaste breast*
> *and quiet mind,*
> *To war and arms I fly.*
> *True, a new mistress now I chase,*
> *the first foe in the field.*
> *And with a stronger faith embrace*
> *a sword, a horse, a shield.*
> *Yet my inconstancy is such as*
> *thou too shoulds't adore.*
> *I could not love thee dear so much*
> *loved I not honor more.*

—Richard Lovelace
"To Lucasta, on Going to the Wars"

*This poem says, in so many words, that love is tied up with honor and duty, as well as romance . . . . I will, after Olivera comes back from his emergency leave, try to get a visitor's pass so that if you came down to see me you could stay on camp in the guest houses. I'll come home whenever possible, but if I can't, we'll see what we can do.*

*Three hundred and fifty miles is nothing. I would go a million miles to see my baby for one second. That food of yours the other night was eaten to the last morsel. The cookies were delicious. I left almost the whole box of fudge in the corporal's car and haven't had a chance to ask him about it yet. Actually, he deserves anything I can give him, after getting that impossible pass for me last weekend.*

*I could use a few dollars, honey, just in case. We won't get any money till the 11th of April, and then it won't be much.*

At the end of the day, I was wearily polishing my boots when Kenney, a fellow Bostonian from Needham, came over to my bunk and said, "Some day, huh?"

I nodded. "And some dew. On the grass, that is."

"And some don't." Kenney chuckled.

"Sit down and be my guest. My bunk belongs to all taxpayers."

"Thanks. Don't mind if I do. My feet are killing me after today."

"My whole body's killing me. I'm not cut out for this kind of living."

"This is living?" Kenney grunted.

"They don't lay off on us for a minute, do they?"

We chatted a while about our views on Army life and did a little review of the scene we had just witnessed out on the drill field. I said, "I think Mario's biggest problem is that he hasn't figured out how to bug out." I continued to buff the boot I had been polishing.

"Did you hear where he ended up today?"

"Yup. The grease trap."

"Do you think he'll smarten up now?"

I shook my head. "Nope. Extremists rarely smarten up. But what the hell, he's getting an education. He's learned all about digging six-by-sixes and doing low crawls in the mud, and now he knows all about grease traps."

Kenney chuckled. "Did you see him yesterday when the cadre made him run around his helmet liner till he got so dizzy he fell flat on his face?"

"He asked for it, but I still feel for him. I understand his hatred of the Army."

"I do too, but he's so self-destructive. Hey, they're gonna let Mendez out on a medical, you know. His heart. It's a great Army if you don't weaken."

"It's shit for the birds," I said, "But the weird thing is my wife and I agreed I should let myself get drafted so I can get the GI Bill later on. I wanted this?"

"Well, you're in now. If you fight the system, you get shafted."

"The next best thing is bugging out of stuff. It helps you keep your sanity."

"But what about the ethics of it?"

"Well, I've given a lot of thought lately to the relative morality of screwing the Army and I've come to the conclusion that it's not immoral."

"How do you justify your thinking?"

I laughed. "By rationalizing, of course. Isn't that how everybody justifies everything? Here's my logic. The Army's like a huge corporation that can't think and can't feel, so morality doesn't apply to it. Actually, A-R-M-Y is just a four letter word anyhow, and how can you act immorally toward a word? The Army's unreal."

"You mean it doesn't exist? I see a flaw in your logic, Tom. If the Army doesn't exist and we're in it, then we don't exist either."

I grinned. "Now you're making sense. The first time I've existed since the Army took my ass was last weekend at home with Mary. I sure don't exist when the Army has my warm body. How's this syllogism? An intelligent man can't accept an insane situation. The Army is an insane situation. Therefore, an intelligent man can't accept the Army."

"Is that your Jesuit logic?" Kenney chuckled.

"Well, my profs at B.C. might not share my views about this organized chaos called Army, but to prove me wrong they'd have to prove that the Army's sane. Can anyone prove that?"

"Nope. But there's another thing they could try to prove. That you're not an intelligent man. That would screw up your syllogism."

"Good point. If I were really smart I'd still be a civilian."

"Please don't mention that word. It brings tears to my eyes."

"The word Army brings tears to mine. I was a patriot before I was inducted into the Army, but now I say screw the Army and all it stands for."

"But it stands for America the beautiful."

"Bullshit! The only thing the Army stands for is itself. It's a self-perpetuating organism."

"Why get upset about an organism?"

"I hate organisms that separate me from my wife."

Kenney chuckled. "You've got that glint in your eye. Had quite a time last weekend, huh? Hey, how's chances of some of us other guys coming along with you and Olivera on your ride this weekend?"

"There's room for you guys, but it's up to Charlie and the corporal, and I don't know if the deal's gonna be on if Charlie doesn't get back here from his phony fire. As for me, tonight I'm gonna pray to Christ, Mohammed, Buddha and every prophet of God I can think of who can help me get out of here this weekend. I'm also praying we don't end up in Indo-China. I'm like a walking prayer book lately."

"Me too. Maybe it takes unholy places to bring out holiness."

"Yup, it sometimes seems . . ." My comment was cut off by a burst of confusion from downstairs in the first level of the barracks.

"Let's check it out," said Kenney.

"You go first and let me know if it's worth hobbling downstairs for. My feet are in rough shape." As he headed down the stairs, I said, "Hey, those guys down there are always raising one kind of hell or another. Some of them think the Army's a circus, but I've never been much for circuses or mob scenes. I don't need crowds to prove to me that I'm alive. All I need is . . ."

"You've gotta see this, Tom! The muscle man's walking on his hands."

As I put my well buffed combat boots under my bunk, I muttered, "Yup, I need to see someone walk on his hands. Maybe the idiot will inspire me. I can hardly walk on my feet, never mind my hands."

Just as I reached the bottom of the stairs, a burst of applause resounded through the barracks. It wasn't for me. It was for Darrow, the muscular athletic recruit from Utica, who was finishing a backward somersault. He landed on his feet, proudly grinning.

I whispered to Kenney, "His Narcissus complex is showing. He's in love with that picture of himself he's got hanging inside his wall locker, right?"

Darrow flexed his muscles and addressed the crowd observing his feats of physical prowess. "This man's Army's a damn breeze when you're in good shape like me."

I laughed. "You could go through the Army standing on your hands, right?"

Kenney followed up my comment by saying, "Yup, you can go through the two years standing on your hands, Darrow, or maybe on your little finger! You're in shape!"

Darrow had no sense of humor. "Bet your ass I'm in good shape. I believe in being physically fit."

"Good for you, Darrow," I said.

Darrow swaggered toward me. "You don't believe in physical fitness, O'Connell?"

"Hey, it has its place, but I'm more interested in mental fitness, Darrow. I'll take brain-power over muscle-power anytime."

"Shit, O'Connell, just 'cause a guy's got a good build it don't mean he's got no brains."

I nodded and winked at Kenney as I mimicked Darrow. "Yup, just 'cause a guy's got a good build it don't mean he's got no brains." I kept a straight face.

"Ain't that what I just said, for Christ's sake?"

Knowing I was pressing my luck with him and could easily end up with his fist in my face, I said, "Maybe I was just sort of agreeing with you, Darrow. I've got an open mind and it could be that you've got a point."

"Sure as shit I got a point." He examined me carefully and then pointed at my ring finger. "Hey, you're married, right?"

"Right."

"Well, shit, you got to believe in physical fitness. What the hell you gonna do if you get all pooped out and can't get it up?" The other recruits laughed and I blushed.

The last thing in the world I was interested in doing was discussing my sex life in public. "That's never been a problem for me, Darrow."

"Well, I'll tell you something, O'Connell. When me and my broad get hitched, this man ain't gonna be pooped out. I stay in good shape for getting laid. Me and my girl are engaged. Engaged to get laid." The other recruits laughed.

"So you're engaged, huh?"

"Sure as shit." He nodded. "But that don't mean we gotta get married, ya know. I mean if we don't make it too good in bed the next couple of months, then it's no go."

"In other words, you're gonna have a trial marriage?"

"You said it, brother." Darrow slapped me on the arm as he laughed. I drew back and caressed my sore arm. "We're not taking no chances of being unsuited to each other in bed after we tie the knot, ya know what I mean?"

"You're a hot shit, Darrow." Somehow I knew I was getting in dangerously deeper with him, but I pressed on. "I think you've got a pretty cold philosophy. Do you think marriage is just sex and nothing else?"

"You mean sex ain't the most important thing in a marriage?"

"As far as I'm concerned if two people love each other the sex part just falls right into place."

"I'm taking no fucking chances."

I could not resist the impulse to ask another question. "Uh, tell me, Darrow, whose idea was this trial marriage bit?"

"Mostly mine."

I laughed. "It'd be funny as hell if the time came for you to get married and you couldn't get it up anymore." The other recruits on Darrow's floor laughed, but not Darrow.

He shoved his face up close to mine. "You better watch your mouth, wise ass." Then he turned to his audience. "Anyways, I don't have to worry about getting it up. I got a twenty-four-hour instant hard-on going for me." The recruits laughed loudly and Darrow was very pleased.

Unable to hold back my argumentative tendency, I said, "Tell me, Darrow. If you and your girl make out great in bed, do you think you'll have some kind of a guarantee you're gonna live happily ever after?"

"It'll sure as hell help the odds!" Darrow's people laughed again, and again he was pleased with his progress in the verbal fencing match.

Not knowing when to stop, I persisted. "I'm all for sexual happiness, but if you're gonna marry just for sex you might as well just shack up on a steady basis with a whore or a nymphomaniac."

When several of the listening recruits laughed, Darrow's face reddened, his pale blue eyes narrowed, and he put his hands on his hips. "What's that shit supposed to mean, O'Connell?"

"All I mean is if you only want sex, you probably should forget about marriage. There's a helluva lot more to marriage than sex."

"Far as I'm concerned, it's mostly sex."

I shrugged my shoulders. "It takes all kinds to make a world, Darrow. Some people marry for love. Others want a sexual guarantee. Money back if you're not satisfied with the product, right?"

Darrow reached out, took hold of my shirt collar with his left hand, and began to twist it. "You're a wise bastard, aren't ya, O'Connell?"

I knew the dialogue was over, and when I saw him clench his right fist, I shouted, "Down, Darrow. Down boy! You wouldn't hurt a 162 pound weakling, would you?" Darrow still didn't relax his grip. "Hey, we're just talking philosophy! Why get so upset?"

"I got a good mind to mop up the damn barracks floor with your warm body, O'Connell."

"And get a court martial for assault and battery?"

He finally let go. "Shit on you and your philosophy, O'Connell. Up your ass with your philosophy!" He turned to the audience of recruits. "I said it before and I'll say it again. I ain't getting married without a sample first."

His fan club applauded, and I knew for sure that it was time for me to back off instead of wasting my breath and risking my neck. "Just a difference of opinion," I said softly, extending my hand. "No sense getting all shook about it, right?" As he ground my knuckles together I said, "Would you give me my hand back in one piece?"

"I forget my own strength sometimes."

"Mm."

As we climbed the stairs to our bunks, I rubbed my sore knuckles. "Now I've got a sore hand to go along with the rest of my sore body."

Kenney said, "You're lucky you don't have a sore nose and a sore jaw."

I nodded. "I was pushing my luck, I guess."

Kenney said, "You were using the right ideas on the wrong person. Darrow thinks marriage is nothing but a steady piece of ass."

"Well, I gave it the old Boston College try. I'm surprised I could work up the energy to shoot off my mouth like that, but Darrow's type frosts my ass. The man-woman relationship's gotta be higher than the animal level. Otherwise, we've come nowhere since the Stone Age."

"Sometimes I think we haven't come very far," said Kenney as we reached my bunk. "Wow, you guys grabbed a good location here. Right next to the stairs."

"Charlie picked it out. He claims it's the best bug-out spot in the whole barracks."

"Well, I hope little Charlie gets back here on the double. I want out of this Fort for the weekend."

"Did I hear you guys using my name in vain?" It was Charlie.

"Well, if it isn't the devil himself." I put out my hand for a shake. "Glad to see you're back."

"What about my front?"

"Front and back, Charlie."

"The sooner I get the hell out of here the better. They don't give out emergency leave like Santa Claus. They subtract it from the time you've got coming to you." He lowered his voice and addressed his next remark to me. "I figured I'd come back in time to bug out of here for the weekend."

"Great."

His charcoal eyes beamed. "Life outside is what's great. It's the cat's ass." He turned to Kenney. "Do you and your pals want in on the trip?"

"You said it, brother."

"You know the deal, huh?"

"Tom told me about it. Twenty bucks for the round trip ride, we get signed in and out, we get taken off the duty rosters, and we get passes in our little hands even though nobody else gets one till after the fourth week of basic. That's the deal, isn't it?"

"Yup." He whispered. "But it's just between us and the corporal. If one word leaks out we've had it. We could be court-martialed. The passes look good, but they're only valid for a hundred miles from here, and that doesn't mean Boston. But there's not much chance of us getting stopped by MPs."

"When do we bug out?" asked Kenney.

"Tomorrow morning after we get back from the stupid First Aid lecture. Don't forget to bring your dirty laundry so you can get it washed while you're home."

Kenney and Charlie shook hands. "It's a deal." Then Kenney went to tell his two friends Lavoie and LeBlanc. They had been admitted to the small select group of recruits who would gain a brief but illegal respite from I Company that weekend. As he hung up his uniform in his wall locker, Charlie turned to me. "Tough week?" There was a glint in his eyes.

"You bastard. Yuh, it was tough. How was your phony leave?"

"Beautiful. Hey, I'm a born bug-out."

"Well, I'm learning fast. I joined the chapel choir this week. I may never get to sing on Sundays if we get out of here on weekends, but I'll be showing up at practice every Wednesday night."

Charlie pointed to himself. "You're looking at another new choir member. Hey, what a time I had. Holy shit. I slept with her every night. Jee-sus! It was really something."

"I thought you told me you and your girl were saving yourselves for marriage."

"We don't go all the way. It's killing me, but we're still holding out till we get hitched."

"You're pressing your luck. How much will power do you think you have?"

He laughed. "We don't need any. We play a little game that helps us out. Mutual masturbation."

We both laughed and a couple of nearby sleepy recruits groaned. I told him, "You really sucked me in on that one. When will I learn to stop playing your straight man? Maybe you could ask Darrow to do the honors."

"Darrow? I just saw him downstairs flexing his muscles and looking at himself in his mirror, the asshole."

After I filled him on on my conflict with Darrow, he said, "You know what? Maybe Darrow has the right idea about trial marriage. Maybe that purity shit's on the way out anyhow."

"Aw, come on, Charlie. I thought you were more civilized."

"Look, if a guy's gonna marry a girl, what's a little piece of ass now and then for a warm-up?"

"Listen, Charlie, if you and Darrow feel like living on the animal level, what the hell do I care? I'm not a damn missionary."

Charlie responded that living on the animal level might not be all that bad, and this led to a philosophical discussion on the relative merits of dodging higher values. Since Charlie had just experienced a high dose of sexuality, and wanted more sexual gratification instead of increased self-restraint, he was on the side of lowering standards, so after a bit of dueling with words and ideas we prepared for bed without really resolving any major issues. I held my ground and he held his.

As Charlie climbed up to his bunk he said, "I feel like I been sliced down the middle by this man's Army. Sliced from the top of my head to my nuts. Coming back here tonight was one of the shittiest moments of my life. Fort Dix and I Company are shit for the birds."

"But we'll bug out again tomorrow. That's a positive thing to look forward to."

"Bet your ass."

"It's a bet."

I closed my eyes and thought, It's hard to believe I'll be seeing Mary again tomorrow. Last weekend seems like a century ago. It's sort of unreal thinking about it. It's like remembering a movie. There I was, looking down at her face while she slept, and she was so pretty. Like an angel. When she felt me next to her in the bed she thought she'd been dreaming. She was so surprised, and it was so good. Like a second honeymoon. No Army. Just us. Together like we're supposed to be.

She didn't quite understand about me bugging out with Charlie and the others. She's afraid I'll get caught. But if I didn't take the risk we wouldn't have been together. I hope it all works out smoothly tomorrow. You can't plan on anything in the Army. My soul may be my own but they've got my body.

Mary couldn't imagine some of the things I told her about this place. I guess you have to go through it to understand it. Like the way she's experiencing pregnancy. All the words in the world couldn't explain what she's going through right now. It's no picnic with all the physical problems she's been having. I wonder how much attention she'll get at that Murphy General Hospital outpatient clinic. Army hospitals aren't famous for their quality. But with no money for private insurance we have no choice. Hey, with a bit of luck everything will work out fine.

Turning from my back to my right side, I thought, I'm so tired right now, but the thought of getting out of here tomorrow has me all wound up. Bugging out of this place on weekends is my major goal now. A few weeks ago I didn't know what the word bug-out meant and now I'm thinking like one.

What other choice do I have? From the Army's perspective I'm just a warm body with a serial number. I'm supposed to keep my thinking at a minimum and just follow orders. But thinking is a habit I'm finding hard to break. Well, up to a point I'll play the Army's game, but when opportunity knocks and opens a door that lets me bug out I'll go through that door. And when I can get away with it, I'll build my own doors for opportunity to knock on. Warm body, huh? Yeah, sure. Well, the Army can think I'm a warm body but I've got some other ideas on that subject. Yup. I've certainly got . . . some . . . other . . . ideas.

The thoughts faded away and deep sleep took over.

# 4

During my second week of basic training my ankles were so painful I could hardly walk. It felt like both of them were sprained. Actually, it turned out that they were over-trained! I went to sick call and received some relief from the stress:

**INDIVIDUAL SICK SLIP, 7 April 54**
**O'Connell, Thomas, US51305178, Pvt 1, Co. I. Line of duty: Yes**

*Remarks:*

*No marching over 4 miles, no double-timing over 100 yards.*

**Letter, April 7, 1954, Wednesday**
**Well, I went on sick call and they taped up my ankles. It seems that I have a couple of stretched or pulled tendons or something . . . . This afternoon was stifling hot down here . . . A couple of days ago it was freezing. We marched a lot through the woods, had a class in compass reading, one in judging distance, then some more marching, then a class in guard duty, then some more marching. Boy, what sweat!**

We learned about the various court martials, including Summary Court, Special Court, and General Court. We learned first aid and how to treat shock, heat cramps, trench foot, frostbite, wounds in stomach or head, fractures like broken necks and broken backs, and we received instruction in the use of various dressings and pressure points.

Around this time my own feet were swelling and the skin was becoming infected, but if I went on sick call about them I might be recycled and have to start basic all over again. So I was keeping the problem to myself, crossing my fingers that my ailing feet wouldn't interfere with my progress in basic.

Part of my progress and Charlie's was volunteering for the church choir. Is there anything we wouldn't have done to get out of duties in our own Company? No. And although we had no intention of being around on Sundays to sing in the choir at services, there was choir practice during the week. "Ave maris stella, Dei mater alma. Atque semper Virgo Felix coeli porta . . . ." My years of Latin at Dedham High and Boston College helped with the pronunciation. Did I feel guilt about this kind of bugging out? No.

We had an abundance of physical exercises to do every day, and we had to take physical fitness tests that challenged my ability to do chin-ups, push-ups, and squat jumps. I had never been much good at physical exercise and so you might be inclined to conclude that I had never admired the physical way of life. If so, what did I admire and respect? The use of the brain.

Charlie, a physical animal, tried so hard to become the outstanding PT contestant that after coming in third he was carted off to the hospital in an ambulance. He had overdone it. He was a great achiever when it came to music and exercise, and I knew he was certain to recover soon from his exhaustion. As a fringe benefit, while he was laid up he bugged out of some grueling 6-mile hikes with full field packs and M-1 rifles weighing us down.

I was seated on a splintery wooden bleacher bench in an open amphitheatre, trying to absorb a lecture on the care and feeding of my M-1 rifle, but my mind was concentrating on the coming weekend. At this point I had spent three weekends in a row with Mary and I was hoping for another. "The M-1 is a gas-operated, air-cooled, clip-fed, semi-automatic rifle."

The pot-bellied training sergeant paced back and forth, addressing his captive audience of tired recruits. "It weighs nine-and-one-half pounds, it's forty-three inches long, and with a bayonet it's fifty-four inches. You men better damn well know this stuff I'm telling you or your asses are gonna be reamed."

Good, I thought. That's exactly what I need right now, a nice thorough ass-reaming. As if just being here isn't ass-reaming enough. That PT test we took just about wiped me out. The sit-ups weren't so bad and the squat jumps I could do, but if our bug-out chauffeur corporal didn't give me a little boost I'd never have made it on the chin-ups. My arms aren't much for lifting my body. Strong mind, weak arms. Not like Charlie. What an athlete! He gets a high score and then he's carted off to the hospital. Was he faking it? I wouldn't put it past him.

Faking it or not, I hope he gets back here pretty soon. Doherty wouldn't even let me go see him in the hospital. Imagine not letting a guy see his buddy. That Doherty's strictly for the birds, the dirty . . .

A body shoved against mine, filling the next space in the bleachers, but I didn't look to my right. The punishment for looking to the right or the left, or closing the eyes for more than a blink, was a hard and very noisy whack on the helmet with a two-by-four. A knee pressed against mine, and from the small size of the leg I knew it was Charlie.

What a relief, I thought. What would I do without him? Now we'll have a good chance of getting away from this trap. This second week of official basic training has just about pushed my head down to my belly button. The captain's too chicken shit for words. Combat Infantrymen types like him really go for this physical stuff. He wasn't kidding when he said if we didn't shape up, our asses would be sucking broken glass.

Actually, right now my ass feels like it's detached from the rest of my body. My head feels that way too. Maybe the damned

Army's separating my component parts. This body of mine is really screwing me up. Even on the weekends with Mary I spend most of my time recuperating from my ailments. As if her pregnancy problems aren't enough for us to cope with. Last week it was my tooth that had to be pulled. What will it be next week? Brother, I wish I could ask Charlie right now what's up for this weekend but my ears are still ringing from the last two-by-four that sadistic Pfc slammed down on my helmet. And all I did was yawn!

Eventually, after the drone of the M-1 lecture and a kindergarten session on First Aid, the troops were marched back to I Company, where we fell out for the noon meal.

"What's the score on the weekend, Charlie?"

"No sweat, pal."

"Tonight or tomorrow morning?"

"You and the other guys will be going tomorrow. I think I might shag ass out of here tonight with the gang from Rhode Island."

"How come?"

"It's a long story."

I chuckled. "A story or a tale?"

He laughed. "A big piece of tail. Hey, did you guys miss me around here while I was taking the rest cure?"

"We always miss your sunny smile, Charlie. How come you knocked yourself out on the PT test?"

"I'm gung-ho all the way."

"Sure you are. You were faking the exhaustion, right?"

Charlie shook his head. "Nope. I broke my ass on that test, for insurance. Know what I mean? Like if they catch me bugging out they'll see something good in my 201 file."

"Good bug-outs don't get caught."

"Sometimes I press my luck."

"I know. Why don't you play it safe tonight and wait till tomorrow morning? They're never strict about security on Saturdays."

"I'm sick of playing it safe."

I shook my head. "I know what you're saying, but after that performance you gave at the Post Theater the other night you've got a crack at Special Services. Why take a chance on screwing it up? There's been talk about a surprise inspection some Friday night when we least expect it. They're getting suspicious about guys like us bugging out on weekends. And a good bug-out watches his odds. Isn't that what you taught me?"

Charlie nodded. "Maybe I'm not a good bug-out. I've got only one thing on my mind. My girl."

"I know." I decided to change the subject. "Tell me about the hospital."

"I suffered." He chuckled. "It was a real bitch flaked out there reading all those Esquire magazines. My eyes are killing me."

"I bet they are," I said as we neared the Battalion Mess Hall. "Have you given any more thought to the Company I Marching Band idea?"

"Oh, I thought I told ya. We got the okay on it." He grinned. "I said I'd get it through, didn't I? I talked to the C.O. about it this morning after I got back from the hospital. We've got it knocked. Me on the sax. LeBlanc on the trumpet. Lavoie on drums. Kenney on the trombone. And last but definitely least when it comes to musical skill, you on the cymbals and triangle. You're our percussionist."

I shrugged. "Last and least? Well, I'll have you know this isn't the first time for me to play a percussion instrument. Hey, I was an overnight sensation with the triangle in the second grade at the Cornelius M. Callahan School in Norwood. Sort of like you at the Post Theater. Maybe someday I'll do a Carnegie Hall performance."

"Did you like my Satchmo Armstrong imitation?"

"You did Blueberry Hill better than Satchmo. You're show biz all the way."

"That's me. So you like the bug-out band idea? It's the bug-out brainstorm of the century. Whenever there's a GI party or a rat race I'll call practice. That rat race we had the other night was our last rat race. What a ball buster."

"Just one more invention of the sadistic military mind. But for every way they think of shafting us we'll think of a way to bug out. It'll be our own law of physics. For every action force from them there'll be an opposite reaction force from us. I even bugged out of part of that rat race the other night.

"Remember when they told us to run in the barracks and put on our full field packs and haul ass right back to the formation? Over and over? Endlessly? Until we would be ready to collapse? The second time I just ran into the latrine and sat on a john for a half hour and had a nice little rest for myself. You didn't even miss me in formation, right?"

Charlie shook his head. "I was so bushed I didn't know what day it was. I guess I was too bushed to bug out." He nudged me with his elbow. "Hey, maybe the pupil's getting better than his teacher. Maybe I'm losing my touch."

"Maybe you are." I laughed. "Seriously, I think you should stay till tomorrow instead of chancing it tonight. I've got a kind of premonition."

Charlie shook his head as we climbed the cement steps leading to the Battalion Mess Hall. "Screw your premonition! I can't stay here. I have to get the hell out because I'm getting a wicked case of lover's nuts. And you know what I'm like when I get lover's nuts. I go ape shit!"

I laughed. "Well, I'm not available! Yikes, my swollen feet are killing me from that speed march." Charlie was moving fast. "Slow down, okay?"

"Okay. Look, I feel for ya. But I've got my own health problems. For example, my eyes are aching from all those Esquire magazines at the hospital." He chuckled as he dunked his canteen cup and utensils into the large barrel of liquid with the layer of scum on top. "Look at this. And they wonder why we all get dysentery?"

I dunked my own eating and drinking equipment. "Maybe Uncle Sam wants us to have the runs instead of constipation. Could a constipated soldier shoot straight?"

Charlie laughed. "There's no such thing as a constipated soldier!"

Inside the Mess Hall, after standing in long lines with our trays and being served cafeteria style, we consumed the rations of canned franks and beans left over from World War II. Each can was dated in the early 1940s. I wondered what miracle of preservation kept them edible for all those years. And the strange thing is that they didn't taste bad at all, compared to my grandmother's cooking.

After chow, we returned to I Company for an afternoon of rifle instruction, dis-assembling, cleaning, and reassembling our M-1s. Before we were released for our evening meal, Sergeant Doherty announced, "In honor of you assholes, we're gonna have another little GI party tonight. The linoleum's been getting a lot of black rubber heel marks on it so we're gonna shape it up."

The dejected recruits walked away, muttering obscenities, but later when it was time to do the chores in the barracks, Charlie pulled on my sleeve. "Watch this."

He went up to Doherty who said, "What's your damn problem, Olivera?"

"Me and O'Connell and three others are going to band practice in the Day Room."

Doherty scowled and his heavy face reddened. "Band practice your ass."

Charlie retorted, "The CO said we could do it, and he asked me to run it. He said we can practice as much as we need to."

"Well, I'll be dipped in shit. I'm gonna go check that out, Private, and while I'm gone you can play a tune on one of them mops." Doherty laughed derisively.

Charlie wielded his mop and I found myself on my knees with a scrubbing brush trying to remove black rubber streaks from the dark green linoleum that dated back to the early 1940s. After a half hour of mopping and scrubbing, with hours more in store for us, Doherty appeared and shouted, "Where the hell is that little Olivera guy?"

"Here, Sergeant! Working my ass off."

"Never mind what your ass is doing. Get the hell over here on the double."

Charlie complied and Doherty said, "The first sergeant says the CO gave you permission to have your marching band, so you and the others can shag your asses to the Day Room and practice till lights out. Oh yuh, when we're marching and you guys are helping with the troops' morale, the other soldiers will carry your rifles."

Charlie and I grinned, but not too broadly. The score for the day: bug-outs seven, Army nothing. Touchdown! And the point after.

A while later we members of the newly formed I Company Marching Band gathered in the Day Room for our "organizational meeting." The so-called Day Room was designed for the recreation and relaxation of tired soldiers, but for recruits being trained it was off-limits. Its television, card table, magazines and Coke machine were reserved for use only by the permanent cadre.

Charlie passed out the battered instruments he had obtained on loan from Special Services. Then he went to the Coke machine and bought us a round. So there we were, the members of the new bug-out marching band. While the troops back in the barracks were exhausting themselves scrubbing and waxing the floors the members of our quintet were enjoying our brief guilt-free escape. To entertain us, Charlie did a perfect imitation of the first sergeant and the platoon sergeant. We gave him a spontaneous ovation.

Then, after a lengthy bull session about basic training in general and the possibility of ending up in Indo-China in particular, we tried to learn the one tune that Charlie believed we could master: When the Saints Come Marching In.

During several practice renditions, I clanged my cymbals with gusto as I enjoyed my role as percussionist in the I Company Marching Band. Part of that enjoyment was the fact that on future long marches I wouldn't even have to carry my own heavy M-1 rifle. I would carry only my two cymbals while rifle bearers carried the weapons of the band members along with their own. The bug-out potential of our band was many faceted.

The time passed rapidly as we alternated band practice with bull sessions, and then it was time to return to the barracks. Before heading for our bunks we discussed the upcoming weekend and we tried to talk Charlie out of leaving that evening. But his repeated reply was, "Forget it, fellas. I'm taking off out of here like a big-assed bird."

"What if they have one of those famous midnight inspections tonight, Charlie?" I asked. "I'm not kidding about having a premonition."

"That's the way the ball bounces."

I said, "And the way the spheroid rebounds."

Kenney said, "Yup, and that's the way the cookie crumbles. If Charlie's got his mind made up, that's it."

Lavoie said, "Charlie, I think you ought to wait and go with us first thing in the morning. Half the camp bugged out over Easter and they're sure as shit gonna do an inspection one of these Friday nights."

Charlie laughed. "They can shove their surprise inspection up their ass. I'm gonna get the hell out of here and hoist my ass into my girl's bed for two nights in a row instead of one." He held out the palm of his left hand and hit it hard with his right fist. "My balls are screeching for love and you think I'm gonna hang around this place? Like hell. Hey, if they have a roll call, yell out my name, okay Tommy?"

"Sure, Charlie, if I can get away with it."

We left the Day Room and went to the barracks, and just as we were about to climb the flight of stairs leading to the second level, a familiar Syracuse voice rang out. "Where the hell were you guys during the GI party?"

"What's it to you?" Charlie challenged the obnoxious little redhead.

"I asked where the hell you was when the rest of us were working like a son of a bitch here in the barracks."

"Why don't you mind your own damn business?" suggested Charlie.

The little redhead's face flamed. "You looking for trouble, you little greaseball?"

Charlie sneered and chuckled. "Watch out, Red, or I'll make mincemeat out of your stupid freckled face."

The redhead charged in at Charlie without another word, but Charlie ducked the redhead's left, let a hard right go to the redhead's gut, and stepped back to view the result. The redhead doubled up and threw his body on the nearest bunk. Charlie had pushed the wind out of him, and his freckled face was now the color of spring grass.

Looking at the redhead, Charlie said, "When I say mind your own business I mean mind your own fucking business, Red." Then he turned his back on the redhead and we went upstairs.

I said, "For a little guy, you pack a helluva wallop."

"It's all in the timing," he said, his charcoal eyes beaming. "Punks like him never bother me. Funny thing about little redheads. They think they're King Shit. They're always looking for trouble. But I've never seen a redhead I couldn't kick the shit out of."

After we had all commented on his prowess with his fists, Kenney, LeBlanc and Lavoie went to their bunks at the other end of the barracks. Then Charlie quickly packed his bags and a few moments later he was tiptoeing out of the barracks to fulfill his sexual destiny in Massachusetts.

I flopped on my bunk, and wondered what the redhead downstairs might do to get revenge on Charlie. I hoped he wouldn't see Charlie sneaking off for the weekend. Then my mind shifted suddenly to the thought of taking a shower, but my eyelids were heavy and I could not picture working up the energy to lift my body from my bunk again. Without even removing my uniform, I fell into a deep sleep.

The voice of Doherty seemed to come at me from out of a distant valley. "Fall out, you guys!" I turned over and kept my eyes closed and hoped I was only having a nightmare. But the voice persisted. "Okay, you assholes, fall out of the damn barracks . . . on the double!"

It was no nightmare. It was the dreaded midnight inspection. As I sat up, I muttered, "Insane. Totally ridiculous."

Doherty kept yelling his message and I felt like telling him what to do with his midnight inspection, but even in my near dream state I knew better. So I fell out as ordered into a very brightly lit Company Area.

The first sergeant announced that we were having "a dog tag inspection" per order of the battalion commander, a major. "I'll call out your name, and when the major and the lieutenant come to you, state your name, rank and serial number."

Uh-oh, I thought. There's no way to cover for Charlie. Not with this kind of inspection. He gambled and lost.

As the first sergeant called out names, the major and the lieutenant marched along the ranks from one man to the next, shining flashlights at dog tags and hearing recitations of names, ranks, and serial numbers. Eventually, the two officers were standing near me.

The name "Olivera, Charles" was called out. But there was no answer, and nobody could conceal the fact that there was an empty spot next to me where Charlie usually stood. The silence was deafening. Then the first sergeant announced, "Olivera, Charles. AWOL."

As I waited for the rest of the inspection I thought, When Charlie arrives home the Military Police will be there to greet him. Too bad. But why would he go home first? Nope. He'll go straight to see his girl friend. Maybe I can get to that phone outside the Post Exchange and call his folks and they can get in touch with him and somehow he can get himself back here without being arrested first. Yes, that's what I'll do. I hope it works.

On a more selfish note, I began to wonder if the inspection might mess up my chances of getting a ride home from the corporal on Saturday. Then I thought about how low my bank account was because of our weekend escapes. But how could I place a monetary value on being with Mary? It was worth every dollar.

I wondered how Mary was doing with the latest in a series of uncomfortable pregnancy symptoms. Now it was severe headaches. Yup, I thought, we're both suffering from our own choices. We chose the pregnancy and we chose the Army, and as Granny would say, now we're paying the piper. But I'll see my honey tomorrow. I know I will.

In a burst of confidence I reminded myself that the corporal was greedy for money. Therefore, early in the morning the gang of us would be on our way to Massachusetts regardless of the midnight inspection. Look, the powers that be had done their inspection. They had discovered that a soldier was missing. They would be happy now. As for bugging out the next day, we would be in the clear. And that would be that.

# 5

It was twilight in the bivouac area and the men of I Company had just been informed by the first sergeant that our promised weekend pass would not be granted. Fourth weekend or not, we would be restricted to the I Company area. In his own inimitable way, our leader had explained the nature of our military errors.

When Charlie and I returned to our pup tent and started digging a drainage trench around our compact living quarters, we were depressed for different but similar reasons.

"I've had it up to my eyeballs," he said. "This place is driving me ape shit."

"A shitting ape would be very happy here," I said as I took a shovel full of mud and slowly let it run off to the side of the narrow "hasty trench" that was supposed to channel water away from our tent. "Charlie, you didn't have time to finish telling me about your court martial. What did they hit you with?"

"Fifty-buck fine, seven day restriction, and extra duty every night when we get back to I Company."

"It could be a lot worse. Anyhow, the rest of us will be here this weekend to keep you company."

"But you won't be having your ass reamed."

"Who knows what our esteemed leader has in mind?"

Charlie was engrossed in his own situation. "You know what, Tom? I've got a good mind to go over the hill."

"Nice way to self-destruct, Charlie. You want a double shafting?"

"That's exactly what I don't need." He paused. "Guess what?"

"What, Charlie?"

"The corporal paid my fine."

"How come?"

"Well, he probably wanted to reward me for not blabbing about the pass racket."

"If you spilled the beans about the ride and the weekend pass racket do you think somebody might end up in Leavenworth?"

"Bet your ass. But what frosts my ass is I'll have a fat chance of getting into Special Services now. Not with a court martial on my record."

"Don't sweat it. They say summary court martials are no big deal. That's hardly even a real court martial. It's the specials and general courts that shaft a guy. Come on, let's get out of the rain and into our home sweet home." I motioned toward our pup tent.

We squirmed into the small tent and tried to make ourselves comfortable. Then I handed him a piece of chocolate. "Have some."

"Where did you get it?"

"The cadre had a little charity food sale. Nickel candy bars for a dollar. Sub sandwiches for five bucks. Small Cokes for two bucks. They're real opportunists, these guys. They make it on us for our weekend rides home and they make it with their little food sales. Hey, a few bucks to pay out for favors makes a big difference around here."

Charlie replied, "A guy can buy anything he wants in the damn Army or anywhere else if he's got the scratch."

"Having no scratch is the story of my life." I squirmed into my sleeping bag and tried to find a comfortable position. Charlie did likewise.

"Hey, I almost forgot something," he said. "I haven't had a chance to thank you for saving my ass. If you didn't call my folks I would have been out like Strout. They'd have put me in the stockade."

"I owed you a favor like that."

"I thought you were the guy who said nobody owed anybody anything in this world."

"I exaggerate sometimes. All my remarks about life in this world are relative, Charlie, and subject to revision."

"I'll tell you one thing that's relative. This half-assed Army is relatively shitty!"

I laughed and then coughed. "You still have your sense of humor anyhow." I coughed again. "Damn throat. It's getting sore as hell. But as Bob and Ray used to say on the radio, 'It only hurts when I laugh.'"

"Go out in the rain and cough. You're prob'ly catching." He chuckled.

"Thanksalot, buddy."

"Anytime, pal." He shook his head. "You know, after seven days restriction, I'm gonna be a candidate for the birdcage."

"And if I don't find a way to bug out of here this weekend I'll be right there in the cage with you. Do you realize we haven't spent a weekend at Fort Dix since that first one when we came here to I Company? It's been a good deal getting those passes."

"Hang onto your pass if you still have it. It's your only proof there's a pass racket going on here. Guess what? I found out the corporal never signed us out and in like he said he did. That was nothing but a snow job. They took us off the duty rosters but our names never got into the sign-out book."

"Which means we've been AWOL every weekend?"

"You might say that."

I shrugged. "It's been worth it, Charlie. And we'll be getting legitimate passes soon; then we won't have to worry."

"Wrong, Tom. If you get put on weekend KP you'll still want the pass racket to get you off the duty roster and drive you home."

"You're right." I moved to a sitting position and fished into my field pack for a small bottle, which I opened. Charlie asked me what I was doing, and I said, "Picking lint out of my navel."

"Come on, what the hell's in the bottle?"

"Terpin hydrate for my sore throat. There's codeine in it. Good. It's got a real kick to it."

"You're probably getting addicted."

"Hey, I need this! Look, I'm not in what you'd call great shape. Sore throat. Pulled tendons in my ankles. Feet getting badly infected from all the marching in wool socks. They feel like sandpaper. I used to wear only white cotton socks after getting a bad skin condition on my feet in high school. Now it's practically crippling me. But I'm not going on sick call about it, Charlie. I can't stand the idea of being recycled. I need to stay with the outfit and out of the hospital."

"It's a great life if you don't weaken, pal."

"Yup. If it isn't physical harassment it's emotional or spiritual. Like that sadistic corporal at the gas chamber telling us to take off all our rings. So I covered my wedding band with a Band-Aid and told the jerk I had a sore finger. I promised Mary I'd never take it off intentionally." I slipped back into my sleeping bag.

"Christ, it's only a hunk of metal."

"It's more than it appears to be, Charlie. It's a symbol of our togetherness."

"Know what a good symbol for the Army would be?"

"What?" I was his perfect straight man.

"A piece of shit."

We both laughed. "I won't argue that point, Charlie. Oops, I almost forgot to do my daily letter."

"Skip a day. She won't divorce you."

"Nope. I have to write. It's a must." I sat up with my head touching the sloped canvas of the pup tent, took out my penlight and my writing pad, and began to write. When I was done I said, "Goodnight, Charlie," and an almost inaudible grunt told me my friend was nearly asleep. Then I scrunched down into my sleeping bag to face the impossible challenge of finding a comfortable position on the cold damp ground.

My body was exhausted but my mind would not let me sleep, and I thought, A bed of nails would be better than this. At least there would be a point to the bed of nails. Mind over matter. But there's no point to anything in the Army. I don't think I've ever experienced anything that got on my nerves as much as this kind of life. And to think that I volunteered for it! I have to bug out of here this weekend, but I wonder how I can carry it off. There has to be an angle. I'll pray about it. Why not? Maybe I can get inspired.

I gave myself the Sign of the Cross and prayed for some bug-out inspiration, and no sooner had I said my prayer than my mind began to fill with memories of Charlie's phony emergency leave due to the fictitious fire. Hey, maybe I can use Mary's pregnancy problems to get me home. Her blood pressure's up and she's getting dizzy spells. The doctors at that Army clinic aren't too concerned with her condition because they minimize everything. But maybe I can maximize it and make it seem very dramatic. I'll call her as soon as I get back to I Company and I'll ask her to send me a telegram saying she's having a setback and needs me home this weekend. Better still, I'll ask her to word it like it's from her mother. That'll be more effective.

Turning on my back I breathed a sigh of relief as I thought of being with Mary on the weekend. I also fantasized about the 14-day leave I would be having after basic training was over in another month. The thought of 14 days with her was more than I could conjure up. It seemed so long ago when we had shared each successive day with no thought of separation. Finally, with some hope in my heart, I slept.

"No!" I shouted. "I can't let it! They can't do it!" There was a sea of wet leaves all around me, smothering me. They kept coming in waves and they were pressing on my chest so heavily that I could hardly breathe. They were pulling me into their soggy mass.

I threw my arms in front of my face and pushed against their sogginess, but they still kept coming at my face, sticking to me, and they were sealing off my air supply. Soon I could see no leaves at all. I saw only darkness and I could hear my heart pounding hard and fast. "I have to get the hell out of here!" I screamed. "Out! I want out!" I flailed my arms and pushed against the layers of leaves above me, and the barrier finally seemed to be opening. I could breathe a little better now.

"Son of a bitch!" I heard Charlie's voice in the distance but I still could only see darkness. Charlie grunted, "I'll be damned!"

I responded. "Where the hell am I?"

"I'll tell ya where the hell you are, Tommy. You're in the middle of the woods at Fort Dix, standing up with our pup tent draped all over your head, you hot shit."

Raising my hands, I felt the canvas, pushed against it, and finally saw two small hands in front of my face. They were the familiar hands of Charlie Olivera. As he and I lifted the canvas together I could see the dark sky above and the shadowy outline of the trees in the bivouac area. And there was Charlie shaking his head as I removed the remaining canvas from my back and shoved a tent peg and string away from my shoulder.

"Some night, Charlie, right?"

"What's going on? You losing your marbles or something?"

"Guess I had a little nightmare. Sorry."

Charlie started talking to the trees. "He says he's sorry, the hot shit. He rips the stupid tent right out of the ground and he stands there with it over his head like the Count of Monte Cristo and he's sorry. Jesus! I would pick a nut cake for my buddy."

Another voice entered our environment. "What's going on here, soldiers?" It was the recruit on guard duty.

Charlie replied, "Nobody here but us chickens, pal. Seriously, sometimes I like to get up in the middle of the night and get out in the rain and tear my tent down and then put it up again, ya know? Just for the fun of it." He let out a loud laugh.

"Okay, wise guy, what's going on?"

Charlie said, "I bunk with a sleepwalker. O'Connell just tried to walk off with the whole tent on his back."

The recruit said, "I didn't think they took sleepwalkers in the Army."

"They took this one." Charlie pointed at me. I said nothing. I was about halfway between sleep and full consciousness. Very groggy.

The guard said, "Better get your tent up again fast. It's gonna rain even harder."

"Good," said Charlie. "Looking forward to it. Thanks for stopping by to say hello and give us the weather report."

The guard did an about-face and said, "I got no time for wise guys." He started beating his way through the brush on his way to his post.

Charlie muttered, "I got no time for assholes like you either."

The guard stopped. "What the fuck did you say?"

"I told my friend here there's no times like old times."

"Oh." The recruit went about his business.

Charlie turned to me. "I didn't know bunking with you in the field was gonna be such an excruciating experience."

"Didn't I tell you about my sleepwalking?"

"Yuh, but I never thought you'd rip our tent right out of the ground."

"Just a little nightmare, Charlie, that's all."

We put the tent back in place just in time for the next heavy downpour to drop on us from the saturated skies above. So we slipped into our sleeping bags, and without hesitation, regardless of discomfort, we slept.

The next day, back in I Company, the predominant thought in my mind was the possibility of bugging out of Fort Dix over the weekend, but I couldn't reach a phone to call Mary and implement my plan. We were restricted to the Company Area.

When evening came, in a burst of daring I decided to ignore the restriction and slipped quietly away to use the pay phone at the Post Exchange. I knew I was risking Company Punishment but I felt it was worth the risk. When I got Mary on the phone my very hoarse voice gave her detailed instructions on how to send the emergency telegram to the Commanding Officer.

Back at the barracks, Charlie asked, "Where the hell were you?"

"Why do you ask?" I chuckled. "Was President Eisenhower looking for me?"

"Nope, but Sergeant Doherty was wondering where the hell you were."

"What did you tell him?"

"I told him you were in the latrine taking a long shit."

"Well, that's where I was." I lied to maintain my privacy in a place where privacy was a rare commodity, and I also wanted to avoid jinxing my bug-out scheme by spreading the word before the event came to pass. If there was one thing in life I had already learned it was that it was unwise to share future plans with most people because of their tendency to feed doubtful remarks back to you such as "Oh really?" "What makes you think you can carry that off?" "How are you gonna do that?"

Charlie accepted my lie. "I'd have called band practice, but it doesn't look like we're in for a GI Party tonight, or a rat race."

"Let's just rest then. My throat's all inflamed. My head's aching. I've got shooting pains in my back muscles from carrying the full field pack. And my feet are breaking down into what's beginning to look like trench foot. I'm in great shape."

"Sounds like you're coming down with laryngitis. You better get some rest."

"Yuh, I better." I threw myself onto my bunk and thought about the telegram I had asked Mary to send, and I said a short prayer that my plan would not be aborted. Then my eyes began to close and I was off to dreamland.

On Saturday morning as I tried to focus my sleepy eyes on bits of paper and cigarette butts we were supposed to pick up during police call, my mind was on the telegram. During the morning meal consisting of leathery fried eggs and hard bacon, my mind was on the telegram. At the morning First Aid lecture my mind was on the telegram. While watching the film on Asian guerilla operations, my mind was still on the telegram. But when noontime arrived the telegram had not come, and as I stood in formation, awaiting the order to fall out for chow, I thought, It's my first major solitary bug-out attempt, and where the hell is the telegram? Maybe it won't come until tomorrow and that'll be too late for going home. I should have thought of it earlier. I guess I had the right idea but . . .

"O'Connell, Thomas F." It was the field first sergeant.

"Here, Sergeant." My almost inaudible voice just about made it to where he was standing.

"Report to the Orderly Room, O'Connell."

"Yes, Sergeant."

"The rest of you guys fall out and get ready for chow."

Charlie nudged me. "What's up, pal?"

"Maybe my Congressional Medal of Honor came through."

Charlie laughed. "See you in a while."

"Right. See you later. Much later." My heart was pounding hard and fast as I made my way up the Orderly Room steps. The Company Headquarters which housed that function was a small building, but it had a large and powerful presence. The very mention of the Orderly Room struck fear into the hearts of recruits.

As I knocked on the door in the prescribed manner, I thought, I won't have to pretend I'm nervous because I'm terrified that I won't get out of here this weekend. I'm really shook up.

The first sergeant shouted me into his office and as I stood at attention before his large oak desk he shifted his ponderous girth, shoved the telegram at me, and asked, "What's this, Private?"

I was tempted to say it was obviously a telegram, but I contained myself and took the piece of paper and read it slowly. As I read it, my eyes misted over. It was word for word as I had dictated it to Mary, and it was signed by her mother. In reading my own creation I became caught up in the drama and

I was captivated by the urgency of the message. I said hoarsely, "It's . . . uh . . . about my wife, Sergeant. Sounds like she's having trouble. Her mother says I'm needed there and . . ."

"There's no passes this weekend, Private." My heart leaped. "But you can take this up with the CO and see what he thinks."

"Thank you, Sergeant." As I threw myself into the mood of the moment my hand trembled and the telegram rattled.

The first sergeant instructed me to knock on the CO's door. "Tell him you got permission from the first sergeant to speak to the company commander."

I nodded, knocked, entered, and followed the ritual demanded of recruits reporting to our supreme leader, the captain. He was seated behind his mahogany desk, lean and muscular, like the image on an Officers Candidate School recruiting poster. He acted as if he didn't know me, and perhaps he didn't even though he must have been in on his corporal's illegal weekend excursion racket. But regardless of what he knew or didn't know, he was playing his role of Commanding Officer and I was playing the nervous private requesting permission to go home for the rest of the weekend.

"What can I do for you, Private?"

I pushed the telegram toward him with a trembling hand. "Uh . . . It's my wife, sir. This telegram's from her mother. My wife's expecting, sir, and she's having trouble."

He examined the telegram, handed it back to me, rose, and left the room. I could hear him talking with the first sergeant. When he returned he asked, "Do you want to go home this weekend to see your wife, Private?"

"Yes, sir, I do, if it's at all possible."

"Well, the first sergeant says you're a good soldier and you've stayed out of trouble so far, but you know we aren't giving out passes to anybody this weekend."

"Yes, sir, but . . ."

"But you think I should make an exception?"

"Yes, sir." My heart skipped about three beats.

He surprised me with a smile. "I'll make an exception then. You'll be authorized to go on pass and you'll have your ass back here tomorrow night by midnight."

A faint smile came to my lips. I knew a broad smile would contradict the urgent tone of the telegram. "Thank you, sir," I said hoarsely.

"You're welcome, Private. I hope your wife feels better soon."

"I hope so, sir. Thank you, sir."

"And take care of that throat. Sounds like strep."

"Yes, sir."

The first sergeant gave me my pass, and I went to the barracks with an uncharacteristic bounce in my step. I felt like leaping in the air and clicking my heels together as Gene Kelly used to do in movies. My ailments, including my dangerously infected feet and throat, were in the background now. Being secure in my escape plan made all the difference.

"Time for chow," said Charlie back in the barracks.

"To hell with chow. I'm bugging out of here until tomorrow night at midnight. I got myself a pass from the CO."

"You're shitting me, Tommy. Nobody, but nobody, is getting out of here this weekend."

"Nobody except yours truly." I grinned.

"How'd you swing it?"

"I'll tell you sometime."

"You bastard, it looks like you're out-bugging the master."

"I'm still just an apprentice, Charlie."

"How'd you do it, Tommy? Come on, tell me."

"It's all in the timing. Ha!"

"That's what she said."

"When?" I enjoyed playing his straight man.

"When the bed broke and the spring went up her ass."

"Don't make me laugh, Charlie. It hurts my throat and my chest." We both laughed as I packed my small bag and got into my dress uniform. A few moments later I shook Charlie's hand and was on my way to the outskirts of Fort Dix. My wallet was nearly empty, so I was going to hitchhike. As I stuck my thumb out at the first passing car, I had a sore throat, congested chest, aching ankles, and very infected feet, but I had a broad smile on my face and a sense of freedom in my spirit. In my personal bug-out game of O'Connell vs. Army I had scored a home run.

# 6

The Dermatology Clinic was a barren place. Plain cream-colored walls. Oak waiting benches. No framed paintings. No decorative drapes. No decor! I was sitting there waiting, with my arms folded across my chest, gazing at the cream-colored walls, and wondering where my diseased feet would lead me in the medical context of events.

I had glanced at a magazine for a few minutes, reviewing the international scene. Early in May the French had suffered a major defeat in Indo-China. Now it looked as if they would be pulling out of that conflict soon. Some of the career soldiers at Fort Dix said we were financing the French military operation, so they wouldn't be surprised if our own government got us more heavily involved there. But it was all speculation. Nobody knew for sure. And it was enough of a challenge for me to get through each day in basic, never mind figure out the international intrigue.

In an amazing streak of luck, with illegal passes, legal passes, and persistence, I had managed to get home every weekend since early in basic training, and I didn't want any hospitalization to change that trend. So I wasn't trying to be a hero who would ignore his physical problems in order to be patriotic. Nor was I trying to keep my body in good shape so I could prepare for a tour in Southeast Asia. I just wanted to finish basic and get it over with, without complications. That's all.

On the previous weekend at home in Franklin, Massachusetts with Mary, much of my time had been spent lying flat on my back ministering to my ailing feet. Recalling what the doctor had advised during my high school bout with the same condition, I had doused them with Absorbine Jr., a solution high in alcohol content and very painful when applied. "Very" was not the right word about the pain. "Excruciatingly painful" would be more accurate.

However, despite all the pain, the Absorbine treatment hadn't seemed to help so we had tried an alternate mixture of iodine and water. The iodine pain made the Absorbine pain seem trivial! On application my legs would stiffen and my whole body would go into spasms. But I told myself that at least I had been attacking the infected area, and that should make a difference.

I knew my feet needed more expert attention than they were getting, but I was very strong in my own logic in those days. Hey, wasn't I the one who had gotten a grade of 100 percent in the Logic final exam at Boston College? Didn't I know how to figure stuff out? Yeah, sure.

When Charlie pressured me to go on Sick Call because of the horrifying condition of my feet, which now appeared to be an advanced case of trench foot, he was sure I'd get a medical discharge, but my own logic didn't fit with that approach. I still intended to finish my two years in the Army, no matter how much I disliked it, because I planned to use the GI Bill to complete my senior year at Boston College. My logical brain insisted that nothing should get in the way of that logical plan.

Also, we were still in some critical training weeks, and a soldier who missed too many sessions would be recycled into another outfit to start basic training over from scratch. At Fort Dix that was considered to be a fate almost worse than death. Actually, a soldier in a nearby outfit had chosen suicide as his own way of avoiding that fate.

So I did my best to hold off on Sick Call and served as my own doctor. I had tolerated the pain and throbbing during the infiltration course as we had slid on our backs in the mud under barbed wire with rifles held flat on our chests as live machine guns showered bullets about a foot over our heads and little bombs exploded nearby and showered us with mud that landed on our faces and in our eyes.

I had also put up with the pain when they tested our skills with the M-1 rifle and the carbine. The M-1 had a powerful kick and I wasn't very accurate with it, but I won "expert" status with the carbine and later was awarded a medal to wear on my dress uniform. I have to admit I enjoyed winning the medal.

I was becoming more and more adept at bugging, but I still had a large amount of patriotism in me. I could get very sentimental about my country then, and I still can. After all, my studies in U.S. history at Boston College had often brought tears of gratitude to my eyes while reviewing the sacrifices that were made to preserve our freedom.

Actually, tears have always entered my eyes during the Star Spangled Banner and God Bless America. Hey, even though my feet and every other part of my body pained me, I even got sentimental during our marches when I clanged the cymbals to the rhythm of When The Saints Come Marching In.

However, neither my feelings of basic patriotism nor a high level of willpower could erase my adverse reaction to arbitrary authority or the diseased reality of my ailing feet. I knew I had reached my limit during one of our grueling overnighters in the field. We had acted out simulated night war games, and in the chaos of pretending to be in actual combat with opposing forces we had no idea who we were shooting at.

That stress plus the hiking and drilling in the cold and dampness had tortured my feet incessantly. My infected toes were bleeding, weeping, swollen, and stuck together. The wool socks felt like a coarse abrasive as they fused with the raw flesh inside my combat boots. Due to the swelling, I could hardly pull the boots on or off anymore, nor could I get the socks off without causing more damage to my open wounds. No matter how gently

I tried to take them off, the socks would remove chunks of raw oozing flesh.

There was a good side to all of this though. Now, with most of the important training and testing done, I was qualified for combat, so it was safe to show my feet to the first sergeant because I wouldn't get recycled.

We were out in the field on bivouac when I decided to make my announcement to him. Surprisingly, instead of his usual detachment from the pain of his trainees, our leader had a shocked look when he saw my condition. "I haven't seen nothing like your feet since combat, soldier. We've gotta get you to the medics."

I had been transported back to I Company in a specially allocated truck; then I was taken to the Dispensary. Instead of a doctor, I saw a "medic" who took a quick look. Then he got the doctor to sign a slip for me. "Try this ointment, soldier. If you don't have any luck with it we'll send you to the Dermatology Clinic." I was appalled that they took my condition so lightly, but this was an Army Dispensary, not a private medical facility.

**Individual Sick Slip 13 May 54**
**O'Connell, Thomas F Co. I**

*No marching over one mile for three days.*

**Letter, Thursday May 13 1954**
**(Written from tent late at night with flashlight.)**
*I wish I could write more but conditions don't permit. I'm back on bivouac again after going on sick call for my tootsies. I got some ointment from the doctor, and I'm going to try to stick it out . . . As long as I can walk, I will try it . . .*

I was trying to make light of my situation so Mary wouldn't worry too much about it. But I was concerned about complications and my imagination conjured up a picture of me returning to civilian life with no feet.

The ointment didn't help because it wouldn't even adhere to the oozing wounded flesh, and even a casual glance at the actual condition of my feet gave me goose bumps. If there was one thing I was sure of, this was no case of athlete's foot. But what could I do? Appeal to a higher medical authority?

Besides, I was hemmed in by my own determination to allow nothing to stop me from finishing basic. I would just have to live with the wounded feet. And my buck slip provided three days respite. So I hung around the barracks doing odd jobs and stayed off my feet as long as possible while the other troops were out in the boondocks being harassed to the limits of their endurance.

When the three days were up though, my feet were still raw and swollen, so I decided to go on Sick Call. I was hoping for an extension of the buck slip so I could rest my feet and continue bugging out.

I soon found myself at the Dermatology Clinic in the next phase of treatment. I sat there ruminating about the situation, and wondering if I might still be on a futile pursuit for relief. Although I could hardly walk, I had been allowed to avoid only the long marches. They could still make me march a mile with a full field pack!

After a long wait, I heard the doctor call my name. "Come in, Private O'Connell."

"Yes, sir." As I went into the major's office I slowed my pace to a crawl, went into a foot-dragging shuffle, and gave him a quick salute which he didn't return.

"What's your trouble, Private?" asked the white mustached physician.

"My feet, sir. I've been treating them myself so they're in a little better shape than before, but they're still swollen and the Dispensary medic said I should come here for a check-up." I was still trying to minimize the seriousness of the condition.

"Let's have a look." He curled his mustache as I slowly removed my combat boots and socks. He examined my feet. "Have you had prior foot trouble of this kind?"

"Yes, in high school I was laid up with it for several weeks one summer."

"I see." He nodded. "You've probably contracted now what you had then. A case of contact dermatitis."

"Contact dermatitis?"

"A severe case of athlete's foot. What have you been doing for it?"

"Dousing it with a mixture of iodine and water."

"You've probably worsened it with that stuff. Didn't they give you our ointment at the Dispensary?"

"Yes, sir, but it just ran off the fleshy spots."

"I see." The major nodded. "When you leave here go down the hall to room number three and they'll peel off the dead skin and give you a mild solution to apply. I'll give you a three-day light duty slip. The swelling should go down soon." He began to scribble on the slip before him. "Also, I think we'll have you wear your low quarter shoes for a while." He handed the slip to me.

I thanked him and he scheduled another appointment for Friday. When I rose I had an impulse to leave without saluting. After all, he hadn't returned my salute before. I guess I was testing the system. But the major noticed.

"Did you forget something, Private?"

"Do you have some more medicine for me, sir?" With a burst of inner confidence that had been generated by many successful bug-out attempts, I started playing my own little game with him.

"No, Private, I don't have more medicine for you. By the way, don't you salute an officer when you're leaving his presence?"

"I didn't think you cared, sir. You didn't return the salute I gave on my way in."

He got a little flustered. "Are you trying to put me on, Private?"

"Why would I do that, sir? What would be the point of it? You didn't return my salute, and that's all there is to it. If you want me to salute you now, fine. I'll do it."

"I want a proper salute from you, Private. Remember that I'm an Army officer."

"Yes, sir!" I put my hand to my forehead and gave the major a limp salute. "I salute you, sir!" I risked a sarcastic inflection in my voice.

The major shook his head, returned the salute, busied himself with his paper work, and waved me away. As I shuffled out of his office I grinned, which indicated an odd mindset because even though my feet were aching my sense of humor hadn't disappeared. I was amused at the way I had gained a few points from the major in my game of O'Connell vs. Army.

I was still grinning when I shuffled into the room where the medic was waiting to scrape dead skin from my infected toes. The medic was frail and dainty. "Are you the fellow we have to scrape the skin for?"

"Right you are."

"Sit on the table, Private."

"Gladly. I'd sooner sit than stand." I grinned but the medic did not return it. I said, "Funny day. The major didn't return my salute and you didn't return my smile. Oh well, hey, just one of those days I guess."

The serious medic didn't respond. He quietly scraped the dead skin, and produced an unveiling of fresh pink tissue beneath the scrapings. It was a relief to see that some healing was going on despite the awful appearance of the feet I had presented to him.

The medic said, "Now isn't that new skin pretty?" He ran a finger along a toe.

I said, "When you've seen one skin you've seen them all." Then I thought, If I'm too friendly with this bird he'll probably start feeling me up. Maybe that's what he's doing with my toe. It's a good thing I don't have a rash on my ass.

When the medic was done he gave me a bottle of calamine lotion. "You may coat the affected area with this, Private."

"Yup, I'll do that little thing." I figured I could get away with some levity with another enlisted man in a medical setting, so I kept testing my limits.

"What did you say?" The medic looked perplexed.

I repeated what I had said and explained, "It just meant that I'll do what you said. You told me to apply calamine to the affected area, right?"

"Right."

I rose to leave and turned to the medic. "I think I might become an Army doctor after I get through basic training."

"Do you have medical training?"

"You mean you need medical training?" I laughed. "Hell, I could give out APCs and terpin hydrate and calamine lotion without medical training."

"Not according to Army regulations," replied the medic, still very serious.

I nodded. "One mustn't forget Army regulations." The medic looked at me blankly and did not reply. "Well, thanks a lot for the calamine." I chuckled. "How many times a day am I supposed to drink it?"

"It's for external use only," said the medic.

"Okay. I'll keep that in mind. I better get back to serving my country now."

"Yes, I think you better, Private."

I said, "I've appreciated both your hospitality and the calamine." For reasons I couldn't fully understand, I was returning to the lighter hearted person I had been before entering the Army.

The medic said nothing as I walked away, forgetting to shuffle as slowly as I had done on my way in. Outside, I had a slight sense of relief. The feet had begun to look better after the dead skin had been removed, and I was glad about that. Also, I had a new buck slip which I carefully examined.

**Office of the Post Surgeon, Outpatient service**
**Fort Dix, New Jersey**

**21 May 54**
**Subject: Temporary Light Duty for Thomas O'Connell, Pvt.**
**US51305178**
**TO: Commanding Officer, I Company**

*The above named individual is being returned to your unit this date. Recommend EM be excused from the military duties initialed below, from 21 May thru 28 May inclusive.*
*Speed Marches*
*Long Marches (Over 4 miles)*
*Drill and Parades*
*Physical Training*
*Kitchen Details*
*Guard Duty*
*Infiltration Course*
*Bivouac*
*On 28 May 54 he should be directed to report to Dispensary for further examination.*

This is a pretty good buck slip, I thought, but for God's sake, now they're saying they can make me march four miles if they want to. Well, some of the other items are helpful. Actually, I've done everything I've needed to do to qualify for combat, including the infiltration course, so it's okay if I coast a little now. I won't get recycled.

On the way to I Company I took my time because any effort to move fast sent jabs of pain from the sensitive toes into my feet and up my legs. But even if that hadn't happened, I still would have taken my sweet time and chalked up a few bug-out points.

I stopped at the PX for a root beer, and when I got back and showed my buck slip to the first sergeant he said, "You can be the barracks orderly, Private. You know what the barracks orderly does?"

"I think I can handle it, Sergeant." I held back a smile because in basic they would tell you to "get that shit eating grin off your face" if they thought you were taking things too lightly. And they would find something very unpleasant for you to do. Something that would not trigger a smile.

"Then get your ass in there and get the barracks in good shape."

"Yes, Sergeant."

In the barracks, I sat on my bunk for a while, daydreaming about the upcoming fourteen-day leave. Then I heard footsteps downstairs, so I grabbed a dry mop and ran it lightly back and forth across the heavily waxed linoleum floor. I hummed as I mopped. Then the footsteps faded.

Sounds like someone going into the latrine. I wonder if it might be Sergeant Doherty down there, but I know he's out drilling the troops. It must be the latrine orderly tending the pisserie. I'll give him a shout. "Who goes there? Identify yourself or I'll fire."

A deep voice echoed from the latrine. "It's me, for shit's sake. It's Mario."

"Hey, Mario!" I laughed as I descended the stairs with my linty dry mop. "How's everything in the urinals today? A little on the yellow side?"

He met me at the entrance to the latrine. "Whattayasay, O'Connell? What the hell they gotcha doing, huh?"

"Barracks orderly. Shaping up the barracks like an obedient soldier."

"How come you got the barracks detail?" He blinked his dark eyes rapidly.

I pulled out my wallet and showed him my medical slip. "Take a look."

"Hey, you got it knocked up, huh? Christ, I sprain my ankle and they put me in the latrine. How'd you work the deal?"

I told him about my foot condition and the events at the Dermatology Clinic. "The deal is simple. Just keep dragging your ankle around, and make like it's killing you. Fake it if you have to."

"Shit, I don't have to fake it. It's fucking A-one killing me. But those bastards don't give a good shit about my sprained ankle."

"I'm surprised you haven't sprained more than your ankles, Mario. How's your back after all the six-by-sixes you've dug?"

"Shit, I can do them standing on my hands. You think those bastards are gonna break Mario? Not in a pig's ass. Nobody's gonna break Mario."

"Sometimes a guy has to bend a little."

"Bend? What the hell ya mean, bend?"

"I mean if you fight the Army too openly you screw yourself. It's best to bend with the breeze a little. Like a willow tree does."

Mario laughed a yellow-toothed laugh. "I don't bend with no damn breeze. I ain't no willow tree, and Mario don't bend for nobody."

"Then they'll keep trying to break you. Hey, the U.S. Army doesn't appreciate guys who don't fall in line."

"Fuck falling in line." Mario laughed again. "I'm gonna fight 'em all the way."

"It's your ass, Mario. Are you bucking for a discharge? If you get into enough trouble they'll throw you out."

"I'm not bucking for nothing O'Connell. Look, I didn't ask to come in no Army but I can take any horseshit they can dish out, ya know I mean?"

"Yuh, I guess I know ya mean, Mario. I also know that nobody in I Company has had more shit details than you."

"And did the bastards break me?"

"Nope. Not yet."

"They ain't never gonna break me, O'Connell. I'm too tough for these bastards."

"I guess you are, Mario. But I'm surprised you haven't gotten so upset with them that you'd haul off and floor somebody."

"Like your little Portuguese friend did?" He was referring to an outburst that Charlie had when he was under pressure from a chicken shit enlisted man.

"That so-called leadership guy that Charlie hit wasn't that important. What I wonder about is you taking a poke at one of the permanent cadre."

"Sometimes I feel like creaming 'em, but I stop myself, ya know I mean? What did they do to your little pal?"

"He ended up in the neuropsych ward at the hospital instead of the stockade. He said he had amnesia and they believed him."

"What's amanee . . . ama . . ."

"It's when you can't remember your own behavior."

"Like when a guy gets crocked?"

"Sort of, but worse. With amnesia you forget everything. Charlie told them he had no memory of flooring the leadership guy and knocking over wall lockers and some bunk beds and practically ruining the whole upstairs. So they put him in the hospital for observation and decided he was overreacting to stress, that's all. He's back again, acting like a good soldier. Charlie's a great actor."

"Like in Hollywood?"

"Right, Mario. Oops. Do I hear the first sergeant's voice out there? It's back upstairs for me. I've got some dusting and floor mopping to do."

"And I've gotta clean some cruddy latrines."

"This Army's making a good housekeeper out of you, Mario."

"Fuck the Army."

"You have a way with words, Mario," I commented as I went up the stairs.

Then the first sergeant did his inspection while I continued to wield my dry mop with great concentration and dedication. When he had left the barracks and gone back to the Orderly Room, I flopped on my back on my bunk and breathed a sigh. "Too bad I can't be out there with the troops marching my ass off. Yup. Too bad."

I had no guilt. I wasn't committing treason, and I wasn't trying to evade my military obligation. I was only trying to preserve my own integrity as a human being, trying to heal my ailing body, and attempting to be with my bride on as many weekends as possible. So the only emotional burden that came with bugging out was the fear of getting caught, and that sure got the old adrenalin rushing sometimes. But guilt? None. My response to a successful bug-out strategy was pure unadulterated satisfaction. Besides, hadn't the Army messed up my feet? And didn't I deserve a break? Guilt? Nope.

# 7

**Letter, Tuesday May 25, 1954**
**Fort Dix, New Jersey**

*Just 3-1/2 more days and I'll be through here and will spend a week and a half with my loving honey. Then I go to another 8-week grind at MP school. Then I will be stationed some place more or less permanently. Tonight we got paid. I got $29, and due to the fact there used to be a kid named Thomas F. O'Connor here I got gypped out of $5. I was given his pay by mistake but I signed for my own $34. When you sign for something in the Army you might as well forget about it ... the lieutenant said I'd have to wait till tomorrow to see if there is $5. left over-it will be my $5 ...*

The miracle happened. Even in the Army they happen because I got the other $5 owed to me. That same evening we had our last bug-out band practice in the Day Room.

"It's hard to believe this is our last practice," I said as I put down my coke. "Tomorrow we'll be finished with this basic training crap and off to fourteen days of total freedom. I feel like I'm graduating from Purgatory and heading for Heaven."

"Wait till you get to Camp Gordon, Georgia." Charlie laughed. "It won't exactly feel like Heaven in Military Police training, pal."

"Will the MPs be worse than this?"

"I don't like being a pessimist, but it might be more chicken shit. Like the U.S. Marines, for example. Also, it's roasting hot down there, and you won't be able to bug out from Georgia to Boston on weekends like you did here. I think you broke the bug-out record at Dix. You were gone a lot more than I was."

"Well, look who taught me how!"

Kenney said, "Sometimes I think we did more bugging out than training."

Lavoie nodded. "No doubt about it." And Leblanc echoed that sentiment.

I chuckled. "Compared to Mario, we're in a different army."

Charlie laughed. "Compared to Mario, everybody's in a different army. What a sucker for punishment."

I said, "He told me once 'Mario don't bend for nobody.'" We all laughed.

Lavoie said, "He'll end up in the stockade one of these days."

Kenney said, "And he'll probably get a dishonorable."

"I don't know about that," I said. "He seems to draw the line just short of punching the permanent cadre in the mouth."

Charlie laughed. "Yuh, but he may take a poke at a leadership trainee like I did. Basically, I think Mario just likes to shaft himself. If he had a brain he'd be a bug-out instead of getting punished every day in every way."

I said, "I think he's proving something to himself."

"Like what?"

"He's proving that Mario don't bend!" I winked at Charlie.

He said, "What the hell, he's built for punishment."

Kenney said, "Do you guys remember the day they had him running bare-ass around the Company area and everyone was yelling that he was hung like a buffalo?"

Charlie grinned. "I wish I could have seen it but I had this wicked fire at home to take care of, you know what I mean?" He winked. "Speaking of fires, I get a big fire in my pecker every time I think about having fourteen days and nights in the slot, man!"

I shook my head. "And you're the guy who said he was saving himself for marriage?"

"I substituted something else for that philosophy."

"Like what?"

"Like getting laid. To hell with chastity, Tommy. It's no damn fun, and it's going out of style anyhow." The others laughed. "Hey, me and my gal will get married some day, so what's the big sweat about some ass in advance?"

I shrugged. "To each his own philosophy, Charlie." My intention was not to debate with him about sexual ethics. Not after my experience with Darrow and the threatened violence that came my way. To each his own. That was my angle now.

"Isn't sex what it's all about?" he continued.

"Do you mean life equals sex?" I retorted, not being able to restrain myself. "If that's the case, we sure waste a lot of time on other activities."

"Not me." Charlie laughed. "From now on it's one steady piece of ass for me and no other activities."

Lavoie said, "Some day Charlie's gonna get so skinny he'll disappear right up the crack." Everyone laughed.

I added my own comment. "Or maybe he'll be like the Frenchman on his honeymoon. Every morning after hours of sex he went over to the window and raised the shade, and he got weaker and skinnier, and one morning he went over and pulled on it and went up with it! He got rolled up in the shade and they never found him."

Charlie said, "Never mind going up with a shade; I'm gonna die with my boots on. Speaking of boots, Tommy, when they get you in Georgia that temporary buck slip won't help much. They'll probably put you in combat boots again. The MPs are big on shiny boots. They don't wear low quarter shoes."

"No skin off my feet, right? Well, all good things have to end, don't they?"

"I still think you could have gotten a medical discharge if you went in for treatment when they were at their worst," said Charlie. "You'd be out of this man's Army now."

"Or I'd have been recycled. Look, if I got discharged that early in the game I wouldn't have been eligible for the GI Bill, and that's important to me. Uncle Sam's gonna help me get that last year at B.C. under my belt. Speaking of belts, I had to take another notch in mine. This Army food goes in one end and runs right out the other. But why complain? I get out in the fresh air and I'm learning a trade. Except for my foot trouble and strep throats and damaged ankle tendons and chest pains, basic's been no big deal."

Kenney said, "You're not exactly the rugged type. Lucky you didn't end up with pneumonia like half of C barracks did. The poor bastards were moved over to A barracks and they're starting basic from scratch. Isn't that why the recruit up the street hung himself? To avoid getting recycled?"

For a while we speculated on how much abuse it would take to get a person to commit suicide. Then, to change the subject, I went back to the situation in C barracks where so many did get recycled. "Hey, look at it this way," I said, "they'll get to eat all the more creamed chipped beef on toast."

Charlie said, "SOS? Shit on a shingle? Excuse me while I go outside and vomit. I'm so sick of that crap and those World War II rations I could shit."

Kenney said, "You mean you haven't shit lately? I thought everybody in I Company had the shits."

The conversation centered on the lower portions of the anatomy for a while and then Charlie talked about his mother's Portuguese cooking, the others boasted about the good cooking in their homes, and I commented on my wife's cooking which I had only experienced for a few months. "She's pretty good at it, but when I lived with Granny O'Connell in high school and college she just figured food was something you had to put in your stomach for survival. Granny would hand me a cereal bowl filled with canned string beans and she'd say, 'Fill up on the beans, Tommy.' But I was lucky to get them. She didn't charge me board and I had a roof over my head and something to eat, so I couldn't complain."

"No wonder you don't mind Army food."

"It's a balanced diet, isn't it?" I winked. "You can't win though. I used to be constipated all the time. Now it's the opposite."

"I think they put Ex-lax in the chocolate pudding," said LeBlanc.

"No shit!" said Charlie, laughing.

"Plenty of shit," said Lavoie.

The conversation of the members of the I Company Marching Band descended to the topic of excrement for a while. Then it moved to Senator Joseph McCarthy's Army hearings which had become daily television fare for the cadre and people like us who had access to the Day Room when we went there for band practice. We discussed how our bug-out weekend fares had subsidized the corporal's purchase of a new Buick. And we speculated on our Army futures, including the possibility of ending up in Indo-China.

"You'll end up in Special Services sooner or later," I said to Charlie.

"Bet your ass I will," he said. "When I'm not bugging out I'm a good soldier, right? Hey, I'm gung ho all the way. I even made marksman on the M-one. This soldiering shit's a breeze."

I said, "I won an expert medal for the carbine, but I don't have to consider myself a good foot soldier, do I?"

Charlie chuckled. "Maybe you won't be a foot soldier, but you're sure as hell gonna be a spit and polish MP, pal! You think your feet are sore now? Wait and see."

"Don't remind me. But at least it's not the Infantry."

"Nope." Charlie laughed. "It's worse than the fucking Infantry."

I said, "Hey guys, did you notice how Charlie's one-word vocabulary has returned? Whatever happened to our cursing and swearing boycott?" We had made a deal a few weeks earlier to curtail the vulgarity which had rubbed off on us from the cadre's foul mouths. It had been a kind of emotional outlet for us, but it reached a point where we were overdoing it. So in recent weeks we had been consistently avoiding the word "fuck."

Charlie laughed hard. "Fuck the cursing and swearing boycott!"

"The Jesuits at B.C. taught us that swearing was the sign of a lazy mind," I said.

"Fuck the Jesuits," said Charlie. "And so what if I've got a lazy mind?"

We all laughed this time, and Lavoie said, "You better fucking A-one knock off that swearing, Charlie."

I mused, "I remember the first time I heard one of the cadre call someone a mother-fucker I almost had a shit hemorrhage from the shock. Now the vulgarity pretty much goes in one ear and out the other. It's amazing what a human being can get used to, isn't it? Like bugging out, for instance. It's become a way of life with me lately. I'm getting so I even bug out of things that don't bother me, just for drill. But sometimes bugging out is harder than doing what you were told to do in the first place!" I chuckled.

"Once a bug-out, always a bug-out," said Charlie. "Don't forget our motto, Tommy. When in doubt, bug out."

I responded, "Remember The Lost Generation? Are we The Bug-out Generation?"

"Let's hear it for The Bug-out Generation!" shouted Kenney. "Three cheers for bugging out! Hip! Hip! Hooray!" All the members of the bug-out band joined in and the word 'Hooray' became a rousing cheer.

I grinned. "It's only right that on our last night at I Company, we're bugging out of a GI party. But I feel sort of bad for those guys back at the barracks down on their knees scrubbing floors. No fun. But I don't feel bad that we're here taking it easy."

"What a prick that Doherty is," said Kenney. "Imagine giving the troops a send-off like that on the last night of basic."

Charlie said, "Yup, Doherty's a real pecker head. I'm gonna miss him something awful, and Jesus Kee-rist am I gonna miss our fearless leader. 'The men that fucks up we're gonna fuck them up!'" We laughed at his perfect imitation of the first sergeant.

"The men that's gonna watch TV in the Day Room, fall out!" Charlie paused. "Wouldn't it have been something else if he said 'The men in the I Company band, fall out and go shoot the shit with each other while everyone else is working their ass off in the barracks! Atten-hut! Fall out!'" We laughed.

Then it was time for us to practice a little music. On the next morning during formation, by request of the first sergeant, we were going to give one last rendition of our one and only piece of music that actually sounded good: When the Saints Come Marching In. So we decided to practice it one more time under the direction of our maestro Charles Olivera, and we gave a passable rendition of it before he said, "Enough practicing for tonight. We sound like the cat's ass!"

I put away my cymbals, the others put away their instruments, and we sat and sipped cokes and exchanged commentaries on our days in basic training together. We speculated on our futures in the Army, and we dreamed out loud about our upcoming fourteen days of leave before going on with another eight weeks of advanced training. We displayed one basic attitude. Optimism.

Despite our dislike of much of what the Army stood for and its dehumanizing ways of getting group uniformity, we believed the worst was behind us and things would be better for us in the days and months ahead. Sharing a bond of connectedness that comes with difficult group experiences, we knew we would miss each other as we went our separate ways, and we were grateful that we had found such compatibility during our weeks together.

As I faced my last day of basic training my feet were on the mend, my body was in pretty good shape, and my mind was fairly well balanced. I was confident that I could handle whatever challenges Army life would present to me in the months ahead.

# PART II

**(June to July 1954)**

# 8

My confidence continued during the 14-day leave with Mary at the Killorens' house in Franklin, Massachusetts. Since my feet had healed considerably, I was able to immerse myself in civilian life and marital togetherness. You might say that in the civilian world during my leave with Mary, I was making up for lost time and actually living in the moment. That was a healthy thing for me.

After all, the bad dream of basic training at Fort Dix was behind me now, and I was temporarily free. Also, despite being an anxious person I was certainly not a confirmed pessimist. So I used my imagination to conjure up pictures of a better Army life as a military policeman. The horror of being an infantryman slogging through mud with a heavy M-1 rifle and infected feet was replaced by the image of me in a role of authority, with my MP armband and a .45 on my hip.

It seemed to me that I would be in a position of respect during the balance of my military sojourn, and life would be easier now that basic was over. But I had no way of knowing that my ideas of the future were straight from the world of fantasy. As I floated around on my dream cloud during that 14 days at home in early summer the images I created had no resemblance to the conditions that I was soon to face down South.

**Letter, early June 1954**
**(on train to Georgia)**
*We just passed through Perryville. I think it's in Maryland.*
*Then we crossed over what the boys think was Chesapeake*
*Bay . . . We just passed through Aberdeen, Maryland . . .*
*You're so much a part of me, honey, I can hardly believe that*
*you are not with me now . . .*

*Company B*
*1st Military Police Training Regiment*
*8801-6 Technical Service Unit*
*Camp Gordon, Georgia*

**ITEMS ISSUED:**
**Jacket, Field, M-1943, Men's**
**Poncho, or Raincoat**
**Overcoat, Wool, OD**
**Bag, Barrack**
**Bag, Sleeping, Wool**
**Belt, Cartridge, Cal, .30**
**Brassard, Arm**
**Can, Meat**
**Canteen**
**Case, Water Repellent, Bag, Sleeping**
**Cover, Canteen**
**Cup**
**Fork**
**Helmet, Steel, M-1**
**Liner, Helmet, M-1 etc.**

On and on went the list of all my earthly military needs. Field pack. Tent shelter half. Tent poles. First-aid packet. Intrenching shovel. M-1 rifle. Bayonet. Blanket. Pillow. Pillow case. Cotton mattress. Cotton sheet.

At the bottom of the sheet: *I assume responsibility for all items issued to me on the date indicated. O'Connell, Thomas F., Jr. 11 June 1954*

To me, this was a very disillusioning batch of supplies. Intrenching tool. To dig foxholes with? Shelter half. To sleep out in the field? Poncho. Helmet. Bayonet. These were exactly like the Infantry basic training supplies. And if they were issued to us here in MP training, we were bound to use them sooner or later. Shit!

It was not just the new supplies that ran counter to my previous fantasies of pleasantly respectable Military Police life. Within hours of arriving at Company B my pipedreams had been rapidly erased by the hot, humid, exhausting reality of the environment.

I've always been unusually sensitive to heat, possibly because in early childhood I experienced a collapsed lung and almost died. Expert medical care brought me back to life, but I believe the body never forgets traumatic events. And throughout my life, extreme heat has been one of my enemies. My lungs are not tropical lungs. I think I was given a Temperate Zone body, and the tropical June heat at Camp Gordon was oppressive. The temperature relentlessly remained around 100 degrees, with extremely high levels of humidity.

During the first few days of Military Police training, my chest heaved in search of suitable air to inhale and my head ached constantly, both from the heat of those humid sun-drenched days and the overdose of physical and psychological harassment that came with MP training. Inevitably, because I was back in combat boots marching and drilling, my partially healed feet began to swell and throbbed painfully from the intensity of the training program. Charlie Olivera had been right. MP training was about spit and polish. If Fort Dix had been a kind of Purgatory, then for me Camp Gordon was a descent into the hot center of hell.

## Letters, early June 1954
## Camp Gordon, Georgia

*This MP school is worse (I wish I didn't tell you but I need you to know the truth) than the second eight weeks of Infantry training could ever be. I have only one thought in my mind. I want to get out of this school and out of the MPs.*

*It was 97 degrees here today and the humidity was over 100 percent, I think. Eight weeks here would be an eternity. The same old marching, the same old rifle, worse discipline, more physical exercises, and besides that I can't see you weekends. Without you near I don't know what to do. I'm going to see the Chaplain as soon as possible . . . Be brave and pray that I will be brave too . . .*

*Today, Sunday, we worked all day. We drilled in the hot sun for hours during the hottest part of the day. This Company B is known throughout the whole camp as the worst and the roughest place to train. Everything here is miserable. To tell you the truth, I don't think I'll be in the company much longer. My feet have broken out again, a little worse than ever. Two days in this Georgia heat in this crazy company have done a job. I think I'll be going to the hospital. All I know is I'm having a tough time walking. Just say your prayers and I know everything will be okay.*

Much of the time during my early days in B Company remains a blur. But I will never forget my sense of despair at being trapped in such awful climate in such a chicken shit branch of the Army. Obviously, the personal harassment that goes with all military training went completely against my independent grain. So between the heat and the training, there was only one word that summed up my desires: Out. That was the single thought that I could entertain on a regular basis. Out. O-u-t. Out. I had to get out of the latest hell hole I had found myself in. One way or another.

Lying in my bunk that night, obsessing about the heat, I asked myself why I had never connected Georgia with heat. Alabama yes. And Mississippi. But not Georgia. Well, if it was this hot in June, what was it going to be like in July and August?

On the long train ride southward along the East Coast, it wasn't until the train hit South Carolina that I had gotten the first clue about the oppressive heat. And when we reached Augusta it was like stepping into one of those Finnish saunas back in Norwood where I had practically collapsed once. I am not, and never have been, the sweltering sauna or Turkish bath type.

"Y'all get out here for Augusta and Camp Gordon." Y'all get out for hell on earth, the conductor should have said. On the bus trip through Augusta my eyes were so full of sweat I could hardly see the scenery along the way, including the red clay that was the most obvious feature in the landscape. Was I just sweating? Or was I crying? Probably a blend of the two. I was definitely not in a heroic mood.

Now it was only a few days later, yet that ride out to the camp seemed like an old dream. I vaguely remembered the bus ride past the shanties in "the colored section," and how the houses had gotten larger and more impressive as we went up the hill. Along the highway I had seen revival meetings in huge tents, crowded trailer parks, busy gin mills, and houses in various stages of decay. Although I had always wanted to travel, I was not thinking like a tourist on this trip.

As I lay there on my bunk, the whole bleary picture seemed unreal to me, except for one thing. I remembered a guy on the bus saying, "Inland Georgia is one big hell hole, man. It's the hottest, stickiest place in the whole world." He was right. The word "Georgia" to me was a very beautiful name for a very shitty place.

I wiped my sweaty forehead with my right hand. Then I took in a short breath and my chest tightened. So I exhaled and let myself lie limp. Then I sighed and thought, this school is about as much like a school as basic training was. We lug the same damn M-1 rifles and we get the same perpetual harassment and endless work details and no sleep.

If a guy passes out from the heat when we're drilling, we just step over him like you'd step over a fallen tree. I had a streak of bad luck getting assigned to the sharpest outfit in the Training Center. Sharp outfits are a steady shafting. Even the mops and brooms stand at attention here, and the coal bin looks like a hospital operating room.

If Captain Young sees a scrap of paper on the ground he comes down with a migraine, and if the first sergeant catches you spilling something on the Mess Hall tablecloth, you've had it.

Yuh, this is some school all right. Double timing with full field packs in the hot sun. Back-to-back rifle drill so we crack each other's heads if we shoulder our rifles a little out of line. Low crawls till you feel like your ass is where your head should be.

Brother, they know how to get a message across here. Especially the message that we're the lowest of the low. Is this supposed to make us proud to be MPs? This outfit's worse than advanced Infantry training would have been.

Rolling onto my side I turned my pillow over, so the cooler underside of it was next to my head, and I thought, When we break our asses to do something right the first sergeant tells us we're "all fucked up like Hogan's goat" and when we're up to our ears in harassment he tells us we've got "assholes for brains." And that National Guard Sergeant is about one notch higher than the apes. When I told him my feet were infected he gave me that wise guy look and said, "My ass bleeds for you, Private."

They're soft as grapes, these training cadre, I reflected. These drop-outs from civilized society get their kicks messing with non-soldiers like me. I guess I screwed up when I loaned that National Guard idiot a buck. I'll never see it again. Too bad I didn't find out sooner how he sucks in privates with that money-borrowing routine. But why should I care about money? Hey, I've got food, clothing, and shelter. What else can a draftee ask for? And I'm getting an advanced education here at the MP Training Center. With the training I get here I'll be all set for Korea or Indo-China.

Bullshit. I'm gonna bug out of this place they call Company B. My feet are really swollen now and pretty soon they'll be as raw and infected as they were in basic. Putting medicated powder on them makes no sense. Why should I take preventive measures? If I keep my feet in good shape I'll shaft myself. The hospital's my best way to bug out, and that's inevitable, considering the way my feet are deteriorating now.

Do I have one good reason to stay out of the hospital? They don't give out passes for three more weeks and even if I got one where could I go? Augusta is in the middle of nowhere. If I had the money I'd fly home, but there's no money left. Besides, how could I get there and back between Saturday afternoon and Sunday night? Anyhow, my mind is made up. My feet are going to become the Army's problem, and I'm going to aim for an exit from the kind of training they give in the Infantry and the Military Police. I'm just not cut out for it. There are other ways I can serve my country and complete my two years.

I turned over on my back and a large mosquito came in for a landing on my forehead and began to feed himself. I raised my right hand slowly and slapped myself and thought, There goes one more mosquito. But there'll be another dozen to replace him. They're as big as birds down here. When you squash one you get showered with your own blood. There's nothing missing here in Georgia. Gnats. Flies. Mosquitoes. Snakes. Maybe I should pull the sheet up over my head for protection but that would keep out the air. It seems like months since I breathed fresh clear New England air. Was it only last week when I was lounging around with Mary pretending I didn't have a care in the world?

Fourteen days. It was like a second honeymoon, but better. We're perfect with each other now. Now? Is this now or was last week now? Maybe there's no such thing as now. Now only makes sense when I'm with Mary. God, I feel so trapped down here. It's so depressing. Worse than I could have imagined. But I can't let myself get too depressed or it'll be the end of me. The problem is that it's not like back in basic when I could bug out on weekends. I'm in complete isolation here.

I should try to concentrate on positive thoughts. Like bugging out of Company B and lining up a deal where Mary and I can live off-post together after the baby comes. I can't visualize myself as a father, but she thinks I'll make a good one. I think she'll be a good mother too. I hope the birth doesn't get too complicated. The doctor at the clinic warned her about her weight, and while I was home with her she complained about swelling in her ankles.

But she's strong. Imagine that six-month creature tossing around inside her. What a sensation it was to feel the baby kick.

I just hope he or she doesn't kick Mary too much. What a mother she'll make. She's all woman. I couldn't get enough of her during those two weeks at home. The more I got the more I wanted. I hope she didn't think I was oversexed. I was like a camel filling up on water at the oasis before a long trek across the desert. One thing's sure. I'm in for a long dry sexual season down here in no-man's land. But between now and September when the baby's due we couldn't be together much anyhow. They don't recommend it.

She thinks they won't let me get a leave to be with her until after the baby is born. Well, I'll be double-damned if the Army's gonna keep me away from Mary when the baby comes in September. If they ship me to Korea, Indo-China, or Tibet I'll find a way to bug out. But first things first. Right now I have to bug out of B Company because I'm definitely not cut out for this kind of Army living. I deserve something better.

My chest heaved and I breathed in and out slowly. As I tossed and turned, I thought, I've been away from her for a few days, but only my body's here in Georgia. My soul's still with her. When I turn over in my bunk I half expect to touch her, but I know there's nothing there but humid air. I didn't reach out for her last night. Nor tonight either. Am I getting adjusted to this torture? Let's face it. There's no such thing as adjusting to the Army. Tolerating it, or suffering it out, maybe. But adjusting to it? Shit! Only a total moron could adjust to this. If I were stupid I'm sure the whole thing would seem very reasonable to me. But it's organized madness, that's what it is.

I slapped another mosquito and thought, It isn't like me to squash a fellow creature. For all I know that squashed mosquito left a widow and family behind. Too bad he sucked on the wrong body. He should have picked someone who was asleep. Right in the middle of his feast I wrote finis to his existence. But what a way to go! Feasting to the end. Strange. I call myself a peaceful guy, but another creature comes along and without blinking an eye I raise my hand and open my palm and wipe him out because I think he's a pest. Well, I guess the commandment Thou Shalt Not Kill doesn't include mosquitoes.

Speaking of commandments, prayer might be appropriate. He's answered my bug-out prayers before. Why not try again? Is there a divine law that says I have to passively accept whatever shit I find heaped on me? Hell no. God helps those who help themselves, Mrs. White used to say at her group foster home. In the name of the Father and the Son and the Holy Ghost, amen. I'm getting very sleepy right now, but I've got a little message for you, God. I plan to bug out of this torture they call B Company, and I want your help. Most of the graduates of this so-called school end up in the Far East, and for me to be in the Far East while Mary's sweating out her last months of pregnancy with the Killorens would be a very punishing strategy on your part, Infinite One.

Hey, we're not asking for Utopia. We just want to be together when the baby comes, that's all. The first step is for me to bug out of Company B, and that may not be easy. I don't ask you for many favors, but Mary and I are gonna need you on our side in the months ahead, so don't give us your deaf-ear routine, okay? I got enough of that when I was in the group foster home for nine years. No matter how many times I asked you to get me out of there it never happened until I was age fourteen. I thought I'd be there forever! So how about a little break now, for a change?

# 9

Letter, Monday June 14, 1954
Ward 22, U.S. Army Hospital, Camp Gordon, Georgia

*Today I went to the hospital for my feet. I was taken by ambulance and admitted to the Dermatology Ward . . . . There are only about a dozen guys here. There are about 30 beds. The food is delicious compared to the stuff they feed us in the mess hall. The day drags in this heat though . . . .*

*The letters I wrote over the weekend about doing anything to get out of here are true, but I didn't have to do anything. The drilling that the sergeant had us do yesterday really made my feet swell, etc. . . . They gave me a little sedative about a half hour ago and I'm beginning to get drowsy now.*

*When I arrived in the South my feet were almost perfect. Now they're in tough shape. I don't think they'll make me stay here in the South long. My foot trouble would keep recurring and I'd spend most of my time in the hospital. I have a feeling that God is bringing us together in this odd way . . . .*

Letter, Wednesday, June 15
Ward 22, U.S. Army Hospital, Camp Gordon, Georgia

*I don't know when I'll get out. I don't know what they'll do with me when I get out. I hate this place. At least, if my feet didn't go bad, I would only be here 8 weeks, and I'd know where I would be stationed after MP School. But now if I am sent to MP School that will be 8 weeks plus the time in the hospital before I can see my only love, my wife. I am so disturbed. I saw the doctor this morning and she asked me all sorts of questions . . . She didn't mention anything about a discharge. If only I could get out of the Army and back to my honey . . . . Could you write to the chaplain (Catholic) at this hospital and tell him everything about my case and ask him, with God's help, to bring me back to you soon.*

My first week in the Dermatology Ward at Camp Gordon Army Hospital was drawing to a close. Yes, my feet had rapidly deteriorated into the same terrible condition they had been in at Fort Dix and I had helped that condition along by keeping my wool socks on inside my boots even when I was resting in the evening in the barracks. The wool against my sensitive skin in that hot humid weather was a constant irritant. Finally, I had asked to go on Sick Call where the instant decision was to admit me to the Post Hospital.

Now I was lying flat on my back in a bed in a large ward that had only a few men residing there. My infected feet were pointing upward for all to see, and I was avoiding looking at them. I had seen documentaries on trench foot where feet like mine had to be amputated. In my case, gangrene hadn't set in, so amputation was not an option, but even after nearly a week in the hospital my foot condition was still very ugly.

I had one major goal now, and that was to get out of MP training and away from Georgia. A medical discharge seemed to be too much to hope for, but I was going to try for one anyhow. No longer was I concerned about staying in the Army and completing the two years. The important goal now was getting out of Georgia.

Because of the oppressive Georgia climate and the harassment at Company B, I could now think of nothing but total escape from Georgia. In moments of realism, I told myself that if I couldn't get a medical discharge, maybe I could get a "compassionate transfer" up North and stay in the Army. But I could not envision staying at Camp Gordon under any conditions. So I had asked for a chaplain to visit me. I wanted to see if he could help me achieve my goal, and I hoped he would be sympathetic.

"How's the foot trouble coming, Boston?" The question came from the sergeant in the next bed, who had jungle rot on the soles of his feet.

"Seems like they're healing very slowly, Oklahoma."

"Don't let 'em heal, man!" shouted Mississippi from across the aisle. "Y'all ought to worsen 'em up, man. Them feet could get y'all's ass out of this man's Army." He pointed to his splotched face. "These hives are gonna get my ass out of here." Mississippi put down his girlie magazine, strolled over to my bed, and turned his hive-patched face toward my feet. "Them feet is one God awful mess, Boston."

"They're itching me to death."

"Did they give y'all something for the itching?"

"They gave me some blue capsules. But even with the medication this heat makes them itch so much I feel like tearing them apart. At night I rub them together in my sleep and they're always worse when I wake up in the morning."

"The worse they get the better your chances." Mississippi nodded. "Y'all think this heat is bad around here?"

"Yup, I think a hundred-and-three in the shade's pretty warm. But at least this hospital beats MP training."

"Down home we think a hundred's cool, man. Look who all's coming to call." Mississippi pointed toward the far end of the ward. "It's the Catholic Chaplain."

"I called him."

"I wish y'all luck." Mississippi leaned over and whispered, "I heard he can be a real hard ass." He returned to his bed across the aisle.

The major with the silver Chaplain's cross on his lapel stopped at my bed. "Are you Private O'Connell?"

"Yes, sir . . . I mean Father."

The Chaplain was middle-aged and heavy set. He had a very serious demeanor and his light blue eyes seemed to focus on everything but my face. "Just what is your problem?"

It didn't take any great flash of genius to realize that Mississippi was right to indicate that this was a hostile priest. But I decided to go into my act anyhow. For the next several minutes, while the Chaplain paced the floor and avoided looking into my eyes, I related the story of Mary's complicated pregnancy, my recurring foot trouble, my depressed state, and my wish to be transferred closer to Boston.

At the close of my dissertation, Major Mahoney cleared his throat and said coolly, "All women have physical problems when they're pregnant, and as for you, Private O'Connell, I've never heard of a father being lost in childbirth."

After reeling from the shock of his retort, a burst of intense hatred filled my being, and although I'm basically a peace-loving person, I really wanted to smash this priest's complacent face. I asked myself, Did he really say that to me? Or was I having persecution delusions? Nice going! I ask for the Chaplain and I get a religious prick instead. Either he's got a very weird sense of humor or he's off his religious rocker. But whatever his problem is he's managed in one sentence to give me the message that he's about as sympathetic as the first sergeant in Company B.

"Father," I said very slowly, "your concern for my predicament is heart-warming. Thanks a lot." Chaplain Mahoney responded to my sarcasm with silence, turned abruptly on his heel, and walked toward the Dermatology Ward exit. I shook my head in utter dismay and growled loud enough for him to hear, "There's some kind of a lesson in this experience for me. I don't know what the hell it is, but there's a lesson." The Chaplain left the ward without turning his head.

Mississippi commented, "If sympathy's what y'all want, call the Protestant Chaplain." Mississippi laughed, but I found it hard to share his humor. Besides, while Mississippi spoke I was somewhat distracted. I was conjuring up a picture of the Catholic Chaplain standing on a gallows waiting for his turn as a group of heretics got ready to send him to his doom.

Shaking my head in disbelief, I threw myself on my back on my bed, and as I stared at the cream-colored ceiling I was very frustrated thinking about how my brainstorm about getting the

Chaplain's help had backfired. I reached over to the small table next to my bed, took my writing pad, and reviewed the letter I had started the evening before. I had filled her in then on the state of my foot condition and my optimism about the upcoming Chaplain's visit. But now I had no cause to be optimistic.

Taking my pen in hand, I wrote a bad-news-good-news letter to her. First I told her about the unsympathetic Chaplain. Then I told her about several soldiers in the Dermatology Ward who were on their way toward medical discharges. As I wrote, the idea of somehow achieving a medical discharge grew much larger in my mind, and the more I thought about it, the more delighted I was with the idea.

With more than ninety days of Army service under my belt already, I had learned that by the time a discharge could be processed, I would be eligible for enough of the GI Bill to subsidize my last year at Boston College. So why not try for the big discharge? Why should I volunteer for more Army torture?

In mid-letter I told Mary my new tactic would be to aim for a medical discharge if a transfer didn't seem likely. The reasons could be either the foot trouble or my overly sensitive nervous system. I asked her to send a long letter to Doctor Wammock, the Chief of Dermatology, and asked her to mention not only my foot trouble, but my adverse reaction to hot weather and my tendency to have my nerves play tricks on me when under pressure. I also told her to fill the doctor in on her own pregnancy difficulties, but I warned her not to mention the word "discharge." That would be overkill. I figured her letter would plant that seed, and that would be enough.

I had just finished my letter when the swinging door at the end of the corridor opened and the middle-aged gray haired Doctor Wammock came in for her morning rounds. She went from bed to bed in the sparsely occupied ward and talked with each patient. Stopping at my bed, she leaned over, examined the infected feet, and muttered, "Mm-hmm."

What the hell does that mean, I wondered. I can't seem to translate medical grunts into recognizable language.

"Are you using the yellow salve?"

"Yes, Doctor."

"And you're keeping up with the soaks?"

"Mm-hmm." I tried the doctor's own language on the doctor.

The doctor examined my feet again. "Come down to my office when I'm through here and we'll do a progress report on you, Private O'Connell."

"Yes, Doctor."

Dr. Wammock continued her rounds and when she was done I carefully placed the loose-fitting blue hospital slippers on my tender feet and wrapped my blue hospital robe around me and shuffled after the doctor, who ushered me into the office and weighed me in. "Mm. One-fifty-nine. What did you weigh when you were inducted?"

"One-seventy-two."

"I see." She scribbled both weights into her folder and then took my blood pressure. "Mm." She made a notation and then gazed into my eyes, nose, throat, and ears. When the physical was done, she directed me toward a chair next to her oak desk. "Sit down and we'll do your medical history." I sat. "You've had this kind of foot condition before?"

I related the details of my treatment for the condition during basic training, and told her of the similar condition that had laid me up for several weeks during high school. Then I said, "When the doctor at Fort Dix said I had contact dermatitis, I didn't argue with him. My feet were healing and I only wanted to get basic over with and not get recycled. It wasn't Athlete's Foot! My feet have always been extremely sensitive. Before I got drafted I always wore white cotton socks and covered my feet with baby powder."

"Well, you still have a strong tendency toward dermatological foot trouble." She peered at me through her rimless glasses and then wrote something in her folder. Again her penetrating blue eyes fixed on me. "Did you have any other physical problems prior to entering the Army?"

"Uh . . . yes." I related every physical problem I could remember from my civilian existence and then I told her about the variety of "nervous" problems I had experienced during my junior year at Boston College.

"Were you having difficulty with your studies?"

"Just the opposite. I was a Dean's List student."

"What do you think prompted the heart palpitations, nervous twitches, chest pains and dizzy spells?"

"Poverty and hunger maybe. I was always broke and hungry."

She scribbled in her folder and then asked, "Have you had similar nervous symptoms since you've been in the Army?"

"Yes."

While the doctor scribbled in my file folder again, I thought about how the "nervous" route could be my alternate approach toward a discharge. And perhaps this session with Dr. Wammock was the beginning of my opportunity to build a case.

"Have you reported any of your nervous problems?"

"No, Doctor, I've kept them to myself. I didn't want anything to interfere with me completing basic training." This is me, I thought, playing the noble dedicated soldier role. I should get an Academy Award for this performance.

"Mm." The doctor wrote a quick notation and then closed the manila folder labeled O'Connell, Thomas F., Jr., Serial US 51-305-178. "Well, we now have your medical history. As for your feet, just go on with the yellow ointment and the soaks and stay off your feet as much as possible during the next several days."

"Yes, Doctor."

"Do you think you'd be able to walk to the Hospital Mess now?"

I nodded. "We'll take you off tray service then." Doctor Wammock rose. "We'll be seeing you again Monday when I make my rounds, Private O'Connell."

"Thank you, Doctor."

I returned to my bed in the ward and Mississippi asked, "How'd y'all make out?"

I shrugged my shoulders. "I don't think she figured me for a candidate for a discharge."

"Y'all never can tell. How much y'all bet if it ain't a discharge it's gonna be a compassionate assignment?"

"I wouldn't bet on it, Mississippi."

He winked. "Y'all's gotta play the game, Boston."

"The bug-out game?"

"Y'all said it, man."

"Yuh, I all said it." I threw myself on my bed, wiped my sweaty brow, and sighed.

"Look who all's coming with the mail. It's the Pony Express." Mississippi announced Mail Call in his own particular regional fashion.

I received five overdue letters which had been postmarked before my hospitalization, and as I began to read Mary's familiar longhand a mist came into my eyes. I arranged the letters according to their dates and in one of them I found a note my grandmother had given to Mary for forwarding. I set it aside for later reading. Most of Mary's letters were optimistic in tone, but in the most recent letter she told me her Army doctor at Murphy General in Waltham had said her blood pressure was high and she would have to work on weight control. She also told me her severe headaches had increased, and she closed with a request for my prayers.

I'll pray for you, I thought. I'll pray for both of us. If I could only see you and touch you and talk to you I know you wouldn't find your ailments so hard to take and I know this heat and even the Army itself wouldn't be so frustrating for me. But you're a thousand miles away and I'm stuck in this Army oven. It's ridiculous how hot it is here. The air's hot. The floor's hot. Even the bed sheets are hot. A glimpse of hell. That's what Camp Gordon is. Infernal, that's the word. Not my kind of place.

There's only one place for me. With my Mary. If my feet don't get me out, maybe my nerves will. Doctor Wammock seemed concerned about my weight loss and my nervous problem. I don't have to fake being a nervous wreck. I am one. I'm losing weight every day and my nerves are raising hell with me. Maybe I should help things along and go on a quiet hunger strike and lose a lot more weight and let my nerves go to pot instead of trying to pretend I'm adjusting to this insanity. I should go into my psychoneurotic routine. What the hell have I got to lose?

That afternoon, I consciously worked myself into a deeper level of depression, and the temperature assisted me. One hundred and six degrees of humid oppressive heat turned the Noxzema on my night stand to white liquid and transformed the yellow ointment for my feet into a murky solution.

I drifted into dark imaginings. My feet would become gangrenous and have to be amputated. I'd be in a wheelchair the rest of my life. Or I might even die from the intolerable heat and have to be shipped home to Mary as a footless corpse. I also pictured Mary dying from shock at the sight of my remains. The more I dwelled on negative thoughts the more depressed I became. Then it was time to eat my evening meal in the Hospital Mess Hall, and I began my own private hunger strike by eating only half of the excellent hospital food on the tray before me. My mind was made up. If I had to turn myself into a walking skeleton to get out of the Army, that's what I'd do.

On my way back from the Mess Hall I stopped at the Hospital Library, looked up Mary's symptoms in a medical book, and depressed myself all the more by concluding that she was in the initial stage of severe toxemia. Leaving the library with tears in my eyes, I hobbled to the Red Cross recreation room where I halfheartedly played a game of pool with a patient from the Neuropsychiatric Ward.

My pool partner's eyes had a vacant, frightened look. When the soldier told me he expected to be released soon on a Section Eight Discharge, I wondered if perhaps the soldier might have played his escape-the-Army game too seriously and brought on a mental state that could psychically cripple him for the rest of his life.

My concentration was definitely not on the pool game, which I lost by sinking most of my opponent's balls instead of my own. As I shuffled back to the Dermatology Ward, I thought, I don't want to end up like that guy, but I want to get the hell out of the Army. The question is, can I play the weight loss game and the nervous wreck game and get out without screwing myself up too much in the process? If I put my mind to it, I'm sure I can carry it off.

As I shuffled along the corridor, several patients passed me on their way to use their weekend passes. When I saw them leaving I thought, This place will be a ghost town this weekend. I wonder if I'll be the only one left in the ward. Who cares? I hope they all get lost. I don't feel like talking to anybody. I just want to be alone with my depression. Strange process. If I pamper my depression and feed it with more negative thoughts it'll get me out of this mental institution they call the US Army.

Back in the ward I found only Oklahoma, who was dozing. Mississippi and the others were gone for the weekend. I went to my bed with Mary's letters and read them again. Then I took Granny's letter and when I read her comment "The Army is no easy matter," I almost laughed, but my depression was taking hold now and my sense of humor was disappearing. I could not bring myself to laugh.

No easy matter, I thought. It's no easy matter, Granny. It's mental and physical torture. It's strictly for the birds. There's nothing reasonable about it. Only a nut or an idiot would ever be able to cope with it. So I'm gonna bug out of it, come hell or high water. I wish there was some high water here right now. I'd dive into it and cool off. But there's nothing here but this smothering humid heat. I really screwed up back there in basic training. I screwed up but good.

Charlie was right. If I had gone to the hospital when my feet were at their worst, I might have gotten out of the Army completely. I wouldn't have been in long enough to get the GI Bill, but on the other hand I wouldn't have had to put up with this chicken shit existence either. It's funny how the idea of trying to get out of the Army never entered my mind back in New Jersey. My basic goal then was doing my time and getting the GI Bill. Well, the goal of getting out has entered my head now, and planted itself firmly, and I can't get rid of it. All I want is out of this Army. Nothing less. No compromise.

Out! O-U-T! Out!

# 10

**Letter, Tuesday, June 22**
**U.S. Army Hospital**
**(American National Red Cross stationery)**

*I received a letter from you this afternoon about 4 p.m. I must have cried for two hours. I didn't go to supper. I really broke down. I can't stand the thought of you waking up frightened at night and being nervous. I'll be with you soon, honey, one way or another.*

*The doctor wrote something on my card as she stopped at my bed. Well, I saw what she wrote and it was something about getting me an appointment with the NP Clinic. NP means neuropsychiatric . . . I am almost positive that I can get a discharge because of my nerves . . . . but I would much rather be discharged because of my feet.*

Because I didn't fully trust that Doctor Wammock would okay a discharge based on my foot trouble, I really threw myself into a campaign to qualify for a Section Eight. I nourished my depression with negative thoughts, and just as a well fed infant grows in size, my depression grew in depth. I willfully stoked my psychic fires with mental exaggeration of the thousand mile distance between me and Mary, and soon my private depression became a public event.

Intentionally, I displayed a downcast facial expression at all times. Also, my body weight steadily decreased. Losing a pound or more a day during my own little hunger strike, I rapidly dropped to my premarital bony state of about 145 skinny pounds. Also, I withdrew from other people and into myself, usually giving only single word replies when anyone tried to engage me in conversation. Assisting me in my psychic plunge was Doctor Wammock's casual attitude toward my problems. The more casual she got the more furious I became.

By the time Friday morning of my second hospital week arrived, I was completely surrounded by the dark side of my own mind. My physical body and the world of people and places no longer seemed real. Although at first I was the master of the combination of anxiety and depression, they soon became the master of me.

Anxiously, I asked for a private discussion in Doctor Wammock's office and the request was granted. The doctor looked at me with her piercing blue eyes and adjusted her rimless glasses. "What can I do for you, Private O'Connell?"

Wringing my hands nervously, I glanced downward at the floor and muttered, "I . . . uh . . . well, I was just wondering . . . I wonder if . . ."

"I can't hear you, so you'll have to speak up."

"I was wondering about getting a discharge from the Army because of my feet, Doctor." I spewed the words out as if to be rid of them.

Emotionally, it was much like when I had asked my father if I could live with him and Granny after six years in the group foster home. My father had told me I needed to stay three more years at Mrs. White's, and this had been one of the major disappointments of my early life. That episode, and others like it, had led me to believe that at critically important times the people I depended on the most would let me down. So I had a difficult time mustering up the confidence that my wishes would be granted by the doctor.

She looked at the folder marked O'Connell, Thomas F., Jr., and said, "You completed basic training satisfactorily and your feet are healing steadily. So you don't have grounds for a discharge. You finished basic with your group at Fort Dix, and if we can get you a position where you don't have to spend much time on your feet, you can be of use to the Army."

On the spot, at that moment, I decided to go the mental health route, and my next comment was designed to move me in that direction. I exploded out of my previous shyness. "The Army needs me like I need a new hole in my head!" I had made an instant decision to lose all my inhibitions and to act out at the level of a madman, shedding all semblance of a being with reasoning power, and defying all authority.

"The Army will decide that, Private."

I'll be damned if I'm gonna put up with her bullshit. I'm not gonna pussyfoot around with her anymore. "Look, if I didn't finish basic training, I wouldn't be in this shit hole they call Camp Gordon."

"I don't know as I'd describe it that way, Private O'Conn . . ."

I cut her off by shouting, "I'll describe it any damn way I feel like. Are you gonna tell me how I have to describe things? Are you pulling your authority on me? Is that the game you're playing?"

"I'm not playing a game, Private. I'm your physician."

I let out a loud sarcastic laugh. "Oh, you're my physician? The Army screws up my feet in basic and it screws them up again down here in Georgia and you tell me I'm in such good shape I can be useful to the Army, but you discharge a guy who has a few hives on his face. Nice going!"

"What happens to other patients is no concern of yours, Private. I'll be the judge of who can be useful to the Army and who can't."

"Well, it looks like you judge my foot trouble as something trivial, but you let other guys out of the Army because they've got a few pimples. I don't even get the right time when my feet are practically rotting off." My lips began to quiver. "I'll be a son of a bitch . . ." Tears of self-pity filled my eyes. I was on an emotional roller coaster.

The blue eyes of the dermatologist drilled into mine. "I'm not minimizing the condition of your feet, but I don't think it's your feet that are bothering you so much, Private. Why don't you tell me what's really on your mind?"

I wondered if she was sincere. I didn't need another routine like the Chaplain had given me. Well, what did I have to lose? Why not tell her all?

For several minutes, I related my difficulties with the heat, my general frustration with the Army, my various nervous problems, my increasing lack of appetite, and my steady loss of weight. Then I told her about Mary's pregnancy problems and how she needed to have me at her side when the baby arrived in September. When I was finished with my monologue, I heaved a big sigh, slumped back into the chair, and waited for the doctor's reaction. Even though I had been giving the doctor a hard time I assumed her response would be sympathetic.

"Private O'Connell." The doctor paused. "I think you should try to put things in perspective. You aren't the only lonesome soldier with a pregnant wife, you know."

I couldn't believe my ears. Was this the same person who led me on and asked me to tell her my problems? Was she giving me the same kind of routine the Catholic chaplain had given me? Instead of a strategy for getting out, the whole episode was turning into a psychological nightmare.

"You'll just have to adjust, like other soldiers do."

To hell with it, I thought. I'll let her have it right between the eyes. "I don't give a good shit what other soldiers do!" I shouted. "I'm not other soldiers. I'm me! Other soldiers don't think like I do and they don't love their wives like I do."

Doctor Wammock remained unruffled by my outburst. "Oh, I don't know about that, Private O'Connell. I'm sure other soldiers love their wives and want to be with them the way you do. But one of the problems of marriage is learning to be self-sufficient so you won't depend on one another totally. I don't think you've learned to do that."

"Oh you don't, huh?" If I had been furious before, I was now in a rage. Even if I was digging my own grave with her, I didn't care. I wanted only to vent, and that's what I did. "Well, you can take your marital theories and peddle them someplace else, Doctor. Look, Mary and I didn't get married so we could be self-sufficient and practical. We got married because we love each other. And I don't need your little marriage lecture. I know what marriage is." I glared at her and just sat there eyeball to eyeball with her.

"I think you've said enough, Private O'Connell."

"Oh you do?" I laughed. "It's easy for you to sit behind your desk and talk about being self-sufficient and adjusting to this hopeless mess they call the U.S. Army. It's easy for big shots to give out with all kinds of advice for us privates. What the hell do you know about . . . ."

The doctor's face flushed and she rose. Her voice rose too. "You're finished with your visit, Private."

"But . . ."

"No buts!"

"I'm finished," I muttered, staying with my pretense of being demented. I turned and started talking to the wall. "It's easy for her to say I'm finished." I kept muttering like a madman as she wrote the words NP Clinic on my manila folder and I knew then and there that my act had been successful. How else do you end up in Neuropsych if you don't act like a nut cake?

While she was scribbling I realized I now had a chance for a Section Eight discharge that would get me out of the organized chaos they called the U.S. Army. The doctor closed her manila folder and rubbed her chin thoughtfully. "It's too bad you and your wife didn't postpone having your family till after you completed your tour of duty."

I'll be damned, I thought. This woman never learns, does she? Here she goes again with her cheap advice. I need her advice about as much as I need to be part of this insanity they describe as the Army.

"You could have prevented this, you see," continued the doctor. "Family planning is quite necessary . . ."

I cut her off. "We don't believe in birth control."

"What I meant was . . ."

"Even if we weren't Catholics," I shouted, "we still wouldn't believe in it! We don't believe in tampering with nature. So you know what you can do with your little family planning theory."

"Enough!" Now she was shouting too because I had finally succeeded in shattering her composure. She dismissed me with a wave of her hand. "You've said enough!"

I laughed again, knowing that I was possibly digging my own grave as far as she was concerned. "It's easy for you to say I've said enough while you sit there like some kind of divinely inspired medical oracle. I can't believe this. Back home this madness is happening too. Those Army Clinic doctors that are supposed to be caring for my wife don't even know she's got symptoms of toxemia. Those doctors are just dropouts from civilian life and they don't even know the time of day! The truth hurts, right, Doc? Well, as far as I'm concerned . . . ." I knew I was going much too far but I couldn't stop myself.

"Enough!" she shouted. Then she said softly, "Later in the morning you are going to visit the Neuropsychiatric Clinic. In the meantime, take two of these. She handed me some green capsules. They may help calm your nerves."

I continued with my routine. "My nerves and I are eternally indebted to you."

"You're excused, Private O'Connell."

"Thanks, Doc." I rose and moved toward the doorway. "Yuh, thanks." I reached for the door knob, opened the door, and as I stepped out I grunted, "She's made my day complete." Then I slammed the door hard and shuffled back to my bed, knowing that I was very efficiently moving myself toward the NP Clinic, but also aware that I might be royally shafting myself when it came to Dr. Wammock's report on my foot condition.

As I stretched out on my back on my bed I thought, God, I was hard on her, but if this warm body is gonna get the hell out of here it may take a Section Eight to do it. And they don't give those out to guys who act nice and polite. I'll put on an act until I'm blue in the face if I have to. All the Army means to me is sweat and frustration and misery. The idea of getting out is the only thing that's keeping me sane!

Later in the morning an orderly told me it was time for me to go to the NP Clinic. Slowly complying, I paused to wipe some of the sweat from my face, took my appointment slip, and was shuffling out of the Dermatology Ward when Mississippi called out, "Hey, Boston, where the hell's y'all going?"

I said nothing. I was angry at him because he was getting out of the Army and I wasn't. I was self-righteous, judgmental, jealous, and outrageously determined to have my own way. And the possibility that Mississippi would succeed and I would fail had me nearly in a total rage. But I didn't think I had enough energy for a real rage, so I just muttered, "You're a pain in the ass, Mississippi," and I pushed the swinging door so hard it crashed into the wall and chipped off some of the plaster.

As I went into the corridor and headed toward the NP Clinic, I thought, That Mississippi can go fry his ass. Him and his damn pimples that are getting him out of the Army. I'm sick of that shit-eating grin of his. He's got it made, the bastard.

I hunched up my shoulders and looked downward toward the shiny linoleum floor as I shuffled along the corridors of the Camp Gordon Army Hospital toward my destination. This was my big chance to get out of this man's so-called Army. It was now or never.

Inside the NP Clinic, in a small anteroom, an overweight nurse told me, "You wait right here and Doctor Holyoak will call you in a minute."

"Sure he will," I muttered, seating myself on a hot plastic-covered divan and opening a copy of Life Magazine. I stared at one page blankly and wondered if the head shrinker was watching me through a peephole. If so, I should provide some involuntary reflexes, at least. Something visible. Something more than my rotten frame of mind.

I relaxed myself almost totally, and my head jerked involuntarily as I began wringing my hands, trembling, breathing heavily. I was simply relinquishing the control I ordinarily exercised over the motor actions of my body. And I was sure that this spastic enhancement would help qualify me for a Section Eight discharge.

After what seemed a long time, the hefty nurse left me alone in the anteroom, stepped into the doctor's office, and returned with the announcement, "Doctor Holyoak will see you now."

Purposely throwing the Life Magazine onto the floor, I got up and said, "I can hardly wait for this momentous occasion."

As I entered a pastel green office with several diplomas on the wall, a swarthy face greeted me with a smile that seemed painted on. "Well, Private O'Connell, come right in, won't you?"

"Maybe I won't," I muttered.

The doctor was not amused. His dark brown eyes fixed on me and they were magnified by the thick lenses of his horn-rimmed glasses. I avoided his gaze. I didn't want to outstare him because that might seem too hostile. So I just stood before the doctor's desk and waited silently.

"Tell me, Private O'Connell, how do you feel today?"

To hell with you, I thought. You figure out how I feel. You're supposed to be a psychiatrist. So earn the money Uncle Sam's paying you. I won't even answer your question. See what you can do with my silence, pal.

Doctor Holyoak picked up a manila folder and examined it. "I see your first name is Thomas. Why don't I call you that?" I shrugged and said nothing. "Uh, why don't you sit down,

Thomas?" I took a seat on a hard oak chair. "Do you mind if I call you Thomas?"

"Call me whatever you want to. Since I've been in the Army I've been called everything from a mother-fucker to a horse's ass so I don't think being called Thomas will be too hard to take."

He nodded. "Undoubtedly true, Thomas. The Army has a language all its own, doesn't it?" The doctor chuckled, but I didn't. I had made up my mind that I would not allow the psychiatrist to be very friendly with me. I tapped my fingers nervously on my knees and jiggled my feet, while clamping down hard on my jaw repeatedly to give an external display of inner tension.

"Just what is your problem, Thomas? Tell me all about it."

I shook my head. "I don't have anything to tell you."

"Then why are you here in my office?"

"Ask Doctor Wammock. She's the one who sent me."

"I see." He looked at the manila folder and muttered to himself as he read. Then he said, "Thomas, I think you have a few problems we should discuss. I'd like to know what's bothering you."

"Oh you would, huh?" Trying tried to sound as paranoid as I could, I said, "Well, how do I know you're not just trying to suck me in and then when I tell you my story you'll shaft me?"

"I'd never do a thing like that, Thomas. I'm your friend, not your enemy. I have no desire to harm you."

"That's what everybody says." I was listening to myself as I talked and I was doing my best to sound like a psychoneurotic.

"Just what does everybody say? Tell me, Thomas."

"They say they won't shaft me. Then they turn around and ram it up my ass to the royal hilt."

"Mm-hm." The doctor scribbled a notation in the manila folder. "Do you feel as if you're being persecuted, Thomas?"

"Of course not," I growled. "I feel like I'm being wined and dined at a summer resort in the Adirondacks. Me? Persecuted? Hell, no. It isn't like I'm in prison. I have everything a man could ask for. Food, clothing, and shelter, right? Who's persecuted?

Me? Nope. Maybe you are, Doc, but not me." Being my own best audience, I felt like laughing after saying this, but I knew that wouldn't fit my scenario.

"Mm-hm." The doctor nodded seriously and wrote again in the manila folder.

"Tell me how you feel right now, would you?"

"You tell me how I feel. You're the psychiatrist."

"You tell me first," said Doctor Holyoak calmly. "We must have rapport if we are to accomplish anything."

"Rapport, my ass. Did you study French too? Like I did? Rapport? What a nice French word. Hey, I didn't ask to come here. Why the hell should I let you suck me in with your snow job and then let you shaft me after you get what you want out of me?"

Was my act paranoid enough? How much anger should I show as opposed to totally lethargic depression? I decided that I would risk the displays of anger.

"I won't shaft you, Thomas. Please believe that. I'm here to help you."

I stared at the floor and lowered my voice. "That's what they all say."

"That's what who says? Who are they?"

"Who are who?" I thought I'd have some fun with him, like Abbott and Costello with their "Who's on first?" routine.

"Who are they?" he insisted.

"Who's on first? I think you're repeating yourself," I muttered.

Doctor Holyoak ignored my remark. "Is it your wife, Thomas? Is that what's bothering you? Do you find it hard to cope with the Army when she's at such a great distance from you?"

I shrugged. "You're the great mind reader, Doc. Heal my mind. Tell me I'm screwy to think everything's shitty down here in Georgia. Tell me I'm really in paradise and not roasting in hell. Straighten me out, Doc. Change my world view."

Doctor Holyoak rose from his chair, came over and put his hand on my shoulder, and said softly, "There now, Thomas.

We mustn't let our emotions get the best of us. We must retain control. Please, Thomas, would you do something for me?"

"Like what?"

"Would you be very frank with me and tell me exactly what's upsetting you? I'm here to help you. I'm your friend."

"Bullshit! That damn Doctor Wammock said she was my friend, too. Then when I told her how I felt she gave me the business like a real pro."

"I won't give you the business, Thomas."

What the hell, I thought, If I don't tell him my problems he won't have anything for that stupid manila folder of his. I better let go a little and make him think he's reaching me. Then if it looks like he's trying to trick me I'll let him have it with both barrels.

"Tell me exactly how you feel, Thomas."

"What the hell, I've got nothing to hide. I'm depressed and miserable and frustrated. Yuh, I'll tell you how I feel, Doc."

"Proceed." He released his grip on my shoulder and returned to the swivel chair behind his oak desk.

"Well, the way I feel right now is . . . well. I guess I feel very alone. Yes, alone and miserable and very confused. And nervous. My nerves seem like they're standing at attention outside my skin, Doc. I feel like I'm getting one long continuing shafting. I feel like I'm being squashed in some kind of medieval torture chamber. The heat makes my breathing difficult and my appetite's completely gone and I'm losing weight all the time and sometimes . . . I guess . . . I guess I feel like my head has become separated from my body and is operating on its own."

I noticed that the doctor was scribbling rapidly on a sheet of paper. "Go on, Thomas. You're doing fine. Tell me all."

I told him of headaches, chest pains, heart palpitations, dizzy spells, nervous twitches, involuntary trembling, troubled breathing, every nervous symptom I had ever experienced in my whole life, and especially in recent months. Then, with a mist in my eyes, I told about Mary and her difficult pregnancy, and

I emphasized my total frustration with our separation. "I just can't function without her, Doc. I love her so much . . . I'm not fully alive when we're apart. I'm no good to anybody. I'm just half alive, Doc."

I poured out my soul to Doctor Holyoak, who sat impassively listening at some times, and scribbling rapidly at other times. During the soul-purging, I revealed the unvarnished truth. When I was finished with my emotional monologue, I was exhausted. I sat limply in the chair, panting heavily as I waited for the doctor's reaction.

Doctor Holyoak sat back, reviewed his notes, and from time to time he muttered as he read. Then he rose and silently paced back and forth. All the while I was waiting for a favorable reaction. Finally, the doctor stopped pacing and returned to the swivel chair behind the oak desk, and his dark brown eyes narrowed and came at me enlarged like snake eyes through the thick horn-rimmed glasses.

I allowed my own eyes to meet his briefly and then I purposely dropped my gaze to the floor in the most downcast manner I could fabricate.

"Thomas." The doctor spoke my name and paused dramatically.

"Mm?" My heart leaped in my chest and I mentally crossed my fingers. If he said what I hoped for, it could mean my exit from the U.S. Army.

Suddenly he swung and pointed his index finger at me like a pistol and he shouted, "Thomas, you are malingering!"

I felt as if his index finger had sent a large bullet into my heart and I sat speechless. Paralyzed. Stricken. The dirty son of a bitch, I thought. I reveal my soul to the prick and he tells me I'm his friend and he sucks me in with fake sincerity and then he tells me I'm malingering. This must be happening to me but I can't believe it. I don't deserve this!

Doctor Holyoak stared at me for a moment and raised his hand again, and pointed his index finger directly at my face. "I'll say it again, Private O'Connell. You, soldier, are a malingerer!"

What the hell, I thought. I've got nothing to lose now. I'll give this half-assed psychiatrist what he's asking for. "Bullshit!" I shouted, raising my own arm and pointing my index finger at the doctor. "You are the malingerer!" I don't know where those words came from.

"I am?" The doctor was taken off guard. "Why do you say that, Thomas?"

"So now I'm Thomas again. A second ago I was Private O'Connell. Look, as far as I'm concerned, all you Army doctors are nothing but malingerers and goof-offs and bug-outs, and if you knew a damn thing about your profession you sure as hell wouldn't be an Army doctor! You're bugging out of civilian life! You're a civilian malingerer! And when you call me a malingerer, it's just a cover-up for the malingering you're doing."

"You shouldn't say things like that to me, Thomas. I'm your friend."

"Friend? Bullshit. With a friend like you I don't have to worry about attracting enemies. You're my enemy, damn you. You sucked me in with your fake sincerity and then you tucked it up my rectum, you treacherous jackal." Where did the word "jackal" come from? Don't ask me. It just came on its own. I hardly even knew what a jackal was!

The doctor stepped back a bit and said, "Now, Thomas, you must control yourself."

"You don't think I'm controlling myself? Shit, how would you like to see what I'm like when I really let loose? Look at you! Are you controlling yourself? You're shaking like a leaf. I bet you're afraid I'm gonna flip my lid and do something dangerous, you cunning rascal!" The word "rascal" must have come to me from a previous life because it was certainly not part of my 20th Century vocabulary.

I laughed at my own description of the doctor as he moved back another couple of steps and stood beneath the array of diplomas on his wall. Without giving him a chance to respond to what I had just called him, I shouted, "For all I know, those are phony diplomas! Do you know what I think?"

"What do you think, Thomas?"

"I think you couldn't tell a malingerer from a pelican!" Don't ask me how I came up with that one. I have no idea. This guy had stirred up parts of me that I hadn't been in touch with, and the words astounded me while shocking him.

"I don't follow you," he said.

"Who asked you to follow me?" I laughed. Now I was having the time of my life! "Do you know what? There's a connection. You've got a nose just like a pelican."

"There's no need to get personal, Thomas."

"I thought that was why I came here, Doc." I pounded my fist on the doctor's desk, widening my eyes like a raving maniac. "I'm here to get personal! Very personal!"

Doctor Holyoak nodded. "Yes, Thomas, that is what you're here for, isn't it?" He tilted his chin upward and fixed his dark brown eyes on mine and he raised his voice and said authoritatively, "You may try to intimidate me all you wish, but I still hold to my opinion that you are a malingerer."

I shook my head and slumped back into my chair, totally fatigued. "I'm plenty of things but I'm no malingerer." This was about as bold a lie as I had ever told. But there was a poetic justice about it. I was giving him the same fake sincerity he had given me.

"You are a malingerer," said Doctor Holyoak as he sat himself behind his desk and glanced at the notes within the manila folder. "A malingerer is a person who feigns illness in order to shirk his duty. You're feigning illness, Thomas. Therefore, you're a malingerer."

"That's an interesting syllogism, Doc, but I don't buy it. Did you go to a Jesuit college like I did? Well, tell me, oh omniscient one, what illness am I feigning?"

"No need for sarcasm, Thomas. You are feigning mental illness."

I laughed derisively. "Oh really? I'm surprised you didn't say I was feigning foot trouble and pretending I needed to be in the hospital flat on my back. Well, if I'm feigning mental illness, you're making believe you're a psychiatrist. Tell me, Doc, are you just pretending you're a head-shrinker?"

Doctor Holyoak said nothing. I think at this point he was getting as exhausted with my behavior as I was with his. He lowered his eyes and wrote in a notebook on his desk and then looked at the contents of his manila folder and sat back and folded his arms and smiled his best smile. "You are definitely malingering."

"Tell me all about it, Doc. Explain how I'm feigning mental illness."

"First of all," he said, with a smug look on his swarthy face, "you're exaggerating your loneliness for your wife."

"I am? How do you know? Are you inside my soul, Doc? Are you completely identified with me so you can feel exactly what I feel? Still and all, I have to admit that you almost sound like you know what you're talking about."

Doctor Holyoak ignored my comments. "You're also exaggerating your wife's pre-natal difficulties and your own nervous symptoms."

I laughed. "Am I exaggerating my weight loss, too?"

"Yes."

"You mean I'm just pretending I'm down to about one-forty-five, but I'm actually still one-seventy-two?"

"You purposely lost that weight."

"To what end, doc?"

"To build up your case for a discharge."

The dirty bastard, I thought. I feel like smashing him for saying it, but he's one hundred percent right. This bird has me all figured out. I suppose there are thousands of guys like me trying to get out and these docs know exactly how we act. But what choice do I have now except to keep on with the act?

Doctor Holyoak waved his index finger at me. "I've said it before and I say it again now. Private Thomas F. O'Connell, Jr., you are nothing but a malingerer."

I was getting angrier and angrier as he kept smashing my dream of getting a discharge. And I knew I was no longer acting depressed. I was displaying normal anger, and that didn't quite fit in with depression. But I lost all restraint as I moved my chair closer to his desk, leaned forward, and bared my teeth at him like an angry watchdog. "Say that again and you'll find a paperweight in your mouth." I reached out and touched the glass paperweight on his desk.

"Now now, Thomas, we must control ourselves."

"Oh, must we? Then why the hell don't you control yourself and stop waving that menacing finger at me?"

"No need to be hostile, Thomas."

"Damn you, will you stop calling me Thomas?"

"But we're friends, Thomas."

"Bullshit. You're no friend of mine, Doctor Holyoak. Just call me Private O'Connell, dammit. I like that better than being your friend. At least it's honest."

The Doctor rose and came over to my chair and put his hand gently on my shoulder. "Thomas, you shouldn't hold my medical opinion against me. I can still be your friend even though I'm convinced you're a malingerer. I can understand why one would become a malingerer. Army life can be quite dreadful. But you may come here and see me any time you wish, and we can sit and talk and . . ."

I got up and brushed his hand from my shoulder and glared into his dark brown eyes. "Do you know what you sound like?"

"I hesitate to reply to such a question."

"You mean you're afraid to know what you sound like?"

Doctor Holyoak furrowed his brow and smiled nervously at me with his painted-on smile and said, "All right, Thomas. You may tell me what I sound like."

Without being dismissed by the doctor who was an officer and my superior, I strode independently toward the door, gripped the knob with my left hand, opened the door slowly, and turned so that my eyes met Doctor Holyoak's eyes. "You sound like a psychiatrist with a paper asshole!"

Doctor Holyoak's mouth hung open in dismay as I stepped into the anteroom and slammed his door with such force that one of the diplomas fell from the wall and crashed to the floor. I stormed past the overweight nurse and out into the main corridor, and as I walked along I said loudly, "If that's all it takes to be an Army psychiatrist, then I should be one myself, for God's sake. Shit! What a waste of time!"

A moment later, as I was heading away from the Neuropsychiatric Clinic I heard Doctor Holyoak's voice coming down the corridor at the back of my head. "I'm not finished with you, Private O'Connell . . . ell . . . ell." The corridor echoed the last syllable.

My furious laugh echoed through the corridor back at the Doctor as I turned and shouted, "Ah-hah-hah . . . I notice you're not calling me Thomas any more . . . more . . . more."

Doctor Holyoak waved his fist and then pointed his index finger at me and shouted, "Come back here, Private O'Connell, I'm not finished with you . . . you . . . you!"

"Well, I'm finished with you . . . you . . . you!" For emphasis I decided to go all the way with my rebellion, and I waved my middle finger at him and screamed, "Up yours . . . yours . . . yours!"

I reached a turn in the corridor and lengthened my stride. Then I was around the bend and with the newfound energy of unleashed anger I literally ran to the next left turn, took it, and stood flat against the wall for a moment to catch my breath. Then I heard his steps coming, so I got down onto my knees and peered carefully around the corner, past a sand-filled cigarette receptacle, and down the hall. At the far end I saw him come to a stop and stand with his hands on his hips, shaking his head in exasperation. I froze in place and watched as he threw up his hands and went back toward the NP Clinic.

As I rose to continue my journey to the Dermatology Ward I knew a turning point had been reached and I thought, That kills my chance of getting out of the Army. I got the bug-out chance of a lifetime and I went and muffed it. I can't say I didn't try.

But obviously, getting out of the Army on a Section Eight is no breeze. I guess I'm not self-destructive enough to go all the way with it. Strange day. But I had a few kicks today and really blew off some steam. It was good to act like a screwball. Well, I think there's one patient Doctor Holyoak will remember for a while. A private named O'Connell.

# PART III

## (July to September 1954)

# 11

I was soon released from the hospital and returned to Company B of the Military Police Training Center, with a light duty slip in my hand that would keep my feet out of trouble until a return visit to Dr. Wammock several days later for a decision that might involve a permanent buck slip. But I couldn't plan on that. In the Army I couldn't plan on anything. And since my earliest years in the group foster home, that was a status that had always been a serious emotional problem for me.

If you want to torture me, all you have to do is take control over my life and remove my power to plan for myself. So there I was, in that unenviable ambiguous position of having no particular status and being at the mercy of all superior enlisted men and officers who might need a warm body for just about any menial duty that wouldn't strain my feet. I was not exactly what you might call "home free."

The truth is that my negativity was so intense that any duty whatsoever would be an emotional strain for me. My hatred of the Army had escalated to outrageous proportions, and I was even thinking of going completely AWOL, although that was one of the most self-destructive things I could do.

After several days of this mindset, with the record-breaking heat really getting to me, I was on a dusting and polishing campaign in the Day Room with several other troops when a new brainstorm came to me.

My enemy, tropical heat, was eliminating any willingness I might have had to simply wait to see what Dr. Wammock was going to recommend when I went back for my follow-up visit.

In the midst of my mental and physical discomfort, passivity was no option for me. I needed to do something dramatic. So I decided to collapse intentionally, that's all. But it would not look intentional. I would be so dramatic that it would look like I was suffering from a very serious health problem.

I had never heard of self-induced hyperventilation in those days. In more recent times it has been used in therapeutic settings. But way back in 1954, my intuition actually handed that approach to me as a way to get myself back to the hospital again.

Let me explain that my drama didn't require much acting. It was a particularly uncomfortable day, and each breath was difficult. Actually, my chest didn't seem able to take in sufficient air. So instead of just feeling that way and putting up with it I decided to act impaired enough to become an emergency case and get carted off in an ambulance.

I threw myself on the floor and began to let my chest heave, breathing loudly and groaning all the while. I can still recall the crowd of soldiers looking down at me and wondering what kind of a fit I was throwing. I breathed so heavily and so fast that I put myself on the verge of unconsciousness. I also added a batch of trembles and shakes to the display, for a more dramatic effect. It was a very effective presentation.

Soon an ambulance came and I was put on a stretcher and taken with siren screeching to the Post Hospital where I waited for a long time in the emergency area. That really got on my nerves. Here I was, a so-called emergency, and nobody was even coming to check me out. I realized that if it had been a real emergency I could have died there, and that was enough to reduce my confidence in Army hospitals to a very low point.

Because of the long wait I couldn't sustain the heavy breathing pace and slowed it down to a fairly normal level. When I was finally admitted and checked out by the doctor on duty he looked at me matter-of-factly and simply commented, "Heat exhaustion with dehydration."

They fed me water and some pills and had me rest on a bed in the air-conditioned Heat Exhaustion Ward for a couple of hours, gave me another temporary light duty slip to add to my collection, and then sent me back to B Company. I didn't consider myself the winner of that contest of O'Connell vs. Army. All that drama and no substantial outcome? Army 7, O'Connell zero.

As the days slowly passed I hardly had the energy to do any bugging out, but I managed to go on Sick Call on a regular basis and was treated to several doses of Mental Hygiene therapy and Heat Exhaustion treatment. Since I was on the verge of passing out and suffering from severe anxiety and heat exhaustion on a chronic basis, they would approve short stays for me in the air-conditioned ward, where I would calm down and find some peace. Then they would release me once again to the horrors of Company B, which to me was worse than being assigned to Dante's Inferno.

Late in July I went to see the Protestant Chaplain, Rev. Sperry:

**Letter, Wednesday July 21, 1954**
**Company B, Military Police Training Center, Camp Gordon, Georgia**
*Your prayers certainly have helped me. I told you about the Protestant Chaplain, Chaplain Sperry. Well, I saw him today and he gave me a little boost of spirits. He told me he really wanted to help me, and said that as soon as the doctor tells me what my fate will be, whether MP school or OJT or something else, to go see him and let him know. Then he said he will try to get me stationed in the First Army area which includes Fort Devens, Fort Dix, Fort Monmouth and a few other places, all nice and close to home. Keep praying.*

## Letter, Friday July 23, 1954

*My nerves are so edgy down here. When I went back to the barracks I was very hot, and I laid down, and in a while I started sweating like anything, had a heck of a time breathing, and shook like a leaf. Anyway, they sent me to the hospital and the doctor there said it was just my nerves. I already knew that.*

*He was the same doctor I saw at the Dispensary that morning and he remembered me and about my appointment with the NP Clinic. Well, he told me that if my nervous trouble kept up they'd have to discharge me. I told him I wished I could get adjusted. Well, after being in the air-conditioned ward for a couple of hours I was a lot better.*

*This morning I went to see Doctor Wammock about the feet. They're in perfect shape almost. Before I went I stopped at the chapel to pray for God's help. When I got to see the doctor, she smiled, asked how everything was, etc.*

*I didn't get a discharge or a transfer, but I got what a million soldiers would give their right arm for, a permanent L3 Profile with the attached orders that I can do no marching, no prolonged standing, no physical training, and I get to wear only white socks and low shoes, no more boots. But I can still get a discharge if my nervous trouble persists . . .*

There was an improvement in my state of mind starting that day even though I still had the same heat and frustrating ambiguity to deal with. Would I completely melt? Where would I be sent? What would they do with me next? I didn't know, but at least I knew I had to receive fairly light duty and would definitely not be with the Military Police. That was a relief.

That weekend, one of my friends from Fort Dix who was stationed nearby dropped in and invited me to go with him to Augusta to see the movie Gone With The Wind. I said yes to Kenney, and it certainly was a change of scene. Actually, it was a time warp. It didn't really feel safe in that theater. I think my pal and I were the only Yankees there, and the prevailing sentiment in that audience was, "Kill those damn Yankees!" They shouted it repeatedly throughout the film.

**Letter, Sunday July 25, 1954**

*I'm still broke, but Kenney wanted me to go with him and said I could pay him back some other time. We went window shopping for a while, had one glass of beer, and then went back to the show. It was 4:00 p.m. and you should have seen the mob. Everybody in Georgia must have been there.*

*You see, the whole picture took place in Georgia during Civil War days. There were Confederate flags hanging all around the movie. The Civil War is still on, I guess. What a picture. It was the original in color with a curved screen and stereophonic sound. How I wish I could have seen it with you. I'll see it with you again some time.*

*Clark Gable, Vivien Leigh, Leslie Howard, Thomas Mitchell, Hattie McDaniel, Victor Jory, were some of the fine actors in the picture. I guess they never will make another picture so great.*

*The love story was really something. What a mixed up affair. It was nothing like ours where everything was beautiful from the first minute. But it was interesting and parts were very exciting.*

*I never dreamed the picture was so long. By the time we got back here it was after 10 o'clock. I fell asleep in the bus on the way back. I decided I'd write to my honey first thing in the morning.*

*I'm going to 9 o'clock Mass and Communion in about 20 minutes. I will pray and offer Communion for our speedy reunion and for your health and baby's.*

*I love you and miss you so.*

As the hot days and nights passed, both Mary and I were in a state of anxiety. In our exchange of letters I tried to be honest with her about my own condition, but I also had to calm her fears about my future in the Army. One of her fears was that I would get shipped overseas and not be able to take her with me. Checking with Personnel, I learned that a soldier with an L-3 Profile like mine couldn't be sent overseas. And that was reassuring to Mary. At least we knew we'd be in the United States.

At the Service Club I found a book of poetry and some of my favorite poets were in it. I copied a Richard Lovelace poem in my next letter to Mary:

**Letter, July 28, 1954**
**Camp Gordon, Georgia**

**"To Lucasta, on Going Beyond the Seas**

*If to be absent were to be away from thee*
*Or that when I am gone you or I were alone*
*Then, my Lucasta, might I crave*
*Pity from blustering wind, or swallowing wave.*

*Though seas and land betwixt us both,*
*Our faith and troth like separated souls*
*All time and space controls.*
*Above the highest sphere we meet,*
*Unseen, unknown, and greet as Angels greet.*

*So then we do anticipate our after-fate*
*And are alive in the skies.*
*If thus our lips and eyes*
*Can speak like spirits unconfined*
*In Heaven, their earthy bodies left behind."*

*My honey and I love each other so much that we're never actually separated; we may be separated bodily but never spiritually. We have but one heart and soul. We are one forever. I am yours alone and always your love.*

My loneliness and my challenges with the heat continued. On Friday, July 30, I ended up in the Post Hospital again because I was on the verge of passing out. I spent the afternoon there in a return visit to the air-conditioned Heat Exhaustion Ward. Later, when I got back to the barracks, I felt so weak I immediately fell asleep and didn't wake up until the next morning.

That was the morning when I was called to the Captain's office where I was told to get ready to leave that outfit on Monday morning. I was informed that I would be moving up the street about half a mile.

I was almost finished packing my bags to leave Company B of the Military Police Training Center when Private Leo Gogan's voice came at me from across the aisle. "Where the hell you going, O'Connell?"

"Temporary Duty to the 95th Military Government Group. According to my orders, they're gonna give me eight weeks of so-called on-the-job training, better known as OJT, at the 402nd Military Government Company. I'm gonna be a clerk-typist."

"You've got it knocked."

"I deserve to have it knocked, Leo." I pointed to my low quarter shoes and white socks. "Hell, I'm practically a cripple."

"You're as crippled as my ass," said Gogan. "They gave you a medical profile?"

"Yup. Permanent L-three." I smiled. "No prolonged standing. No guard duty. No marching. No KP. No PT. No nothing. Just me and a typewriter, Leo. That's how I'm gonna serve my country."

Gogan shook his heed. "The bastards think they're recycling me to make an MP out of me. Well, they can pound sand up their asses. I'm gonna bug the hell out of here if it's the last thing I do."

"It might be." I grinned.

"What's that supposed to mean?"

"Bugging out can be self-defeating if you don't play your cards right."

"Listen, the ten days in Jersey after the kid was born were all I needed. I'm not only gonna bug the hell out of the MP Training Center, O'Connell, but out of the damn Army too." His left eye twitched. "I'm going for a Section Eight."

"I tried that route and I wouldn't recommend it." I told Gogan about my attempted exit from the Army.

"Shit," grunted Gogan. "That psychiatrist was just testing you. He faked you out, O'Connell. If you kept hollering and went on your hunger strike all the way you prob'ly would have made it to civilian life."

"I also could have screwed up my whole nervous system in the process. It's a hard thing to beat the Army."

"I'm gonna bug out if it kills me."

"I hope you don't really go nuts while you're building a case."

"Forget it. I don't give a good shit if I go ape. Look, I go up to A Company today, and tomorrow morning I go on Sick Call for the headaches till they put me in the NP Ward. I've had enough of this shit they call an Army, O'Connell. This ain't living. Look, even if I crack up trying to get out, it'll be better than having my ass rot in the MP Training Center or ending up in Korea or Indo-China. I'm gonna bug out if I have to walk around bare-ass or start wetting the bed or shack up with another trainee in broad daylight. I've had it up to my eyeballs."

I laughed at the picture he had created, but Gogan did not appreciate the laughter. "I'm not shitting you, O'Connell. I'm serious."

"You're Syrian? I'm Irish."

"Is that supposed to be funny?"

"Look, Gogan, everything's funny. You're funny and I'm funny and the stupid Army's funny. There's no percentage in taking things too seriously. I was doing that when I was depressed. But I'm feeling better now that I'm just thinking the whole damn thing is ridiculous."

"I don't get your point."

"What else is new? Sometimes I don't even get my own point. I talk one way and operate another." I tightened the drawstring on my barracks bag and then straightened up. "Good luck, Leo. I really hope you make it to that great civilian Heaven out there." I put out my hand to Gogan.

"Thanks, O'Connell." I noticed that his hand was trembling as we shook. "Good luck to you too, you damn clerk-typist."

"Even us clerk-typists serve our country."

"Bullshit."

I hoisted the strap of my heavy barracks bag to my shoulder, took my duffel bag in my left hand and my small brown canvas bag in my right, and I stepped out into the late July sun to begin my short walk to the Military Government Group.

It's hard to get used to these low shoes, I thought as I trudged slowly along the sidewalk toward the MG area. The cruddy combat boots are a pain in the ass but they help support your ankles when you carry a donkey load like this one. Brother, it's hot today. Ninety-eight degrees again and one-hundred-percent humidity. The blacktop's so hot it looks like a river. Sweat, sweat, sweat. Tote that barge, lift that bail, get a little drunk and you land in jail. Ole Man River, that Ole Man River . . . Shit, these gnats are gonna drive me bughouse. It's a good thing I've got my clothes on or they'd be up my ass.

Ducking into a barracks doorway, I put down my bags and started waving the irksome gnats from my nose, eyes, ears, and mouth. Then I shrugged and thought, It's no use. I'll have to put up with them like I'm gonna have to put up with the Army and Camp Gordon. They say there are only three ways out of here. A discharge, volunteering for the Far East or Airborne, or being carried out in a box. I muffed the first one and I'm not about to do the others.

But at least I've bugged out of Company B. If I stay at the Military Government Group after the eight weeks are up, Mary can come down here to this God-forsaken place after the baby's born and we can live off-post. She sounded pessimistic on the phone last night about my chances of getting home before the baby's born, but I promised I'd be there no matter what, and I think that made her feel a little better. I've got two months to come up with the right scheme. God, how slowly the time passes down here. I've only been here five weekends and it seems like five years.

On I walked toward my new assignment, pondering the events of my four months in the Army and speculating on the future. Soon, through my sweat-filled eyes, I saw a white sign with green lettering under a gleaming gold eagle. "402nd Military Government Company." I went into Headquarters Building and found two rows of desks with no occupants. The walls were covered with topographical maps and on supporting posts rising from the shiny linoleum of the center aisle I saw white cardboard signs neatly stenciled in black: Legal. Economics. Public Safety. Labor. Public Welfare. Civilian Supply. Food and Agriculture. Public Works. Public Education. Displaced Persons.

I was wondering what the signs meant when I heard a voice coming from upstairs. "Who all is down there?"

"Private O'Connell reporting in."

"The Orderly Room's up here."

I left my bags on the landing, climbed the stairs, and was greeted by a tall sergeant first class with a massive chest. "Y'all on OJT?"

I saw the sergeant's name tag and replied, "Yes, Sergeant Lemmond."

The sergeant examined my orders and said, "Mm-hm. I am acting first sergeant in charge of details and such. The Company's out in the field and won't be back here till Friday. Y'all's gonna start OJT Monday? Don't fret. We'll find something for y'all to do while you wait for the troops to get back here."

Sergeant Billie Lemmond gave me five minutes to organize my gear at my new bunk location, and then ushered me to the shower room next to the latrines, where a fatigue-clad form with a low forehead and a mass of close-cropped curly brown hair and rimless classes was on his knees scraping paint from the peeling gray woodwork.

"Molesko, this here is O'Connell, the new OJT. He's gonna help y'all till Friday when the outfit gets back."

"I see." said Private Molesko, rising to his feet.

I wonder if I should pull my buck slip, I thought. I'm not much for things like peeling paint. But what the hell, I can goof off in here with this guy. I'll save the buck slip till I run into something worth bugging out of.

Molesko switched his putty knife to his left hand as Sergeant Lemmond departed, and he put out his right hand to me. "Private O'Connell, it's my distinct pleasure to make your acquaintance. I'm Norman Molesko. Private E-two Molesko." He had emphasized the E-two which was the lowest rank in the U.S. Army.

I was amused by his formality. "My name's O'Connell. Private E-two Thomas O'Connell." Molesko gripped my hand hard. "Hey, save the hand. You've got a grip like a gorilla."

Molesko released my hand and his narrow brown eyes blinked rapidly. When he smiled he revealed extensive gold dental work. "These work details must be building up my physical strength."

"So your country is shaping you up, huh? Tell me, Norman, what's this outfit really like?"

Molesko shrugged his rounded shoulders. "It's difficult to describe. It's the only Military Government organization in the whole Army, and if you can cope with this sort of environment, you may enjoy it. I'm trying to adjust but I don't think I'm succeeding." He waved the putty knife. "One can derive just so much satisfaction from tasks such as scraping paint. But such is the fate of those who are listed as surplus."

"You're surplus, huh? Does that mean you do nothing but shit details like this?"

"Exactly."

"Well, I'm here for eight weeks OJT as a clerk-typist."

"Did you just finish basic?"

I shook my head. "Nope. I've been over in Company B at the MP Training Center for a few weeks. In fact, I'm still assigned there. I'm just on TDY right now, but if things work out right I'll end up here permanently." TDY means "temporary duty" in the Army and the two words are hardly ever uttered, only the initials.

"That might be a questionable fate," he said. "I came here to function as a clinical psychologist and they have me scraping paint. I'm definitely not working in my Military Occupational Specialty and they've listed me as surplus. But when I ask for a transfer they tell me I'm essential here."

I laughed. "Maybe you're too good a paint-scraper. You haven't told me what this outfit does, Norman. What's the story?"

"I've only been here a couple of weeks myself and I'm totally confused by the Military Government Group. Do you know what I believe? I believe this outfit is a figment of the Pentagon's imagination." He let out a childlike giggle.

I chuckled. "What do people in an imaginary outfit do from day to day?"

Molesko leaned over and scraped off several flakes of paint with his putty knife. Then he stood up, and as he wiped his olive brow his large nose jiggled. "Basically, they pretend they're occupying territory in foreign countries. That's exactly what they're doing out in the field right now. Do you recall the aggressor game from basic? The make-believe battles?" I nodded.

He continued, "They're out there in the woods with flour sacks dropping on them from Piper cubs and they're pretending they're setting up a military government in Southeast Asia. Rafe Ezekiel says they do so much simulating here, he's beginning to think he's simulated too." I laughed and Molesko giggled, hitched up his pants, and went into a step dance.

"Who's Rafe Ezekiel?"

"He gives the Troop Information and Education lectures. He thinks that business about us sending advisors to Vietnam will bring on another Korea. Out in the field they're using fictitious names on the maps, but Rafe says they're maps of Vietnam."

"Well, if Ike decides to make war there, I hope I'll have less then ten months left when it happens. But I've been told that my permanent L3 profile will keep me in the US anyhow."

"I know about the profile, but what's that about less than ten months?" Molesko furrowed his brow.

"They don't ship short-timers overseas. I just want to stay in the U.S. and live off-post with my wife."

"You're married?"

"Married and expecting. The big event's taking place in September."

Molesko congratulated me and shook my hand. "Pardon the flakes of paint." Then he asked me about my personal history which I outlined for him. Also, I told him all about the string of bug-out weekends during basic, the hectic rides at one hundred miles an hour along the New Jersey turnpike, and the bug-out marching band. He told me that he had also gone through basic at Fort Dix in the infamous Fox Company.

I said, "I Company was pretty bad, Norm, but wasn't Fox where the guy decided to hang himself?"

Molesko nodded and said matter-of-factly, "He found it difficult to adjust."

I laughed. "That's the understatement of the year."

Molesko giggled. "I was just trying to be objective. I believe objectivity is the first step toward adjustment in relation to one's environment."

"Good for you, Norman." I chuckled. "You just keep on believing that and you'll see where it gets you. Were you objective about basic?"

"Quite objective," he said as he returned to the paint-scraping job while I just stood there leaning against the wall with my hands in my pockets. "You see, I wanted to understand every facet of basic training from a clinical point of view. I even volunteered for the grease trap."

"You're shitting me!"

"I am not shitting you. I heard much negative talk about it, and I wanted to have the experience. I'm convinced that every experience in life is meaningful."

"How meaningful was your stint in the grease trap?"

"It was quite opprobrious and stifling. The air was heavy and very close. It was difficult to breathe and the stench was almost beyond acceptance." He paused. "And I vomited."

I laughed until the tears rolled down my cheeks, and then said, "You're too much, Norman. Do you think you may have gone a little too far with your experiment?"

"No. One must experience life and one must adjust."

"I don't agree. If everybody adjusted to every experience, we'd still be operating like cavemen. The refusal to adjust leads to progress! As for me, I don't adjust very well to things that go against my grain."

"How do you cope?"

"When in doubt, Norman, I bug out." I explained various ways I had already bugged out and also told him about my attempt to win a Section Eight discharge. ". . . and when I slammed the door on that psychiatrist I guess that knocked me out of my depression, Norman, but I'll tell you something. Even though I didn't succeed, I still don't think trying to bug out was wrong for me. Hey, my goal made sense. But I realized it could be self-defeating. So I've talked myself into going along for the ride in this ridiculous so-called 'peacetime' Army instead of bucking the system openly. I've come to terms with the need to put in my two years, and I'll cope by bugging out."

"You wouldn't consider fully adjusting?"

"Nope. I only try to adjust to reality, and the Army isn't real, so what's the point of adjusting to it?"

Molesko paused and put his putty knife in his pocket. "I wonder if perhaps I should turn to bugging out."

"Maybe you're not cut out for it because you're so committed to adjusting to your environment. But people who try too hard to adjust can end up being committed!"

He giggled and hitched up his trousers and did a step dance. "That's quite humorous, Tom."

"Thanks for the compliment. You know, I almost lost my sense of humor a couple of weeks ago, but it seems to be coming back now. From the way you described this outfit, it looks like I'll get plenty of laughs around here."

"Indeed you may." He told me that most of the personnel considered their MG assignment to be punishment. "The organization is top heavy with majors and captains and lieutenants, and they're as frustrated as the enlisted men. Almost everybody puts in for a transfer once a month, but Major Ivey insists every officer is essential, and you should hear Diamond Jim curse when the enlisted men put in for transfers. He says they're essential too."

"Diamond Jim?"

"Our first sergeant. His name is hard to pronounce and he's always pointing to the diamond in the middle of his master sergeant stripes and saying 'I've got the diamond.' So that's what they call him. But not to his face."

"Who was that other sergeant who waltzed me in here to work with you?"

"Lemmond. Sometimes he boasts about how MPs in Korea used to shoot college boys who tried to run from battle. He's an extreme braggart and also claims he's ridden on the back of a porpoise. But he appears sane next to our first sergeant. Wait till you see Diamond Jim. From what I've seen of him and the stories I've heard I believe he's a manic depressive with a touch of paranoia. Also, he constantly refers to himself in the third person."

"Am I in the right place? Is this the Military Government Asylum?"

Molesko hitched up his fatigue trousers and danced around the shower room, waving his putty knife and shouting, "That's great, Tom! The Military Government Asylum!"

"You like my sarcasm? The psychiatrist at the Post Hospital didn't go for it, but you're a psychologist, not a head-shrinker, right?"

"I'm a clinical psychologist with a special interest in research. I've requested an assignment at the Disciplinary Barracks testing prisoners. I took my B.S. in Psychology at Columbia and my Master's at Fordham."

"You went to a Catholic grad school? Aren't you Jewish?"

"I'm an agnostic."

"Did the Jesuits try to convert you?"

He shook his head. "I got along quite well with them. I think they accepted my agnosticism. Actually, I'm not antagonistic towards formal religion. I simply don't need church membership. I believe life is its own church." He giggled. "Do you think I'll be condemned to hell for my beliefs?"

I shook my head as I picked up a putty knife and began to pitch in. "I always say each man to his own religion, even if it's almost a non-religion. There's not much talk about hell these days, Norman. The Jesuits at Boston College interpret it as a lack of something instead of an eternity of fire and brimstone. As for me, I think hell's a state of mind here on earth."

"You're not a strict Catholic then?"

"Strict enough, but I don't necessarily go along with every edict that comes out of Rome. I believe God gave us minds to think with, and I also believe that God helps those who help themselves. That was a slogan in the group foster home I was raised in. Look, if I expect to get home before the baby's born I'll have to come up with the right combination of praying and divinely inspired bugging out."

"Do you know what you have?" Norman's small brown eyes narrowed as he adjusted the rimless eyeglasses that constantly drifted down his nose on a layer of sweat.

"Tell me." I grinned as I slowly scraped my putty knife over the surface of the shower room wall. A few small flakes of paint fell to the floor.

"You have a psychological syndrome," said Molesko as he scraped paint. "I've observed other soldiers that manifest similar symptoms, and I've come to the conclusion that large organizations like the Army trigger an escapist instinct in many

individuals. I believe I've identified a condition that I now call
The Bug-out Syndrome."

"I think I was born with it, Norman. I've never been much
for organized group activities. I really hate arbitrary authority
and group conformity."

He nodded his head. "You're a bug-out, but bug-outs are not
born, they're made. Essentially, they are fairly moderate rebels
against overpowering systems of authority."

"Why do you call them rebels? Why not just say they're
people with a strong sense of self? To bug or not to bug, that is
the question, and us bug-outs don't have any trouble answering
the question."

Molesko absorbed what I had said, displayed his gold-filled
smile, waved his putty knife, and leaped into the air, all the while
giggling hysterically. "To bug or not to bug! That's great, Tom.
That's great!"

"It is? I thought it was just average."

We returned to our paint scraping, which Norm seemed to
attack with relish while I moved my putty knife very slowly.
As I scraped, he mused, "I think bug-outs are goal seekers and
challenge makers. They're active and aggressive and have no
concern about the odds against them."

"Odds are just mathematical concepts like averages, Norm.
A bug-out considers the odds but he still makes a sincere bug-
out attempt."

"Sincerity and bugging out seem mutually contradictory."

"It depends on what you're bugging out of. If it's something
intolerable that completely goes against a person's grain,
what's insincere about bugging out?" I scraped lightly on the
painted wall. "Look!" I pointed my putty knife at the patch
of wall I had been scraping. "I've created a masterpiece of
flake painting."

Molesko squinted his narrow brown eyes and leaped to his
feet with excitement. "It's great, Tom! It's a profile of Charles
DeGaulle!" He waved his putty knife and giggled. Then he did
his inimitable step dance around the shower room.

I laughed at the supposedly well-adjusted psychologist. When he had calmed himself and returned again to his paint-scraping, he said, "You're a great artist, Tom."

"I didn't plan this creation. It was just a coincidence. But let's preserve it for posterity. We'll frame it with toilet paper and when the painters come to this wall they can paint around it."

Shouting "That's great," he leaped up and danced around, giggling uncontrollably. Then he stopped when he saw me shaking my head. Apologetically, he said, "It's good for a person to work out frustrations in physical activity or emotional outbursts."

I chuckled. "If you had an outburst like that when they were giving you your Army physical, you'd still be a civilian. Forgive me, Norman. I shouldn't have used that word 'civilian' so loosely. It represents another reality. But the more I think about the real world, the more unreal this Army and everything else connected with it seems."

"It must be real," he said, "but it makes me wonder sometimes."

"Let's consider reality, Norman. If this outfit's a figment of the Pentagon's imagination, and I'm scraping paint instead of learning to type, and you're on surplus when you're supposed to be a clinical psychologist, then isn't it possible that you and I might actually be simulated?"

He didn't react as I had expected. Instead of laughing, Molesko lowered his putty knife and looked at me with a serious mien. "Considering us objectively, Tom, as we stand here with our putty knives in hand, perhaps we have crossed the bridge from reality to unreality and perhaps we are indeed simulated."

"Well, if that's the case I'm just gonna sit down now on my simulated ass. My simulated body is hot and tired. The simulated Army has taken my simulated body, made a piece of simulated cardboard out of it, folded it, mutilated it, and spindled it."

I slumped to the floor, rested my head against the wall, and breathed a sigh as I slowly wiped the putty knife against the wall near me. This behavior threw Molesko into another giggling fit. I had found quite an audience for my own zany imagination.

"For God's sake, Norman, will you stop the simulated giggling. I've got some simulated work to simulate here and I don't want any simulated distractions. This simulated Army is a serious simulated business and we don't need simulated guys like you making light of it." His giggling continued. "No shit, Norman, this simulated Army separates the simulated men from the simulated boys, right, and makes soldiers out of them, right? So do me a favor, will you?"

"What?"

"When the simulated men of this simulated outfit get back from the field, please don't tell Diamond Jim what I just said, okay? The last thing I need is getting my simulated ass plunked into a real grease trap."

# 12

After spending time with Norm Molesko, I had a slightly better idea of where I had been assigned for on-the-job training (OJT). The Military Government Group, located on the outskirts of the Military Police Training Center at Camp Gordon, had an unusual peacetime mission, being the only organization in the Army preparing to provide a civil government in a foreign territory during wartime.

MG took up a whole block of barracks and other buildings and was top heavy with officers who represented the major branches of the Army. In most Army outfits there were a few officers and many enlisted men, but in MG there seemed to be as many officers as there were troops.

Periodically, the Group would go on maneuvers out in the field to practice setting up a military government in occupied territory. And that's what the troops had been doing when I arrived there.

When the men of the 402nd Military Government Company came back from the Camp Gordon bivouac area, I was relieved of shower room duty and assigned to Headquarters Building for my eight weeks of OJT.

As my training for my Military Occupational Specialty (MOS) began, I was placed at a desk behind a manual typewriter on the second floor of the nerve center of our organization. I did not know how to operate the typewriter but was told that I would soon have work to do regardless.

Why was I given a job I wasn't qualified for? This kind of personnel behavior was not unusual in the Army during the 1950s. Actually, there was a popular slogan that summed it all up: "The right way and the Army way."

Serving as an additional "warm body" upstairs in Headquarters, my ability to type was irrelevant. Therefore, long before Xerox machines became available to make copies, I found myself operating a hand-cranked mimeograph machine which produced a steady flow of revisions for Standard Operating Procedure (SOP) handbooks.

We used blue stencils and black ink, and after running a supply of printed matter we would hang the stencils up to dry on a wire resembling a clothesline. We didn't call it "recycling," but we used them over and over again until they wore out. Also, as part of the job, I learned to print and collate materials for the steady flow of "simulated" Area Studies of foreign lands.

Another of my functions was to carry messages from the second floor of Headquarters to the various MG teams on the first floor. It was enjoyable to meet the officers and noncoms downstairs. While doing these errands I soon realized that a very effective tool for bugging out was a manila envelope in my hand. Less effective but better than nothing was a folded sheet of white paper, whether blank or printed. The point was to look like you were on a mission. The reality was not important; the image was everything.

The ultimate bug-out tool was a clipboard with just about any kind of paperwork attached to it. But whether you carried a clipboard, an envelope, or a piece of folded paper, having any of these items in your hand made it seem as if you were serving an important purpose. With nothing in hand I was apt to be questioned by superiors who seemed to be irritated by the idea that a private might have nothing to do. And they were experts at assigning nonsensical tasks.

Although I had entered the 402nd thinking I would try to be a good obedient soldier, my lone wolf independent attitude rapidly emerged again, and I soon found myself resenting various MG authority figures. So my tendency to bug out was not solely based on my frustration with the Infantry or the Military Police. Any kind of arbitrary authority would trigger my behavior. And the whole Army was based on arbitrary authority.

Whether I was born with resistance to authority or I became this way because of my feeling of being trapped for nine years in a group foster home during my youth, the tendency was very strong in me. Another factor was that I had experienced an amazing amount of freedom of choice during the years since Junior High School when, at the age of 14, I went to live with my grandmother who was too old to try to limit my freedom.

So you might say that by the time I entered the Army I was both hypersensitive and extremely allergic to authority of any kind. As a result, even though the Military Government Company was far less of an endurance test than my previous assignments, I soon found myself bugging out whenever a chance offered itself.

To qualify for my evasive actions, the task didn't even have to be irksome. When the job was simple, easy, or even pleasant, I still had the bug-out urge. And each time I successfully bugged out I was winning a new game. Small bug-out successes meant O'Connell one, Army nothing. A major bug-out achievement was a home run or a touchdown. O'Connell 7, Army nothing.

As the summer progressed, the Georgia heat was still my enemy. Because the feeling of being in a blast furnace continued unabated, I would try to compensate for the heat by slowing my bodily motions to a point where my lack of speed became so noticeable I got comments on my slow stride.

My rapid response was, "I've never considered speed a virtue." After all, even at Norwood Junior High School the gym instructor used to call me "Old Man O'Connell" because I was so slow. Rushing had never been my preferred way of functioning, and if someone criticized me for it I would slow down all the more. I could relate very well to Wilson, one of the colored soldiers in my barracks, who often said, "I has two speeds: slow and stop."

To escape the heat for a brief while and to obtain a break from the monotony of life in the Company, I went to the air-conditioned Service Club each evening with either Norman or another bunk neighbor, Al DeJohn. That was where I wrote my daily letters to Mary, and then played ping pong or pool.

I also borrowed some of the older novels from the Service Club Library. I had never been attracted to new novels, or so-called bestsellers. My orientation had always been toward stories written at least a few decades before I arrived on the planet. Actually, I had an almost automatic negative response to anything classed as "popular."

Something else that I browsed through at the Service Club was a medical handbook, to keep abreast of the symptoms Mary had described on the phone or in her letters. Thinking she might be understating her ailments so I wouldn't worry, I became convinced that she had toxemia, and I was very concerned about the treatment she was getting from the indifferent Army doctors at Murphy General's outpatient clinic.

On a daily basis I had to do battle with pessimistic thoughts about Mary's fate in the event of childbirth complications. Where did these negative imaginings come from? I believe they emerged from thoughts about my own birth which had triggered my mother's postpartum depression that led her into incurable insanity and gave me the status of orphan even though I didn't have a dead parent.

For my own mental health, as the weeks went by I did my best to think positively and to adjust to life in the 402nd MG Company. And my outlook did improve to some extent. Although I knew I was still classified as a "warm body," and was serving in that transient state known as TDY, or Temporary Duty, I felt that in the MG Group my body was more my own.

As for the officers and enlisted men assigned to Military Government, I soon learned that Norman Molesko's clinical observations about members of the Company being mental cases were not exaggerations. And most other relatively sane observers agreed. So when I voiced my wish to stay with the Company as permanent party, my comments were greeted with disbelief from my sane friends. They just didn't get it. "Why would anybody want to stay here in this insane asylum?"

I had already learned that the career personnel were constantly requesting transfers because they felt out of place in the make-believe of Military Government. They preferred to be with whatever other branch of the Army they had been trained for, and most of them also detested the climate in Georgia.

They would request transfers to Germany or Japan or even Korea, but each time they would be turned down because of their status as "essential personnel." This bred such an intense level of frustration that good morale was a rare commodity. And to me, strangely enough, that was a good thing. In MP training I had learned how awful a spit-and-polish outfit could be. A low morale outfit would suit me just fine.

Therefore, in my offbeat wish to stay with MG, I was practicing a bit of Irish philosophy often vocalized by Granny O'Connell. "Sure, and the devil ye know is better than the devil ye don't know." As weird as my life with MG was, it was far superior to the round-the-clock harassment I had suffered in MP training and in basic.

As I stood in formation on Monday morning of my third week in MG, it was hot and the air was heavy with humidity. We had just finished police call, in search of unwanted objects on the grass and red clay of our Company area, and I had carefully avoided picking up cigarette butts. After all, I didn't smoke. Was I being unpatriotic?

"Y'all smoke if y'all's got 'em," announced Sergeant Lemmond. "The first sergeant will be here in a second. At ease, men."

I thought, What if I ain't got 'em? What if y'all's don't smoke? Well, I guess I'll just stand here at ease with my hands folded behind my back and I'll stare off into space and ask myself if this is some kind of a hot, sticky nightmare here in Georgia, and is there really such an outfit as the 402nd Military Government Company. Here we stand, this motley crew, but we also serve who only stand and wait, as the poet John Donne once said. We're the standers and waiters. Uh-oh. Here he comes. The one. The only . . . Diamond Jim!"

"Atten-hut," shouted Lemmond.

I slowly manipulated my body into a stance of semi-erectness. Yes, my bug-out attitude had expanded to include posture! Even with my slightly rounded shoulders, I could stand at attention if I put my mind to it, but lately I had not put my mind to it. Such things as standing not quite at attention and not picking up butts on police call and taking unauthorized bug-out excursions out of the Company area were my personal ways of retaining a sense of self. Norm could call it a syndrome and think of it as a psychological problem if he wanted to. For me, it was a positive way of life.

Diamond Jim stood before the assemblage of enlisted men with his clipboard in his left hand. His light blue eyes darted shiftily. "Okay youse guys. Stand your asses at ease." A spray of spit came from the space between his large protruding upper front teeth.

I wondered, How the hell do I stand my ass at ease? Do I separate it from the rest of my body and tell it to not quite come to attention? This Diamond Jim's a prize. Yup, they threw away the mold when they made him, and that's a good thing. The world couldn't cope with two of him. Norm wasn't kidding when he said this guy was a badly impaired manic depressive.

Diamond Jim scratched his head with his right hand and examined the data on his clipboard. Then he grunted, "Let me see now." He shook his head and his face showed a scowl as his light blue eyes aimed over the heads of the troops in formation and focused on some trees to the rear of the area.

"You sonsabitches!" he shouted, waving his fist, "Do you damn birds have to make such a racket? Can't ya shut your yaps so a guy can think? I got a good mind to get a shotgun and blow your asses out of them trees." He waved his fist again at the offending birds. Then he looked at the troops as if they should understand his bird problem. "I'm gonna kill those little bastards one of these days."

He called the roll. Then he looked at his clipboard and shouted, "Molipsko! Front and Center." Diamond Jim's fair complexion turned red as Norm marched toward the head of the formation. "What the fuck you going to Personnel for, Molinko?"

"To request a transfer again, Sergeant." Norm aimed an unblinking stare into the first sergeant's eyes. "My name's Molesko, Sergeant."

"Don't you think I know what your fucking name is, Morenko?" Diamond Jim continued to intentionally mispronounce Norm's name while nervously avoiding his gaze. "You're stuck in this fucked-up outfit, Molixko, and you better believe it. I don't give a good shit if you're one of them pisscologists or whatever the hell you think you are."

Norm was unabashed. "I'm a psychologist, Sergeant, not a pisscologist. I'm a clinical psychologist."

"Don't fuck with old Dad, Molanko. If the first sergeant says pisscologist, it's pisscologist." Diamond Jim pointed to his emblem of rank. "I got the diamond, see? Three up. Three down. The diamond in the middle." He looked at the rest of the troops to emphasize his symbol of authority. "I'm your first sergeant and you damn assholes better believe it." He returned his gaze to Norman.

"As long as we can use your ass on shit details, Molipsko, you're gonna be essential around here. How's them for fucking apples?"

"Apples?" Norman kept a straight face.

"When you're talking to your first sergeant you call him Sergeant!"

Norm simply continued to make eye contact with the Diamond. "Apples, Sergeant?"

Diamond Jim blinked his shifty blue eyes rapidly. "Dammit, Molexko, get your damn squinty pisscologist eyes off me, will you? You trying to hypnotize me or something?"

"No, Sergeant, I'm not trying to hypnotize you. I'm not a psychiatrist or a hypnotist. I'm a psychologist."

"I don't give a shit what you are, Molenko. You better watch your ass. I'll tell you this. Pisscologists don't cut no ice with me." He pointed again to his symbol of rank. "I got the diamond, see?" Norman nodded and waited for Diamond Jim to finish his diatribe. "I answer to only two people: Major Ivey and the Post Commander. Youse guys answer to me."

He looked at Norman and then at the rest of us in the formation. "The next time you fuck up, Molipso, your ass is gonna be in the grease trap and it ain't gonna be punishment, it's gonna be extra duty." Diamond Jim peeled back his protruding upper lip, revealed his buck teeth, and burst into a manic laugh. "Heh, heh, heh." But the enlisted men did not laugh along with him. They had learned that laughing with Diamond Jim was sometimes confused with laughing at him, and he had no potential for forgiving acts against him, be they real or imagined.

"Okay, Molenko, take your pisscologist ass to Personnel, and after you get back, report your ass to the Orderly Room. I got some more painting for ya to do. Some more art work." Diamond Jim peeled back his lip and chuckled. "Heh, heh. Art work. Heh, heh. Take off, you pisscologist asshole!"

As Norman silently about-faced and strode toward his destination, Diamond Jim's attention returned to his clipboard. "Wilson, what the fuck's wrong with your ass today?"

"It ain't my ass, Sergeant. It's my head." Wilson's deep Southern drawl came from my right rear. "Seems I has one bitch of a headache. I got it yesterday cuddling wif my girl." The other troops laughed.

"Knock off the bullshit, Wilson." Diamond Jim was not laughing. "So you got a damn headache, huh?"

"Man, has I got a one-each headache." He was applying Army Supply Room language to his symptom.

"Take your black ass to sick call, Wilson." Diamond Jim shook his head. "You're nothing but a black eight ball, for Christ's sake. Never saw so many eight balls in one outfit."

Enjoying his place at the center of attention, Wilson said, "I'll go to Sick Call now." Then he shuffled off. "I is sorry for talking too much."

Diamond Jim ignored Wilson's parting comment and asked who else was going on Sick Call. Some dozen hands shot into the air and Diamond Jim growled. "What a bunch of half-assed misfits!" As he took the names of the others, the sparrows in the trees became more animated. "Damn birds," he grumbled. "They won't give a guy any peace, the little bastards."

When he was finished with the sick list, he told us that a Pentagon inspection team was coming that afternoon to critique the recent field maneuver. Then he instructed Sergeant Lemmond to supervise the shaping up of the barracks. Finally, he ordered the headquarters personnel to go to their posts. Along with about a third of the men in formation, I strolled toward Headquarters while the remainder of the group waited to be assigned to busy-work projects that filled their time between training cycles.

I thought about Norm and how he would be scraping and painting the shower room again, and I hoped he wouldn't paint over my profile of Charles DeGaulle. It would be a shame to have my flake painting masterpiece concealed from posterity.

While I was following Sergeant Faber of the Public Information Team into Headquarters, I noticed that the members of the Food and Agriculture Team were assembling at their desks and Major Dudok Langerak's large blonde head was shaking excitely as he exclaimed, "I contend there's an 'h' on the end." Langerak's head had a striking resemblance to the head of the late Franklin Delano Roosevelt.

I slowed my stride and watched the major pull his rank on the members of his team. "I've always spelled it h-e-i-g-h-t-h," he insisted, "and I know mine is the right spelling." As the major saw Sergeant Faber walking by, he whirled and pointed at him. "Faber, how do you spell heighth?"

Sergeant Faber, a self-described cynic, said very dryly, "Height, sir? Why don't we look it up?" He reached for a dictionary. "Let's see now. Height." He kept emphasizing the "t."

"Heighth," said the major, emphasizing the last two letters.

The sergeant commented, "It says here that common usage is h-e-i-g-h-t and less common is h-i-g-t-h. There seems to be no such spelling as h-e-i-g-t-h, sir."

Major Langerak's face flushed. "Let me see that book." Examining the dictionary with a critical mien, the major shook his head. "I just don't like the look of it without the 'h' on the end and I don't like the look of it with only the 'h' on the end and without the 'e'. It just doesn't seem right to me."

Amused by the whole interchange, I walked slowly by, and as I did so Sergeant Faber winked at me and I winked back. Faber, a one-time civilian newspaper editor in the Southwest, was a reluctant career soldier. His newspaper had gone out of business, so with several years of World War II service under his belt, he had re-enlisted in the postwar Army.

In addition to his willingness to call himself a cynic, he was also very casual about saying he was an alcoholic. He had been divorced by his wife when his business career had sunk to its low point, and he had told me he had served in many posts during his Army tour of duty, but few had matched the Military Government Group for sheer insanity.

As I began to climb the stairs to the Administrative Section I heard the major announce, "Well, we'll print it without the 'h' on the end."

I breathed a sigh of relief because I knew that if that particular mimeographed page had to be changed, I would find myself operating the messy hand-cranked mimeo again. Using that machine was a dull stand-up job and I had developed a fondness for sit-down jobs which required little or no effort and worked up little or no summer sweat.

"Good morning, Captain," I said to Captain Solomon, head of the Administrative Section. He was my direct superior during my on-the-job training even though I was still assigned to the

Military Police Training Center. At the same time, Diamond Jim was in charge of our asses, as he enjoyed reminding us, on a continuing basis. No matter where we worked, no enlisted man in MG could escape Diamond Jim's authority.

The captain flicked the ashes from his fat cigar, lifted his beady brown eyes from his newspaper, shifted his pear-shaped lower body on the cushion he was using to ease the post-operative pain of his recent hemorrhoid operation, and nodded. "Oh, it's you, O'Connell."

He stroked his hawk nose and winked, as if we shared some deep secret. "Yes, it's a good morning. Not bad at all, O'Connell. Hmm-hmm." He pointed to his newspaper and grinned. "I have some paper work to do here. Very important." He was reading the stock market quotations and I saw that he had already completed his crossword puzzle. "Why don't you just go poke around on that typewriter and see if you can figure out the keyboard. Later on I might have some filing to do." I liked his low key manner. You never had to worry about being overworked by Captain Solomon.

"Yes, sir." I walked down the center aisle of the spacious office toward my desk and on the way I passed Sergeant Filer, a former first lieutenant who had not had his officer category renewed. Filer was intensely concentrating on a crime magazine. "Good morning, Sergeant."

The sergeant looked up through his thick glasses. "Oh yuh . . . good morning there, O'Conner . . . O'Connolly . . . O'Connell, isn't it?"

"Yup, it's O'Connell, Sergeant."

The sergeant nodded and went back to his reading. I sat at my desk near Company Clerk Raftery, a National Guard corporal who had been activated for two years at his own request. "Whattayasay, O'Connell?" The blank Morning Report, an all-important document, was on his desk awaiting the first sergeant's return from the formation down below, and Raftery was reading a paperback detective story.

I leaned back in my chair. "I don't say much, Raftery. The less said around here, the better."

"You said it. You have to keep your mouth shut if you want to stay out of trouble. Especially with The Diamond. He's always looking for an ass to shaft." We both heard Diamond Jim's voice echo from the open area outdoors and Raftery chuckled. "Looks like he's doing a little shafting right now. What are you up to today, O'Connell?"

"I'm gonna simulate that I'm typing because I'm taking some simulated on-the-job training. I wish I had a self-taught typing manual. If I could teach myself to type, it might come in handy after I get out of this simulated Army."

Raftery scratched his red head pensively. "I could have sworn I saw a typing manual around here somewhere. Did you try the Message Center? Here comes Kattus now, the damn short-timer. Look at that shit-eating grin on his face. You can always tell it's Kattus. He takes his time. Always the last one up the stairs to Headquarters."

"A man after my own heart, it sounds like. I think I'll go ask him about the manual."

Corporal Kattus, a fair-haired former semi-pro baseball player, had just seated himself in the Message Center cubicle across from the Orderly Room when I stood at the Dutch door whose top section was always open. "What can I do for you?" asked Kattus as he put his feet on top of his desk.

I grinned. "I hope I'm not screwing up your busy schedule."

He laughed. "Maybe you ought to come back later when I'm not so tied up with my daydreams of civilian life."

"You've got that short-timer smile."

"Two years in the Army is two years too long."

"Don't depress me. I've got most of my two years ahead of me." I asked him about the typing manual, and he invited me into his space which wasn't much larger than a walk-in closet.

"You can sit down, if you don't mind getting dusty." He chuckled.

I wiped some dust from a chair and said, "I'll sit instead of stand any day . . . and lie down instead of sit."

"You're the physical type, huh?" Kattus blew some dust from a pile of field manuals stacked on his oak desk. "The red Georgia dust has a way of settling here."

"You'll miss it when you're on the outside." I crossed my legs and leaned back, placing my hands behind my head.

"I pissed two years right down the drain, O'Connell."

"But you've been serving your country as a citizen soldier and defending the nation in time of need. You're a modern day patriot."

Kattus laughed. "And you're a modern day bullshit artist."

"From you that's a compliment."

With his handkerchief he wiped some dust from his fingers. Actually, he was a very neat person, but between the Georgia red dust and the black coal dust that belched out of the furnaces during the winter, it was hard to keep objects such as books dust-free. "The guy that takes over in here when I get out is gonna have a little dusting to do. I'm allergic to it so I try not to stir it up. So you'd like a typing manual, huh? Well, let's see now. Where would something like that be? I know damn well I've got one."

He rose and slowly moved toward his bookcase. "It should be right here. That is, unless my filing system has broken down. I pride myself on my efficiency and my good housekeeping." He laughed. "Now let's see. Typing, Self-Taught? Could this be it? It's so dusty I can hardly see the title. Let's dust it off and check it out. Hey, you're on OJT and they expect you to teach yourself how to type?"

"I don't think they expect a thing, but I'll be better off with a clerk-typist MOS instead of military police. Let's see the manual."

He looked at me very seriously. "You'll have to sign for it."

"Come on, Kattus, I bet you haven't asked anyone to sign for anything since Palm Sunday fell on a Monday."

Kattus winked. "I have to play the game every so often. Sign here."

I signed for the self-taught typing manual and as I was leaving the Message Center, Kattus told me about the US Armed Forces Institute (USAFI) typing course that was given periodically a few blocks from the Company. "Thanks. A course like that would have a built-in bug-out feature. I'll look into it."

Kattus said, "Us bug-outs have to give each other a hand."

"Yup, a hand is good; all we get from the Regular Army guys is the finger."

Kattus laughed. Then I heard the voice of Diamond Jim on the first floor, so I left the Message Center to return to my desk. Just as I sat down, I saw Diamond Jim's form bobbing into sight at the top of the stairs and then he disappeared into the Orderly Room. I sat behind my old Royal typewriter, fingering keys, and closed my eyes to see if I could memorize the keyboard properly before beginning my first self-taught typing lesson.

"O'Connell!" Diamond Jim's voice echoed from the Orderly Room. "Get your ass in here, Private."

I rose and walked slowly toward the Orderly Room. I had made up my mind not to rush for anybody. At the Orderly Room door, I stopped before entering. "Yes, Sergeant?"

Diamond Jim did not look up from the papers on his desk. "Get your skinny ass in here, Private."

As I complied I thought, I'll get my skinny ass into your office, Diamond Jim, but what about the rest of me? Do you want that, or is this request just limited to my ass?

"I want ya to mimeo these here stencils, O'Connell. Is that what your name is? Huh?" He tossed the stencils at me. "Or is it Connors?"

"It's O'Connell, Sergeant." I picked up the stencils and was about to leave the office when I heard Diamond Jim's fist slam the desk.

"Where the hell you going?"

"To mimeo your stencils." My face flushed. "I thought you wanted me to . . ."

He cut me off. "Never mind the 'I thought' shit." He grunted and threw his shifty blue eyes at my face. Then, peeling back his upper lip in a half-smile and half-sneer, he said, "You don't take off from the first sergeant till the first sergeant tells your ass to take off, Private."

I stood before the desk, facing Diamond Jim, and I waited. "Right, Sergeant."

Diamond Jim leaned back in his oak swivel chair, ran his fingers through his sandy crew cut hair, and darted his eyes from my face to a folder marked O'Connell on his desk. "You're another one of them fucked up college boys, aren't ya?"

"Well, I finished three years at Boston College, if that's what you mean."

"Shit. Three years or four years or one year, you fucking college boys are all the same. You're all fucked up, that's what you are."

I felt the blood rushing to my face and my fists clenched, but I told myself it would be self-defeating to let the first sergeant get too much of a rise out of me.

"That's what the hell you are, O'Connell, huh? A fucking college boy."

I couldn't resist saying, "Not exactly a boy, Sergeant. I'm a married man who worked his way through three years of college. When I get out of the Army I'll go back and finish because education is important to me."

Diamond Jim nervously shifted his gaze and pulled his protruding lip down hard against his buck teeth. "Well, if the fucked-up college boys they keep sending here are a sign of what education is, then education's nothing but bullshit. Why don't they send me men instead of college boys, for Christ's sake?"

I decided not to reply. I knew I had already said more than enough. Examining my 201 file, Diamond Jim asked, "What's this here foot trouble you got?"

"It's like trench foot. They call it a chronic tender blistering condition of the feet. I get it from too much standing, or walking."

He sneered. "What the fuck good are you to the Army if you can't walk?"

"I guess they figure I can be a typist. That's why I'm on OJT here."

Diamond Jim shook his head in anger. "Don't you think I know why the fuck you're here? Do you think I'm stupid or something 'cause I didn't go to no fancy half-assed college? Huh? Is that what you think, Private? Are you trying to fuck with old Dad, huh?" I said nothing, and he returned his gaze to the file before him. "So you got this here con-contig . . . uh . . . const . . ."

"I think it says congenital, Sergeant. It's a congenital foot condition."

"I know what the damn thing is. Can't ya see I'm reading about it right now? Them doctors and their six-bit words. What you got is a damn foot problem, that's what you got. Why does the Army take eight balls like you anyhow?"

I grinned. "If a guy can breathe I guess they take him."

Diamond Jim did not return my grin. "You think something's funny, O'Connell?"

"No, Sergeant. Nothing's funny. Was I smiling?"

"You bet your ass you was smiling. Don't ya know when you're smiling, for shit's sake?"

I kept a straight face. "I usually do." I was beginning to feel the danger of any attempt at conversation with him, especially the hazard of trying to defend myself.

He grunted. "Damn misfits is all we get in this outfit. Misfits and college boys." He began to shuffle some papers on his desk. I cleared my throat and Diamond Jim looked up at me and growled. "What the fuck you standing there for, O'Connell? Get your ass to the mimeo and run them stencils off and then go to your damn typewriter and see if you can learn yourself how to type. That's what you're here for, ain't it, college boy? You're on OJT to be a clerk-typist, right?" Diamond Jim drew back his upper lip, bared his buck teeth, and broke into a horselaugh.

I stepped from the Orderly Room without another word and Diamond Jim rose and followed me to the corridor. As I began to walk toward the mimeo machine with the stencils, Diamond Jim's loud voice came at the back of my head, "This here O'Connell takes the cake! Another fucking eight ball college boy, and he's got cruddy feet besides."

The roar of the first sergeant's manic laughter followed me down the aisle, and I could feel my face flushing and fists clenching, but I tried to maintain my composure. I knew that any loss of temper on my part would lead to my own destruction.

I was amazed at how fast he had raised the fury in me, and I thought, That madman! I feel like shoving those stencils up his diamond-shaped ass. Up to now I was doing pretty good with the nut because most of the time he was ignoring me. Now for some reason I'm on his shit list. I better stay calm and keep my mouth shut. If I argue with him there's only gonna be one loser, and it won't be the first sergeant. Hey, I'm just a warm body he can shaft any time he feels like it. Keep your trap shut, Thomas. Swallow the venom you want to spew in the moron's face. Don't answer him. Just keep walking and make like he doesn't exist.

I kept walking, and although my heart was pounding hard with emotion and the blood was coursing full speed through my face, I said nothing and went to my desk to proofread the stencils. Then Diamond Jim returned to his office and said no more. I stared at the stencils but did not see them. I saw only the face of the angry Diamond Jim and I wished there could be some way to eliminate that face from the planet called Earth. As I sat there I shook my head and muttered to myself. "His ass is where his head should be, damn him."

Company Clerk Raftery went "Pst!" and whispered, "Hey, O'Connell, don't let the bastard upset you. It's nothing personal. The asshole hates everybody, even himself." I nodded and forced myself to see the words on the stencils before me. I shouldn't let him get to me, I thought. My hate's wasted on him. But I hate the bastard's guts and I hate the idea that he's got authority over me and there's nothing I can do about his abusive behavior and insane antics.

I shook my head and thought, I hate his very being. He's a non-entity who doesn't deserve to exist. But I better keep my hate to myself because it'll screw me up if he finds out he's getting on my nerves. That really turns him on.

After proofreading the stencils, I ran them off, and nervously brought them to Diamond Jim. He took them, nodded politely, and said, "Thanks, O'Connell."

Well I'll be damned, I thought, this is a totally different guy from the one who reamed my ass a while ago. A psychiatrist would have a field day with this nut.

I went back to my desk, picked up my self-instruction manual, placed my fingers in position on the typewriter keyboard, and pecked out those much repeated words: "The quick brown fox jumps over the lazy dog." As I neared the end of the sentence I muttered, "Shit! It came out l-a-x-y instead of l-a-z-y. That letter 'z' is a tough one to hit."

# 13

**Letter, Monday August 9, 1954**
**402nd Military Government Company**
**Camp Gordon, Georgia**

*There are a few things I want to suggest. Call the local Red Cross chapter or even go there if you can. Find out if there is a certain procedure you may follow in order to get me home with the least amount of time wasted, preferably a few days in advance. I talked to the chaplain today and he was very optimistic about everything. Of course, it's easy for him to be optimistic, but in any case he said the first thing I should do is ask you to get in touch with your local Red Cross chapter.*

*The easiest and quickest way to get the leave is from your end of the line. At my end there's a lot of red tape. Down here, I will talk to the Company Commander and see if he will help me to get off a couple of days early. Don't worry, we'll get everything straightened out in advance. Then all the baby has to do is come on the 17th, as expected.*

*Don't worry about other families, honey. They may look happy but are they as happy and really as contented as we are when we're together? I don't believe it.*

*People are basically the same everywhere, but in certain sections such as the South there are so many circumstances such as the racial problem, the low standard of living, the large number of GIs, the poor schools, etc., that this all breeds lower moral standards.*

*New England is the tops as far as morals in the U.S. are concerned. That becomes obvious as soon as you hit New York and New Jersey, but it really creates a contrast when you hit our poor Southland.*

*There are places around Augusta that you just couldn't find in Boston, dens of gambling, vice and corruption. They are declared "Off Limits" but the crazy kids never learn. "Off Limits" attracts them rather than deters them. There was a town next to Fort Dix that afforded the same opportunities that certain sections of Augusta offer. It's like that everywhere, but it's a little more wide open down here.*

*Vice is one big subject. All I can truthfully say is that for each person who is unfaithful, addicted to vice, corrupted in various ways, there are many others who live good clean lives here in the South as well as everywhere else.*

**Letter, Thursday August 12, 1954**
**Camp Gordon, Georgia**

*Civilians just don't realize the wonderful freedom and blessings they have. They magnify their little problems . . . . The Company is in the last week of a 10-week training period. These last few days they are receiving sort of an overall "proficiency" test. In Military Government, all the problems dealing with Civil Affairs in occupied territory are supposed to be solved by different committees.*

*Well, in the headquarters where I work, the problems are solved by the different groups-economic, public safety, legal, etc. Then they are turning them in to the commanding office, a major.*

*Today I was put in the major's office to pass on the messages that come though his desk. About every twenty minutes or so I'd get up and take a paper from him to the other room, then come back and sit and wait for the next one. In the meantime, all kinds of brass are coming in and out to converse with the company commander.*

*Also in the office is another major, the executive officer. So there I am, private E-2 O'Connell, in an office with the two majors, trying to act nonchalant and calm, while these officers are talking about everything from soup to nuts.*

*In the meantime, the company commander bawls out captains and lieutenants while I'm sitting there watching. Also, a couple of lieutenant colonels pay a visit once in a while and I get quite a picture about the life of an officer.*

*I found out that they are no different from enlisted men except that they are paid a lot better and naturally have more responsibility. But they're always dodging work and trying to beat the Army too.*

*Well, to top it off, in the afternoon a full colonel, the next thing to a general, pops in and everyone goes all out to impress him. He is sent to the outfit from Washington to look things over.*

*There I am, in the office listening to a lieutenant colonel, a colonel, and four majors trying to snow each other. Quite an experience.*

Norman and I had just come back to the barracks from supper at the Mess Hall, where we had dined on limp lettuce with cottage cheese, dry chicken legs, soggy mashed potatoes, shriveled peas, and muddy coffee.

Lying flat on my back on my bunk, I was silent and anxious. Also, I was unusually sweaty because August had already been declared one of the hottest in the history of Georgia. The red clay of Camp Gordon was cracked like a parched river bottom, clouds of fine red dust swirled in the air at the slightest breeze, and busy hordes of irksome gnats had become the masters of the area.

I was anxious about getting to Mary's side before the baby's birth, and the official reception for my idea hadn't gone well. When I had made out an Emergency Leave Application at the

Military Police Training Center where I was still permanently assigned, the sergeant had said bluntly, "Your ass is out if you think you're gonna get leave ahead of time. There ain't no emergency till after the kid comes, Private."

I had pleaded that Mary's "threatened toxemia" was an emergency and I had stubbornly persisted in my request for a leave date of September 13, a few days before her forecasted delivery. The sergeant had failed to bully me out of filing the application, but he had succeeded in accentuating my anxiety state.

"What are you thinking about?" asked Norman.

"The Arctic Circle." I sighed as I wiped the sweat from my brow. "I'm also thinking about bugging out of here before the baby comes. Those Army docs up in Massachusetts won't put anything in writing about her complications, so they won't help me get there in time. But come hell or high water or a flood of chicken shit, I'm gonna be there with her."

Norman smiled his gold-and-ivory smile. "I don't know exactly what your bug-out plan is, but I think it'll work."

"What makes you think so?" I raised myself on my elbow and watched him adjusting his pink, plastic-rimmed, Army-issue eyeglasses.

"The bug-out syndrome involves a highly effective yet negative form of positive thinking, and I'm sure you've mapped your strategy well."

"Now you're beginning to understand the fine art of bugging out. I'm proud of you, Norm. Pretty soon you'll be realizing if you get too well adjusted in this life you can shaft yourself."

"I can agree with you, but only up to a point."

"Up to what point?"

He fidgeted with his sliding eyeglasses, then moved them higher up his sweaty nose. "To the point of avoiding extreme anxiety."

"But anxiety is God's way of showing us we're alive!"

Norman smiled. "I notice you've been referring to your God quite a bit lately. Are you renewing your faith?"

"Did I ever say I lost it?"

"Not really," said Norm. "But you seem to be strengthening it now. Sometimes I envy people with faith because I think they have more than just themselves to fall back on when the going gets rough."

"Aren't you the guy that said life itself was your temple?"

He giggled. "I'm beginning to think my temple was erected by an incompetent architect. Perhaps I'm depressed about my imprisonment in this strange outfit."

"Situation normal, Norm. Depression is an occupational disease around here." I stood up and walked slowly to the large fan at the end of the corridor. "Excuse me for a second; there's something I have to do."

I went to the fan and put my face in front of it and began to whistle the theme from a movie called "The High and the Mighty" which I had watched at the Post Theater a few nights before. As I stood whistling, the strong breeze dried the sweat on my face and my whistling gave out an eerie vibration that echoed in my ears.

Wilson's voice came from the far end of the aisle. "That damn buck slip mother wif the cruddy feet and white socks is bucking for a section eight!"

I shouted, "Wrong, Wilson. I like this Army life. Where the hell else could I get forty-two bucks a month for myself and almost a hundred a month for my wife?"

Wilson's broad white smile, so accentuated by his coal black skin, came up the aisle at me. "You is bucking for somefin' O'Connell."

"Just whistling into the fan, that's all. Try it. It might cure what ails you."

Wilson shook his head. "What ails this mother nothing could cure. I is a hopeless case, man."

"If you say so." I turned to Norman. "Come on. Try some fan therapy." Norm looked at me, blinked rapidly, and shook his head. "Hey, it's no sweat," I urged.

He looked directly at me, closed his eyes involuntarily, and said, "It's very odd, Tom. I've never seen it done before."

"Now you've seen it done. It's therapy! Hey, aren't you the guy who volunteered for the grease trap?" He nodded. "Well, come and try the fan. It's therapeutic and free."

"Free therapy!" He leaped to his feet, danced his inimitable step dance, hitched up his trousers, kicked his legs high into the air, and shouted, "That's great! Whistling into a fan for free therapy! I think I'll try it."

"Be my guest, Norm."

Now the two of us whistled the theme from "The High and the Mighty," and as we whistled, I noticed that Norm had his eyes tightly closed and his face had a radiant glow as he totally absorbed the new experience. When the tune was done, he said with a straight face, "It was excellent therapy, Tom. I feel much less depressed now."

"This ain't no barracks!" Wilson's voice boomed from the far end of the aisle. "This is one-each NP ward."

"You should try fan therapy," retorted Norm. "It might help your headaches."

"Shove your fan, man. That's the fan what the shit hit!" Wilson's laugh echoed through the barracks. There was nobody who appreciated Wilson's humor more than he did himself, which made him all the funnier.

He continued, "There ain't no fan no place that'd help my headaches. Knocking off some ass in Atlanta could help. And I s'pose if I went downtown to Augusta for shacking up my head would be good again, but I likes my Atlanta ass."

"You're a riot, Wilson," I said.

He retorted, "Y'all's the riot with your damn white socks buck slip and your cruddy feet and the nut there what thinks he's a pisscologist." Wilson threw himself back into his favorite position, flat on his back on his bunk with his long legs dangling over the bottom end, and he laughed to himself at his own remarks.

I sat on the edge of my bunk and Norm sat opposite me on the edge of his. Then I asked him, "How's the painting coming?"

"We're almost finished the Day Room. We start on the Supply Room tomorrow."

"How'd your visit to Personnel come out this morning?"

"The sergeant said I should take a trip to the Pentagon and try to find a Columbia or Fordham alumnus to help me toward a transfer."

"Do it, Norm. I'll miss you around here, but do it."

"I'll definitely consider it."

"You know what they say about procrastinators. A good bug-out never procrastinates."

Norm squinted. "My fundamental aim in life is not to be a good bug-out."

"That's why you're scraping paint instead of giving ink blot tests to prisoners at the Disciplinary Barracks. You should take a few days leave and go on a little junket to the Pentagon. What have you got to lose?"

"I could lose my leave time and the funds to transport me there and back."

"Time? Money? Hey, nothing ventured, nothing gained. Go, Norm. Go! Speaking of the Pentagon, that bird colonel from Washington came back to HQ for the follow-up critique this afternoon and you should have seen Langerak. He was one shook major."

"He's a very neurotic man." Norm involuntarily closed his own eyes as they met mine. "Langerak's eye movements reflect his own disturbed emotions. They're always roving about, scanning."

"Yup, he's got jitterbug eyes. I thought his eyeballs were gonna fly out of his head this morning. I was doing some mimeo work for him and he got shook about whether to put three holes in each sheet and put them in a notebook, or to punch two holes on top and use Alco fasteners. Then he made a momentous decision and decided on the Alco fasteners.

"Also, he turned the office upside down trying to find a way to dry off the wet mimeo ink so the report wouldn't smear when he gave it to the colonel. They tried blotters and light bulbs and space heaters and nothing worked fast enough, so I made a wisecrack about holding the pages up to a fan!

"Damned if Langerak didn't get everybody in Headquarters Building to stand in front of the fan with one sheet of paper at a time until they all dried. It was a circus. By accident I've endeared myself to the major. I wonder if I should ask him for help if I get stuck on my emergency leave strategy. Nope. Forget it. With Langerak helping me I'd shaft myself."

"Perhaps. How did the critique come out?"

"You should have seen the majors and captains licking the bird colonel's boots. I was running messages to Major Ivey's office and I saw the colonel basking in the flattery. I've never witnessed such a massive snow job. Maybe that's what the Army is. One massive simulated snow job."

When I called the Army one massive simulated snow job, Norm giggled, leaped off the bunk, hitched up his civilian slacks, and did his step dance. "That's great, Tom. One massive simulated snow job!" He stopped dancing and his face became serious. "But if we're nothing but part of a huge snow job, then we don't exist."

"We'll just have to adjust to that." I laughed.

Wilson's voice came from the far end of the barracks. "I never heard such crazy talk in all my days. My head is aching from it, man. Aching wicked."

"Just stop the Atlanta ass on weekends and you'll be okay," I shouted.

A laugh came from Napoli across the aisle. "Speaking of ass, Boston, you been getting any lately? Me and Medina are going down to Augusta if you want to come along."

"No thanks, Philly. I'm a one-woman man."

"Shit," grunted Napoli, an emaciated yet handsome private who had completed Military Police training. "I'm a twenty-woman man. If I get any more snatch I'm gonna go up with the shade some day. Did I tell you the one about the guy on his honeymoon that knocked off so much ass he got up one morning and dragged his tail to the window and when he went to put the shade up, he went up with it?" He laughed.

I said, "That's an old joke, Philly. And I was the one who told it to you."

"Well, one of these mornings that's gonna be me," he said as he opened a can of pears. "I'm not shitting you, Boston."

I was still lying flat on my back on my bunk. "You might shit on me, Philly, but you wouldn't shit me, right?"

"Hey, Boston." His voice came closer. "Wait till you see the blonde I'm getting into." He came over to my bunk and showed me a snapshot from his wallet. "How's that for a babe, huh?"

I examined the snapshot of the blonde in the brief swimsuit and said, "She looks like she knows more than her alphabet, Philly."

Napoli flashed his bright, even-toothed smile. "Bet your cotton picking ass she does. You sure you don't want to come along for some tail, O'Connell? Medina's broad's got a big-knockered sister on the make. Come on, you hot shit. No sense letting your weapon get rusty."

"I've invented my own rust remover. It's a secret formula. Thanks for the invitation, but no thanks. Why the hell do you keep trying to corrupt me, Philly?"

"I just hate to see married guys suffering from lover's nuts." Napoli laughed. "Hey, how much you weigh now, Boston? You putting some on?"

"Yup, I'm up to one-fifty-five."

"Shit! I eat like a damn elephant and it don't do me no good. Maybe getting too much snatch is screwing me up. son of a bitch, MP training knocked twenty pounds off me and I can't get half a pound back."

I grinned. "That's life, right? Pound on, pound off."

"You're a hot shit, O'Connell." Napoli put his snapshot back in his wallet and crossed the aisle to his own location where he continued combing his hair as he prepared for his night on the town.

I wiped my sweaty brow. "Well, what say, Norm? Off to the Service Club for some cool air?"

Norm adjusted his glasses, which were always sliding down his nose. "We have a tradition to maintain, don't we?"

Nodding, I said, "If you and I don't take off to the Service Club with our books in our hands, Wilson doesn't get to do his running commentary and his day is ruined."

I fixed my sport shirt so it would hang outside my slacks and let the air circulate. Then I grabbed my letter-writing kit and the battered library copy of Fitzgerald's "Tender is the Night." Norm brought along his Menninger's "The Human Mind," which coincidentally had been the title of the solitary psychology book in the bookcase at Granny O'Connell's house. As we headed for the stairwell, I saw Chandler scratching his thigh. "Hey, Chandler, how's your invisible rash coming along?"

He looked up. "It may be invisible but it's itchy as hell. I've been scratching since I got reassigned to this screwed-up outfit."

Norm commented, "You've got a psychosomatic rash."

"Lucky me," replied Chandler, returning to his scratching.

I said, "Scratch your way into the hospital and maybe you'll bug out of here." Chandler nodded as we walked on.

Just as we were about to enter the stairwell, Wilson's voice resounded throughout the second level of the barracks. "There they goes, the nut what think he's a pisscologist and the buck slip what thinks he's got cruddy feet so he wears white socks for the way his feet stink. There they goes!" He gave out a large laugh. "Out the door they goes wif their books under their arms. Where y'all going you mens? To night school or somefin'?" This time Wilson laughed so hard his whole bunk shook.

I said, "Without your send-off, Wilson, going to the Service Club wouldn't be half the fun."

Wilson did not bother to acknowledge the comment. He simply went on with his running commentary, "They sure ain't going after ass. Not wif books under the arms, they ain't. They sure is somefin' those two. The nut who thinks he's a pisscologist and . . . ." He continued talking and laughing at our expense as we went down the stairs, and I was laughing all the way down the stairs too. I was one of Wilson's favorite audiences.

Norm observed, "Wilson is far too vocal for the Army life. He's maladjusted."

"He should have been a comedian, or maybe a preacher."

"Perhaps," said Norm.

We walked out of the barracks and into the Company area, heading in the direction of the Service Club. Norm and I talked about Diamond Jim's continued vendetta against the chirping sparrows in the trees to the rear of the formation area and as we stepped out across the dry red clay, I took in a hot humid breath. "The air's so close. It feels so heavy. Not a breeze stirring."

Norm inhaled. "I believe it will rain."

I saw dark clouds on the horizon. "You're right. Hey, speaking of rain, it was raining abuse up in Headquarters today. I think Kattus is getting on Diamond Jim's nerves because he's on his way out of this man's army. The Diamond was calling him every name under the sun, but Kattus just kept grinning his short-timer's grin and didn't say a word. Real nice guy, that Kattus. And the nicer he is the more The Diamond hates him. Perverse, isn't it? In my letters I've been describing Diamond Jim to Mary and she thinks I've invented him."

"I'll vouch for you that he exists."

"Thanks. Hey, did you hear about the new phrase Kattus coined?" Norm shook his head. "Well, I'll fill you in on the background. The other day Diamond Jim had a very tight hair across his ass, and Gore showed up in his office and asked for a transfer for about the twentieth time, and The Diamond told Gore to shove his transfer request up his Gore. When Kattus heard the Diamond ranting he came up with the new expression. Are you ready for it?" Norm squinted, adjusted his eyeglasses on his nose, and nodded.

"This may be anticlimactic. But here are the three immortal words that are going around the barracks right now: Up your diamond!"

Norm's face was serious at first. Then he squinted his eyes, blinked rapidly, burst into a giggle, and shouted, "Up your diamond! That's great, Tom." He hitched up his slacks and did his step dance on the dusty red clay. "That's great." He began to giggle and laugh hysterically. "Up your diamond! It's perfect." I joined the laughter and when we had purged ourselves at the expense of the first sergeant, Norm asked, "How has Diamond Jim been treating the Headquarters Personnel lately?"

"Same as usual. He still rages about college boys, but he's off my back pretty much now. He's got a new Ph.D. to harass. I try to stay out of The Diamond's way, and when I have to talk to him I use mostly one-word sentences. I made a mistake when I asked him about my chances of getting home to Mary before the baby comes. He gave me a lot of bullshit about college boys expecting too much. I'm working on Captain Solomon now. If I run into any snags at the last minute, I think he may help me out."

"Tell me your plan, Tom."

"It's top secret, Norm."

"You won't confide in me?"

"A good bug-out confides in nobody. Sorry. Hey, look at the trees. I wonder if . . . Yup, we've had it. Look at that black sky." Not a breeze stirred as the sky above darkened. Then the stillness ended and the winds came, swirling red dust around us. I shouted against the wind, "It's a little gale, Norm. Let's head for that barracks!" The darkness deepened, the skies opened, and the rains came down on us while the temperature dropped rapidly as we ran toward the nearest shelter.

"What a whirlwind!" I exclaimed, a little breathless, as we stepped under a small roof. "Look at the basketball court." The dust in the court was spinning in the shape of a small tornado. Then the basketball apparatus tumbled and the trees bent so that their tops nearly touched the ground.

For five minutes we stood watching the rains come down, filling storm sewers to overflowing and soaking every object not under cover. Then, as suddenly as they had come, the black clouds moved on and the sun filtered through the overcast and glistened in dusty small puddles on the dry red clay of Camp Gordon. The storm sewers emptied and it was as it had been before. Hot. Humid. Still.

As we moved on again toward our destination, Norm shook his wet head and said, "I thoroughly enjoyed it."

"Not me." I wiped the rain from my face with a handkerchief. "I like to be high and dry. Not low and soaked."

"One must try to adjust to life's seemingly negative experiences," said Norm.

"Hell, if everyone always adjusted we'd still be bare-ass in the jungle."

Norm chuckled. "You may have a point, Tom. Can you picture us in a jungle running around in the nude?" He giggled. "I think I might like it."

"Watch out, Norm. you're beginning to sound like you know who." I moved a few feet to one side, as if avoiding contact. "Look, you can count me out of your nude jungle. I'll stick with the Twentieth Century, in spite of its drawbacks."

"It's an interesting period in history," he said.

"It'd be more interesting if we weren't wards of the government. Our hillbilly sergeant reminded me of my status this morning. I was walking along on police call, minding my own business and purposely overlooking cigarette butts, and Fulghum in his own inimitable way told me to pick up a butt. He said, 'Take your Boston ass and y'all pick up that mother fucking cigarette, ya hear?'"

Norm grinned. "Did you concur with his polite request?"

"Well, I looked him in the eye and said, 'Wait till I peel this grape,' and he looked at my hands to see if I had a grape, and I told him the grape couldn't be seen with the naked eye. Then he gave me a lot of crap about the way privates should address sergeants, so guess what I did?"

"What?"

"Instead of arguing with him, I agreed with him. I told him he was absolutely right about everything, and I told him I've always believed in the need for politeness in a civilized society, and I even told him I approved of the Army's anti-litter campaign." I laughed. "But I don't think he took me seriously, Norm."

"What gave you that indication?"

"He said if I didn't watch my cotton picking mouth, my ass would end up in the grease trap."

"Fulghum has a way with words, doesn't he?" Norm adjusted his pink plastic, Army-issue eyeglasses, which were sliding down his nose on the slippery mixture of sweat and rain. "Uh . . . tell me, Tom, just what did you mean about peeling the grape?"

"If you don't know, I can't explain it to you. We're on different humor wavelengths, but you're still okay in my book, Norm."

"How fortunate for me."

I laughed. "Are my ears failing me? Was that sarcasm I just heard?"

"Perhaps you're rubbing off on me."

"Maybe in time I'll even make a bug-out out of you."

"I don't think I have it in me. I'm too passive by nature."

"Well, I've never met a passive bug-out. But you haven't exactly been passive with all your attempts to get a transfer. And you weren't passive when you got your higher education."

As we walked on, we discussed the attributes of a good bug-out. Then at the Post Exchange we stopped and I paid sixty-five cents out of my last dollar-and-a-quarter for a Scripto pen. As we left the PX, I said, "I'm almost back to my natural state. Flat broke. But Uncle takes care of my warm body and he feeds, clothes, and shelters me, right?"

"Quite right, Tom. And cheer up. Payday is coming."

"Everything I get on payday goes for my train fare home. I'll have exactly two bucks left for spending money." He said he might be able to loan me some funds, and I said, "I'll work it out. When Mary's allotment check comes, she'll send me a few bucks for my meals on the way home. She's terrific that way."

TOM O'CONNELL

"Are you anxious to see her?"

A mist came into my eyes. "The word is 'possessed.'"

At the Service Club, I went to the mezzanine and sat in a lounge chair. Norm went to the record player. While I prepared to answer Mary's recent letters, I heard the strains of White Christmas. Then I heard Norm's off-key voice accompanying Bing Crosby and I groaned, "Only Norm would play that song in the heat of August."

Norm was standing there before the phonograph with his eyes closed and his arms waving, almost in time to the music, and his mouth was moving as he approximated the tune. Soon there were more groans as other enlisted men became aware of the number, but Norm went on undaunted. He was conducting as if he had an orchestra as he sang along with the record, his eyes closed the whole time.

He's a strange bird, I thought, but he helps keep my mind off my problems. One thing I like about Norm is there's no question about who he is. He's strictly himself, take it or leave it.

Well, let's see now. I've got a magnum opus to write tonight. I'd better get going on it. One good thing is that my last talk with the first sergeant at B Company left me a lot more optimistic than the first time I dropped the idea of an emergency leave on him. Now I can be very specific with Mary about what the Red Cross has to do.

**Letter, August 27, 1954**
**Army Service Club**
**Camp Gordon, Georgia**

*As long as I'm in "B" Company officially, the leave will be given when they receive a wire that the Red Cross verifies the fact that you are under a doctor's care, and that I am needed for morale support, and other reasons.*

*They won't accept any vague talk like "There is an emergency; send Thomas home." They want something like this:*

*"On checking with Doctor So-and-so, we verify the fact that Mrs. O'Connell is in a condition where the presence of*

*Mr. O'Connell is necessary for morale purposes, as well as the need for him to be present for transportation of Mrs. O'Connell to the hospital. Please arrange leave as soon as possible."*

*Tell the Red Cross lady that they won't arrange leave for me until they receive word that the emergency exists from the official Red Cross representative. The first sergeant at B Company said they rely entirely on the Red Cross request, and he told me that if I needed any money for transportation they'd arrange a loan at the Emergency Relief place on the Camp.*

*The procedure is just this:*

1. *Red Cross wires my company (B Company).*
2. *They get in touch with me.*
3. *They prepare my leave papers.*
4. *I go home.*

*I know, honey, the Army is crazy, but when it comes to emergency leave, the Army is usually okay.*

*Bye-bye for now, sweet.*

*Your own loving husband,*
*Tommy*

By the time I was done an hour later, I had completed seven pages and enclosed a verse I had come across that week in a book of poetry. As I sealed the envelope I thought, That verse reminds me of me and Mary. Of course, nowadays every romantic song or poem reminds me of Mary. There was a time when I wondered if I'd ever have this kind of love, and I used to wonder what was going on with other couples. I knew about the sexual urges but I didn't know about how deep love could go.

"How's your letter coming?" It was Norm.

"Oh . . . I . . . good, Norm. Just finished it. I guess I was daydreaming here. Thinking about getting the other half of my soul back."

"The other half of your soul?"

"Mary."

"Oh, I see."

I shook my head. "No you don't. Nobody sees. What's between Mary and me can't be seen. But it's there." I paused and nodded. "Like God, Norm. We can't see God, but he's there beyond what we can see and touch. There just has to be a God, Norm."

"Why?"

"To answer the question why." I laughed.

"Are you going to use your Jesuit logic on me again tonight?"

"Nope. You can find your own salvation, buster. I won't pressure you."

"I believe that's a selfish philosophy."

"Believe what you want to. I relate to freedom of thought. God gave everyone free will, so who am I to impose my will on you? I might make a suggestion once in a while, but your will is your will, period. Come on, let's go shoot some pool. Then maybe we can get some new books to read."

We shot pool for a while and, as usual, I won. Then we played a game of ping pong which I purposely lost. Finally, we turned in the books we had read, took out new ones, and sat reading until the Service Club closed for the night. Then we walked back toward the 402nd Military Government Company in the warm night air, and we talked about the Army, the world, and life itself.

We were halfway to the barracks when a car pulled up beside us. "Hey, O'Connell, you guys want a lift?"

"Sure, Philly. What the hell, I don't have any prejudice against riding with a guy from Philadelphia."

"What about a guy from Chicago?" asked Napoli's hell-raising friend.

"Us Bostonians don't have anything against Chicago. How's it going, one of fifteen?" The Chicago-born Medina was the youngest of a family of fifteen.

Norm and I sat in the rear seat and made ourselves comfortable. Then Medina turned around and said, "I'm pooped from all the snatch we got tonight. My broad had hotpants and prackly gave me a hernia."

"I tossed off a helluva piece, too," said Napoli. "No shit, Boston, I think I'm gonna go up with the damn shade tomorrow." He laughed at his favorite joke. "Hey, Boston, you ain't much for strange ass, right?"

"I don't need any strange ass. How many times do I have to tell you I'm happily married?"

"He's in a state of marital bliss," said Norm.

"Bliss your ass," grunted Napoli. "Any guy that's used to knocking off a steady piece and then he has to do without it isn't in no state of bliss, Molesko. He's either playing around with the lady from five fingers or he's getting something to keep his weapon oiled. Hey, Boston, you gotta keep an instrument tuned up, ya know, or it's gonna go flat on you."

"That doesn't worry me, Philly. A good musician doesn't forget."

Norm nudged me and said to Napoli, "Man does not live by his genitals alone."

Napoli laughed. "You mean man don't live by his balls? You'd never know that by me, Molesko. I'd sure as hell hate to lose them. I'm sort of attached to 'em."

Napoli's comments hit Norman's funny bone and he jounced on the seat and held his sides as he laughed and giggled hysterically. Then he shouted, "That's great! He's sort of attached to his balls!"

As the car pulled into the lot across from the 402nd MG Company, the vehicle rocked with contagious laughter. "Hey, Molesko," said Napoli, "I never thought you could laugh your ass off at a dirty remark. I thought you were neuter!"

"Neuter!" Norm giggled. "He thought I was neuter!"

Napoli turned to me as we left the car. "No shit, Boston. I thought he was one of those things that's half man and half broad."

"A hermaphrodite?"

"That's it. I thought he was a half-assed hermaphrodite."

This really threw Norm into a fit of hilarity, and he hitched up his slacks and went into his step dance in the parking area and shouted, "Napoli thought I was a half-assed hermaphrodite!"

Napoli said, "Shit, Molesko, you always got your damn nose in a book. If I didn't know O'Connell here was married I'd think both of you guys was shacking up with each other." We all laughed and Napoli slapped me on the back. "You don't give a shit if I rib you a little, huh Boston? You know I don't mean nothing by it."

"Sure, Philly. It's all in fun, and you're just a hot shit from Philadelphia, right?"

"Fucking A-one right, Boston." His bony hand slapped me again on the back. "In Boston they really know their beans, right?"

"Right, Philly, and in Philadelphia they know their cream cheese."

We were all laughing as we entered the barracks. "Here they all comes," shouted Wilson when we reached the top of the stairs. "Here comes the two eyetalians wif their peckers drooping from all the ass they been planking and here's the buck slip wif his white socks and his book under his arm, and the damn nut what thinks he's some kind of a pisscologist. These mens are one mess of cruddy feet and pisscologist nuts and bug-outs and ass-reamers."

I responded, "Thanks for your running commentary on the news of the day, Wilson. Tune in again tomorrow, same time, same station, for the Wilson show."

As we neared our bunks, I said to Norm, "Wilson sure breaks the barracks monotony."

An early sleeper shouted, "Come on, you guys. Knock it off!"

"I isn't saying nothing at all," replied Wilson with his naturally loud voice. "I is just whispering is all." The rest of us laughed as the sleepy soldier groaned.

I was soon in my own bunk and as I lay there I thought, With just a couple of weeks to go we're in the home stretch now, me and Mary . . . and him or her, whichever the baby is. Seems like I've been away from home forever. The only reality here is red clay and heat and dust and bugs. Home is about a thousand miles away but it might as well be a hundred thousand.

I hope to hell Western Union can get us together. But what if the powers that be don't pay any attention to the Red Cross telegram? Then what? Will I go AWOL? It would be self-defeating, but I promised her I'd be there. I have to be there when the baby arrives! Timing is everything in this life, and I've planned as well as a guy could.

If the telegram works I'll be on the train and out of this hole with no sweat. Well, where there's life, there's sweat. Nothing comes easily. Especially down here in Georgia. This place would make a bug-out out of the most unlikely soldier. Maybe I better say a little bug-out prayer.

In the name of the Father and the Son and the Holy Ghost. Amen. God, this is bug-out O'Connell tuning in on you. There's something I want to remind you about. Have you got a divine minute? I need your help to get home in time to be with Mary. I can't carry it off without your help, as you know, so I'm reminding you again. I know you're very busy with all kinds of requests, but they say the squeaky wheel gets the grease, so how about it, huh? Your help, please.

I closed my eyes but I was not sleepy, and in my whirling mind I wondered, Why did she have to get those toxemia symptoms? As if being pregnant isn't enough of a problem. Those doctors of hers claim it's just a threat, not actual toxemia, but what about the dizzy spells and swelling in her legs and wrists and even in her fingers?

Are those symptoms just a threat? And not a reality? These Army doctors only react to the sight of blood. If you don't spill any, you've had it. You'd think they'd be more concerned about her blood pressure, but all they've done is tell her to stay away from salt and watch her weight. She's got all the symptoms they list in that medical book, and it says toxemia can bring death to the mother or child or even both when the mother goes into labor.

God almighty, she could end up with convulsions or go into a coma or have her blood pressure go completely haywire or any number of other problems, but I'm the only one who seems to get the seriousness of it. Actually, Mary's more worried about me being stuck here than she is about her own toxemia, and those idiot Army doctors aren't apt to be too concerned about a private's wife. But if I get there before she goes to the hospital I'll stay right on those doctors' backs. I won't keep my eyes off those birds for a minute. The key thing now is getting myself home ahead of time.

# PART IV

## (September to November 1954)

# 14

My persistence, coupled with a relentlessly positive attitude and constant prayer, paid off. With the help of the Red Cross office in Framingham, Massachusetts, I made it home on time to be with Mary a few days before the labor pains came. The woman at the Red Cross had used my revised message for the telegram exactly as I'd dictated it to Mary on the phone. It was a more powerful letter than the first one I had suggested. The thrust of it was that Mary was suffering from last minute medical complications, and because her parents were ill they couldn't drive her to Murphy General Army Hospital; therefore, I was needed at home as soon as possible.

I wasn't sure the Army would buy the logic I had concocted, but I had asked the Red Cross to address the telegram to Captain Solomon who had agreed to be my advocate. At this point I had almost completed my temporary duty in the 402nd and would probably be made permanent party shortly. Captain Solomon sold the idea to Diamond Jim, got the sergeant in the MP outfit to agree, and soon I was being sprung loose, packing my bags, and catching a train for the thousand mile ride to Massachusetts.

## REQUEST AND AUTHORITY FOR ABSENCE
*DATE: 13 September 1954*

*NAME, GRADE, AND SERVICE NUMBER*
*O'CONNELL, Thomas F*
*Pvt-2*
*US 51 305 178*

*TYPE OF ABSENCE: Emergency Leave*
*AUTHORITY: AR 600-115*
*NO. OF DAYS: 10 DATE FROM: 14 Sept Sep 54 DATE TO:*
*23 Sep 54*

*ORGANIZATION AND STATION*
*Company "B" MPTC, 8801-6 TU*
*Camp Gordon, Georgia*

*ADDRESS WHILE ABSENT: 11 Sherman Avenue, Franklin,*
*Mass.*

*[X] I CERTIFY THAT I HAVE (NOT) SUFFICIENT LEAVE*
*TIME ACCRUED TO COVER THIS ABSENCE.*

*SIGNATURE: Thomas F. O'Connell, Jr.*
*REMARKS: I certify that I have enough funds to cover me*
*while on this leave.*

*DATE APPROVED: 13 September 1954*

*TYPED NAME, GRADE AND TITLE OF APPROVING*
*AUTHORITY: FRED VIGIL, Major, MPC; Adjutant*
*SIGNATURE OF APPROVING AUTHORITY: Fred Vigil*
*(Form DA 31 Aug 53)*

The time at home with the in-laws in Franklin passed all too rapidly. First came the ongoing thrill of being home again, and the excitement of watching for Mary's birth signals. Then, after days of waiting while my leave time gradually shrunk, there was the exciting middle of the night ride to Waltham in Bill Killoren's old Studebaker. And finally, after a very long labor at Murphy General Army Hospital, while I rested around the clock on a hard wooden bench outside the labor room as women's screams and moans provided background sound, Mary was wheeled into surgery and little Margaret Mary O'Connell, seven pounds and four ounces, made her entrance into the world on September 18, 1954.

Then it was almost time for me to go back to Georgia, but Army hospitals like Murphy General had a policy of keeping new mothers and their children for a full seven days after the birth. This motivated another request to the Red Cross to come to my aid so I could be on hand to take Mary and the baby home.

Once again, the very helpful woman at the Red Cross in Framingham worded the telegram exactly the way I dictated it to her, and a request to extend my leave for five more days was on its way to Georgia. It was rapidly approved, so not only had I been able to get home before the baby came, I could also be with Mary when she took the baby back to the Killorens' house. Home run with the bases loaded! O'Connell four. Army nothing.

All too soon my emergency leave ended and I had to exit the scene of my new fatherhood and head toward Georgia. South Station in Boston was once again the place of departure, and there I was, checking my duffel bag and heaving my smaller bag on board.

Counting the steel steps, and trying to appear casual, I almost tripped as I reached the top step. Then I turned and saw Mary with the baby in her arms, blowing me a kiss as the train pulled away, and with misty eyes I returned it. We waved goodbye to each other as the train began to move slowly out of the station heading southward. Then the image of Mary became smaller, her auburn hair became a glimmer of sunlit rust, and her spring coat turned into a dab of dark blue. Finally, she became a distant dot and then there was no dot at all. She and little Peggy were gone. And I was alone again.

**Letter written on the train and mailed in Washington, DC: Tuesday, Sept. 28, 1954, 6:00 p.m.**

*The trip back is the hard one. I am only living for the day when you step off the train in Augusta in 5-1/2 weeks and we'll live like we should, together.*

*Be brave, honey . . . we have so much to be thankful for and so much to look forward to. The train just left me off here. I catch the train for Georgia in about an hour. Right opposite the train station is an enormous U.S. Post Office here in D.C. That's where I'm writing to my honey right now.*

*Gee, hon, so far it's a struggle to hold back the tears. When the days start going by and finally when you get to Georgia soon, everything will be wonderful.*

*I read that pocket book "The Sun Also Rises" on the way here. I had a hard time concentrating but it helped pass the time. Tonight I'll try to get some sleep. Tomorrow I'll be back in Georgia, darn it. Already it's hotter, here in Washington. Oh, well.*

*Most important of all, remember that I am yours and can live happily only when you are near. Tell Peggy I love her too. She is a wonderful daughter. I'll see the two of you in a few weeks (I wish it were a few hours).*

*I'm always your loving husband,*
*Tommy*

The train was crossing the state line between South Carolina and Georgia, and the heat was beginning to get to me. There was no air conditioning on most trains in those days, and if you could get a window to open you were just letting smoke and soot in, so traveling by train was not exactly a romantic adventure.

I thought, September's just about over but it's still hot as hell down here. I was getting used to that nice clear crisp air back home, and here I go again, into the inferno. My lungs are in for the heat treatment. My mind is in for a treatment too. For my own sanity, I'll have to make like Camp Gordon is just an illusion. But that poses no great problem. The only reality for me now is that little family of mine: me and Mary and Peggy. Wow, is Peggy cute. She must take after her mother.

I leaned my head back on the hard-cushioned backrest and during the rest of the ride to Augusta, Georgia, and on the bus to Camp Gordon, my mind was filled with thoughts of my days in Massachusetts.

When I arrived at the 402nd, Norm was about to head for the Mess Hall for supper, so I put my unpacked belongings at the foot of my bunk and joined my friend. At the Mess Hall, Norm and I chatted. Sipping his coffee and blinking his small brown eyes, he asked, "Just how does it feel to be a father?"

I grinned. "Different."

"Is that all you can say?"

I was not very adept in those days at sharing my deepest feelings, so I said, "Do I have to go into a dissertation? It's new and different and I'm not quite used to it yet."

Norm nodded and moved away from his tendency to probe my psyche. "You stayed home longer than you planned."

"Right. The Red Cross came through twice in the telegram department, so with the help of Captain Solomon I made it home on time, and later I got an extension so I could be there when she left the hospital. I was very lucky."

"You were anxious about being there with her, weren't you?"

"The word 'anxious' isn't strong enough, Norm. 'Possessed' is better. A real bug-out is always possessed and doesn't stop being that way until the goal is won."

He said, "I don't imagine I could get possessed enough to become a good bug-out. I adjust too readily to situations. But I would certainly like to bug out of here and go to work in my MOS."

"Then get possessed. Look at these canned franks and soggy beans and tell yourself there's something better waiting for you at the Disciplinary Barracks, a job you're really suited for. Then take the necessary steps and damned if you won't make it."

He shrugged. "Perhaps some day I'll make it. I still go to Personnel every week."

I laughed. "Try going every day! Being possessed is more than a weekly thing. I'm already possessed about my next goal. Living off-post with Mary."

"You don't rest, do you?"

"Nope. Resting never got anybody to a goal. A bug-out never rests on his laurels, Norm. The Killorens don't like the idea, but their opinions don't interest us. Our minds are made up. It's strange how a few weeks ago they were bitching about how much it cost to have Mary living with them. Now they're trying to keep her from coming down here."

"You don't get along well with them, do you?"

"That's the understatement of the year. The farther we get from them the happier we are. The Killorens have something in common with Diamond Jim. They don't like college boys. My dedication to my education makes them feel uncomfortable."

Norm squinted at me. "Maybe they think you feel superior."

I laughed. "Maybe I do. They can be pretty hopeless."

"Perhaps you intimidate them."

I shrugged. "Why should a poor guy working his ass off to get through college intimidate them? I've never given them a hard time about anything, but they're anti-youth and anti-love and anti-intellectual. Who needs them?"

"You do."

I agreed. "Yup, right now we do. But we pay every cent of our way, including our long distance phone calls. The Killorens are never gonna die of generosity. I think one of the reasons they were upset when Mary and I got serious was they knew they'd be losing her weekly board money."

"Could they be that crass?"

"Yes, Norm. They used to drive to Walpole to meet her on payday at the Bird & Son factory so they could get her money as fast as they could. Look, you'd never believe the stuff we've run into with them. Sort of like Romeo and Juliet. Brother, when

I think of some of the things they pulled on us I could shit." I swallowed the last of my lima beans. "But to hell with the past. If I spend too much time there it depresses me. I'm better off trying to live in the present with an eye on the future."

"I wish I could put Diamond Jim in my past."

"Make like he doesn't exist. Then he won't bug you."

Norm shook his head. "Practice what you preach."

"Easier said than done, right? Diamond Jim bugs me, the Army bugs me, and the Killorens bug me. The trouble with you, Norm, is you're getting to know me too well."

"It's quite obvious that you bug out to compensate for your frustration."

"I'd rather compensate than incinerate."

"Just what does that mean?" Norm blinked rapidly and adjusted his glasses.

"It means when I'm faced with the fires of hell I believe in trying to cool myself off instead of accepting a fiery fate like a passive piece of very dry wood."

"Do you think I'm passive?" Norm asked nervously.

"No, not really. You're living your life the way you think you have to live it."

"But we don't think the same way on certain subjects, right?"

"My motto is 'Live and let live.' So I don't have to agree with all your ideas."

"In reference to Diamond Jim I do not feel like living and letting live," he said with a frown. "He's been exceedingly difficult to live with in recent days. He has not only excoriated the birds in the trees, he has excoriated me, Tom, and I find it hard to adjust to his verbal lashings." He paused and said matter-of-factly, "I'm afraid I'm allowing myself to hate him."

I laughed. "Welcome to the club. Are you trying to tell me you've been having a hard time hating The Diamond? It's difficult to do?"

When we both broke out in laughter, Corporal Pollard, the cook, looked over at us from his rigid stance behind the food trays and said, "What all's so funny?"

I said, "You wouldn't get it. It's sort of an inside joke that only a draftee would understand."

"If I had y'all's buck slip draftee ass on KP your ass wouldn't be laffing so hard." He grunted and returned to his work, and I decided to let it stop there.

Turning to Norm, I said, "Considering Pollard objectively, I wouldn't think he had enough imagination to picture somebody's ass laughing."

When Norm absorbed my remark he almost choked on the muddy coffee he was swallowing. "It makes a humorous picture, Tom. I can see it now. A posterior immersed in laughter. That's great!"

I grinned. "Watch out or you'll lose your depression and it will come to me and add itself to the one I've been sinking into. I've been depressed since the train hit South Carolina."

"Your timing is not the best. The Diamond is preparing us for an IG inspection, and his testicles are literally in an uproar. He's been checking for dust with his white gloves and obviously he's been finding it. Tomorrow we rise at five, and on Friday we have to get up at four-thirty."

I frowned. "Sounds like Infantry basic and the MP Training Center."

Norm continued, "He found some dust on the back of the TV set so the Day Room is now off-limits. I also believe he's upset about Private Rawson getting off so lightly at the trial. Goldstein defended him so well he only received six months. The Diamond assumed he'd be in for at least a year. Apparently Goldstein is an excellent defense lawyer."

"Maybe he's too excellent," I said. "If he keeps volunteering to defend shafted enlisted men he'll find himself in Korea. Did Diamond Jim testify?"

Norm nodded as we rose from the table and brought our trays to the tray stack. "The Diamond did his best to crucify him." Norm paused. "But Rawson got back at him."

"Oh? How?"

"Goldstein told me that when the court martial was over and they were leading Rawson out of the chamber, he turned and shouted something that angered Diamond Jim to a great degree." Norm adjusted his eyeglasses and blinked rapidly. Then he giggled and said, "Rawson looked at Diamond Jim right in the eye and yelled, 'Up your diamond!'"

"You've gotta be kidding me, Norm. Kattus must have been pleased to have his new slogan used."

Norm nodded and giggled as we left the Mess Hall. "There was no mistake about it. Goldstein heard him yell 'Up your diamond!' It's great, isn't it?" Norm hitched up his pants and did his step dance while giggling hysterically. "Up your diamond!"

"Well, it seems like Rawson looked his enemy in the eye and gave it to him. It's poetic justice, right? I clearly remember the first time I heard the Diamond tell Gore, 'Shove it up your Gore' so now the tables are turned."

Norm said, "The expression has spread like wildfire. Lately all the enlisted men in the MG Group are walking around saying 'Up your diamond' to each other."

As we walked back to the barracks, he filled me in on the most recent events in the 402nd Military Government Company, and I tried to keep my part of the conversation light so I would not dwell too deeply on the depressing contrast between my lighthearted days with Mary and the dismal renewal of an unspecified term of marital separation.

I had my own goal of her coming to Georgia in five to six weeks, but I knew only too well that personal goals in the U.S. Army were subject to arbitrary and capricious authority. I was not overly confident about achieving my goal.

When we reached the second level of the barracks, Wilson was there to greet us. "Look who all's back here." His large white teeth gleamed in his black face. "It's that damn buck slip wif his white socks and what all. He's back here living the good life again. What cruddy book y'all reading tonight, buck slip?"

"It's a book that might change my whole life. I'm gonna read the Re-enlistment Guide. I'm thinking of going gung-ho RA all the way. That's me, Wilson." I laughed. "I'm a Regular Army kind of guy. A twenty-year man." I chuckled at my own sarcasm.

"What was that bullshit about RAs?" An angry voice came at me from a group of career soldiers playing poker in the space between bunks at the top of the stairs. It was Pfc. Pearse, whose unpredictable fury had reduced his rank from sergeant to private. The legend was that he had floored a lieutenant in a fit of temper, and he was now working himself up slowly toward his former rank. Lean, muscular, and very strong, he was a dangerous person to tangle with.

"What were you saying about us RAs, you damn bug-out?" he persisted.

I grinned and replied, "I just said I was thinking of going RA, Pearse." I grinned again, hoping to get across the message that I was only poking fun.

Pearse's muscular frame flew up from the bunk where the poker game was in progress and his large left hand grabbed my collar. "Damned if I'm gonna take any bullshit from a fucking college boy like you, O'Connell." Suddenly I found my long thin body lifted from the floor, and my smile was rapidly fading. In survival mode now, my heart was pounding hard and my face was flushed. "You damn college boys think us RA's are nothing but dog shit, ain't that so, O'Connell?"

As he tightened my collar like a noose, I wheezed and grunted. "Nope. I didn't say that, Pearse, so let me down, okay?"

I felt my feet touch solid ground again but the hand was still clenched hard at my collar. Pearse growled, "You're a wise bastard, O'Connell." Looking like a crazed beast, he drew his right hand back for what I knew would be a very damaging punch in the mouth.

Squirming in his tight grasp, I put my left arm up in front of my face to protect myself. "Dammit, Pearse!" I grunted. "Court martial! Cream me and you'll be in the DB for sure. The stockade!"

"The what?"

I could hardly breathe now, but I croaked, "Assault and battery, you hot shit." At that moment he had a burst of enlightenment, his right fist stopped in mid-arc, and I felt the grip on my shirt collar loosen.

"You ought to watch that wise mouth of yours, O'Connell," he said as he released me. "If I was a damn buck-slip bug-out like you I'd watch my ass around us RAs."

As I pulled myself together I still managed to push my luck even further. "You mean RAs can't take a joke?"

"We can take a joke, O'Connell, but we don't like being put down. You're lucky your face is still on your head."

"I've got your message, Pearse, loud and clear." I was finally ready to surrender.

"You better believe it," he said as he returned to his card game. The expression "You better believe it" was a statement used on a very regular basis in the Army during my term of service.

I was tempted to make another wisecrack but held my tongue. Anyhow, how important was it to get the last word? Instead, I preferred to keep my face in its usual place on my head. Turning toward Norm, who had been watching the action, I said, "Did you enjoy the show? It isn't often you see a near-death experience."

"I believe you asked for it," he said calmly.

"But I wasn't even talking to Pearse, I was talking to Wilson."

"However, Pearse felt you were referring to him."

"In a general way, I was. I guess I haven't completely accepted the fact that I'm back here at cruddy Camp Gordon, Georgia, as a lowly buck private. Maybe I'm still thinking like a civilian."

"Thinking and talking are two different things," said Norm thoughtfully. "At times it is best to keep one's thoughts to oneself."

I agreed with him, accepting his constructive criticism, and then I suggested that we get ourselves out of the barracks and down to the Service Club, to play pool and ping pong for a while.

At the Club I wrote a letter to Mary and filled Norm in on more of the details of my trip to the other world which seemed so unreal now that I was back in the confines of Camp Gordon.

**Letter, Wednesday, September 29**

*Well, I'm back at the grind. I arrived in Augusta at about 10 a.m. this morning. Boy, it's still quite warm down here. I roasted with my winter uniform on.*

*The first thing I did was check on the railroad fare and Railway Express rates. Well, the railroad fare will be $34, less than we expected. That's good because we'll need every cent we can get extra. Right now we have $56, which only leaves us about $20. Enclosed is the schedule you will use.*

*The best train is the one called the Palmetto. You'll make connections just as I did on the way down here this time. I have marked the schedule accordingly. One call to South Station will give you all the information you need about buying the tickets.*

*After arriving here, I didn't want to go right back to camp so I had lunch and saw the "Caine Mutiny" court martial at the Miller Theatre which you will be attending soon. It was terrific. What a picture. Certain parts made me awful lonesome for you.*

*I'm being assigned to the 402nd on October 1st. At last I will be finished my training. I won't worry about anything when you are here, my wife. It's awful away from you. It seems so unreal. I feel so content when I can just blow you a kiss, and hug you for being so cute, and just be your honey. I pray to God that this will be our last time apart in the Army. In a few weeks we'll be praying together and it will be wonderful.*

*Enclosed are pictures of me and my pals. In one picture I'm sticking my tongue out at the Army. In the other I'm waving to you, honey. In both pictures I'm carrying my letter-writing*

*equipment and a book as I head for the Service Club. The*
*pictures are taken right outside the barracks.*
    *I got two cute letters you wrote before my leave. You're*
*wonderful, honey.*
    *I love you.*

                                                *Your own,*
                                                *Tommy*

I didn't tell her that the psycho commanding officer, Captain
Queeg, played by Humphrey Bogart, had mental health problems
that reminded me of The Diamond's behavior. I held back
because I wanted to keep my letter upbeat. Also, I didn't want
to accentuate the negativity I was already feeling so soon after
my arrival back in Georgia.

Later that evening as I lay on my bunk in the barracks, I
reflected on the days of my leave and I reviewed the scenes of
my days in Massachusetts. They had not exactly been relaxed
carefree days; they had been real days filled with real problems.
But handling problems in civilian life was like a vacation
compared to being in the Army.

Among the problems was the rush to the hospital in the
middle of the night in the Killorens' slow-starting old Studebaker.
There was also the problem of trying to hold down my personal
anxiety about Mary's physical condition.

A very dramatic situation arose during the tension-filled
thirty-six hours of labor when the baby presented its face instead
of the back of its head in the final stages. Along the way there was
also the problem of a private trying to communicate with Army
doctors who were majors and colonels. Yes, and there had been
the problem of getting into the labor room to see Mary, against
the wishes of a negative nurse with an eagle eye, a raspy voice,
and an irritating mouth shaped like a torn pocket.

An ongoing problem had been the challenge of trying to
make my sensitive body comfortable on the hard oak bench in

the hospital corridor where I had maintained my vigil day and night until the moment of birth. In addition, there had been the problem of having my leave extended so I could be with Mary a few days after she went home from the hospital.

However, all the problems had worked themselves out, and compared to the problem of adjusting to an Army life away from Mary, they had not been very large problems at all.

Yup, I thought as I lay there in my bunk, we had a few problems when I was home, but Mary and little Peggy survived the birth process. I'll take a life of problems with the two of them any day over the so-called total security of Camp Gordon. I was there by her side like I promised, and she really appreciated that.

After the birth process was over and I saw the sweet look in her eyes as she held our baby, there was no question about it being worth all the bug-out anxiety. Now the next bug-out challenge is getting her down here to live off-post in our own apartment. That depends on whether they keep me as permanent party or ship my ass someplace else.

It's a weird contradiction, isn't it? I hate this place, and I hate the heat, and Diamond Jim is strictly from hunger, but I still want to stay here. I suppose a guy would want to stay in Purgatory a little while if he could have a chance at Heaven and avoid going to hell, so maybe it's no contradiction after all.

There's one thing that's a real contradiction though. This simulated Army's a contradiction from the word go. That's probably why Pearse got so shook and almost rearranged my face. Hey, his whole life is a contradiction, but he doesn't know it. No wonder he got upset when I wisecracked about re-upping. He's trapped in the Army, right between a rock and a hard place as these guys say down here.

Considering the heat and the dust and the gnats and Diamond Jim it's hard for a guy to keep a sense of humor around here. I guess I'll have to try to be more compassionate and diplomatic with these Regular Army guys. They're like rockets ready to explode. And I don't want them going off in my face.

My face isn't a perfect face, but I'm used to it and I'd just as soon keep it the way it is. Even though the Army looks at me only as a warm body with no identity except a number, I'm sort of attached to this warm body. Well, enough philosophizing. I better get some sleep. Diamond Jim expects us warm bodies to wake up at five o'clock tomorrow morning. Five? I can't believe it. But I better believe it. Oh brother . . .

# 15

The enlisted personnel residing in the barracks of the 402nd Military Government Company had been up since five a.m. preparing our living quarters for Diamond Jim's simulated General Inspection. Sergeant Ernest Tucker, who happened to be "colored," as we all said in those days, was the senior man in our barracks since his recent promotion. He had just called us to attention when I heard the first sergeant enter the ground level. We were doing what we had learned to do well, standing and waiting.

My impression was that Tucker was "getting shook." After all, it had taken him a long time to get his three stripes, and now he had the challenge of proving that he deserved them. I was thinking, Hell, he didn't have to call us to attention up here on the second floor until our lord and master climbs the stairs. What was the big rush?

Sounds like Diamond Jim's raising hell with the men downstairs. Maybe he'll be worn out by the time he gets up here. There's no doubt about one thing. I'm living like a soldier again. It's only seven a.m. and I feel like I've been up for a year. I got spoiled sleeping late at the Killorens' house. This Army life is strictly a minus. Who needs it? I'm definitely not cut out for this type of existence. What I'm suited for is the . . .

Diamond Jim appeared at the head of the stairs. "At ease, you idiots. Now I'm gonna check out this rat hole." Starting at the far end of the barracks, near the stairway, he worked his way slowly along the two rows of bunks, inspecting footlockers, wall lockers, clothing, brass, shoes, and any other category of readiness he saw fit to inspect.

With his white-gloved right hand he tested locker tops for dust, along with two-by-four wall braces, and window sills. As he made his way up the aisle it soon became evident to me that he was "gigging" every soldier for one or more infringements of his completely arbitrary standards.

Finally, he reached my bunk. "You got back off leave just in time for the little inspection, huh O'Connell? Are you ready to add your name to my damn gig list? Huh? Are ya?" I thought no reply was needed, so I simply shrugged my shoulders. "I said are ya ready for me to gig your ass?" I nodded. He looked me over from head to toe. Then he reached for my well polished brass belt buckle and flipped it to its back portion which I had skipped. "Uh-huh. It's cruddy, O'Connell, so your ass is gigged for a cruddy belt buckle." He added my name to his gig list.

Then he grunted. "Christ, I almost forgot to check your wall locker." Stepping arrogantly to my wall locker, he ran his white gloved right hand along the top and when he looked at the palm of the glove, already dirty from the dust of many other wall locker tops, he grunted. "Sure as shit, your wall locker's dusty, O'Connell." He added the second infraction to the list on his clipboard.

Then he stood before me and darted his shifty blue eyes into my dark brown ones, and I calmly looked into Diamond Jim's eyes until the first sergeant blinked and looked away and then turned back to me again and grunted, "Two gigs, O'Connell. How's them for fucking apples, huh?"

I had made a pledge to myself to keep my words to a minimum when it came to Diamond Jim, so I shrugged and said nothing, and while I was standing there saying nothing I thought, You can take those non-existent apples of yours and shove them up your non-existent ass. I'm not answering your question because I've decided you don't exist in my life. You're just a military non-entity.

Diamond Jim wasn't satisfied with my silence. "I said how's them for fucking apples, O'Connell. Didn't ya hear your first sergeant talking to ya? Or did ya get deaf on leave, for Christ's sake?"

"My leave didn't affect my hearing, Sergeant," I replied as calmly as I could, although I was seething within.

The Diamond glared at me. "When your first sergeant talks to ya, he wants a fucking answer. I don't need no cruddy foot college boy telling me about his damn hearing problems. I just want a simple fucking answer for a simple question." He paused and my face was now getting red. "Okay, O'Connell, whattayasay? I said you got gigs. As I asked you already, how's them for fucking apples?"

As he spoke, I thought, This guy is a madman. He asks a stupid question and he expects a normal answer. I can't win. If I tell him I don't like the gigs, or if I tell him I do, or if I tell him I question his judgment, I'll only be shafting myself. Well, here goes nothing. "No comment, Sergeant."

Diamond Jim narrowed his light blue eyes and scowled. "No comment? Are you fucking with me, O'Connell? It don't pay to fuck with old Dad, you know. No comment? Well, I'll be dipped in shit." He turned to the other soldiers. "This here O'Connell says no comment. You might know I'd get an answer like that from a damn college boy!"

Turning his attention back to me, he said, "In civilian life you guys think you're the cat's ass, but in this man's Army you're nothing but shit and all's you're good for is shit details." He pulled back his lips against his buck teeth and sputtered, "Hey, that's pretty good. Good for nothing but shit details." I tried not to show my building irritation. "No comment, huh? Well, you better remember something, O'Connell. You're not home on leave no more and your warm body belongs to this man's Army. And don't let your long skinny ass forget it. I got the diamond, see?" He pointed to the diamond flanked by six stripes. "Three up and three down and the diamond in the middle. Your warm body does what the first sergeant says it's gonna do, O'Connell. No comment, huh? Is that all you got to say?"

My face was flushed and hot with anger, but I controlled the urge to lash out at Diamond Jim verbally and I merely nodded and said, "That's all I can say, Sergeant. No comment."

"For Christ's sake!" shouted Diamond Jim with a wave of his clipboard that came close to hitting my chin. "That's all ya can say, huh? When I ask how's them for fucking apples, that's all ya can say?"

"Right, Sergeant."

Diamond Jim threw his hands in the air. "The damn eight ball can't say nothing else but no comment. Well, his ass is gigged and double-gigged and all's he's got to say is no comment. I should of known better than asking a damn college boy a simple question." He shook his head as he moved to the last bunk in the row. "Let's see how many gigs I can give Moresko. You all shaped up today, Motesko?"

Norm nodded. "I believe so, Sergeant."

"You believe so, huh? Heh-heh. He believes so. Well, let's see what he believes so." Diamond Jim went to the foot of Norm's bunk, opened his laundry bag, and peered in. "What the Christ we got here, Molonko? Or Molitzko? Or Moonotko? Or whatever the hell your pisscologist name is? What's this?"

"Where, Sergeant?" Norm stood facing the aisle, looking straight ahead, and didn't want to turn his eyes unless commanded to do so.

"Here, you four-eyed asshole," growled Diamond Jim. "Right here in your laundry bag which is supposed to be used for laundry."

"Is there something in my laundry bag that doesn't belong there, Sergeant?"

"What the hell did ya think I said, that your laundry bag was over at the damn WAC barracks, for Christ's sake? Heh-heh. That's pretty good. Over at the WAC barracks. Okay, Molasko, what the hell you got in your laundry bag?"

"My laundry, Sergeant."

"Oh yeah?" Diamond Jim let out an angry roar. "Then what the fuck is this?" He yanked a bulky object out of the blue laundry bag. "Is this here what you call laundry?" The first sergeant held a large stuffed elephant toy high in the air and shouted, "I thought I seen everything, but this Molapso takes the major's cake!"

When the men of the barracks saw the elephant they all laughed and even Diamond Jim chuckled. "Heh-heh. Yuh, he takes the major's cake, huh? Okay, youse guys, get your laughing asses back to attention. You'll laugh when I tell ya to laugh, you assholes." He looked at the toy elephant, shook his head, peeled back his lip, and sputtered. "Well, I'll be a no good son of a bitch."

That's right, I thought. That's exactly what you are. It's interesting you should admit it to all of us.

Diamond Jim waved the elephant at Norm. "Explain this, you asshole pisscologist. What the hell was this here doing in your laundry bag?"

Norm squinted through his eyeglasses and his small brown eyes blinked rapidly. "I put it there for safe keeping, Sergeant. I bought it in Augusta for my cousin and I haven't had a chance to mail it yet."

"Are you just shitting me, Morasko?" Diamond Jim put his face about one inch from Norm's. "You expect me to believe that goat shit?"

"It's the truth, Sergeant. I assume you want the truth."

"Assume your ass, Molisko!" Diamond Jim looked at the stuffed elephant first, then at Norm. "You think I was born yesterday, huh? Are you fucking with old Dad? You trying to make a fool out of your first sergeant?"

"No, Sergeant." Norm adjusted his eyeglasses, which were slipping down his nose, as usual. "You wanted to know how the elephant got into my laundry bag and I believe I explained it to the best of my ability."

"Oh, you believe that, huh?" Diamond Jim glared at Norm. "Well. I think you're just trying to be a wise bastard, you damn pisscologist. I think you're just trying to fuck with old Dad."

Norm looked at Diamond Jim and calmly asked, "What have I done to make you feel that way?"

"You know what you done, you damn four-eyed goof-off pisscologist private. Molinko, you're a fuck-up and I'm gonna have your ass for this!"

As calm as Norm was trying to appear in front of the first sergeant, he did not want to have his rear end in Diamond Jim's hands. "But what have I done, Sergeant?"

Diamond Jim put his clipboard on Norm's bunk and scratched his head with his right hand while still holding the elephant in his left. "I think you're trying to make me out an asshole, Molexko. I think you're doing some cruddy pisscologist experiment on me or something. Well, you're the one that's the asshole, private. I got the diamond, see?" He pointed to his emblem of rank. "I'll fix your four-eyed ass, Molinko." Diamond Jim scratched his head again and said, "You don't know what you done, huh?"

"No, Sergeant. Other than getting a toy elephant for my cousin and putting it in my laundry bag until I had a chance to mail it, I have no idea what I could have done to get you so upset, Sergeant."

"Upset?" growled Diamond Jim. "Who's upset? You're the one that'll be upset because your ass is gonna be buried in the grease trap."

Although I was supposed to be at attention, staring straight ahead like everyone else in our barracks, I couldn't resist turning my head a bit to get a better view of the proceedings. "What the hell you gawking at, O'Connell?"

"Uh . . . er . . . nothing, Sergeant."

"It damn well better be nothing or your long skinny ass is gonna get reamed."

I fixed my eyes on a window across the aisle and thought, Is this really happening to me or am I having a nightmare about being stuck in this weird Army outfit with this psychotic?

Diamond Jim turned his attention to Norm. "So you think you can put one over on old Dad, huh Molarko? You think you can play pisscologist games with old Dad? Tell me this, Morinko, didn't the first sergeant tell you idiots a couple of days ago your laundry bags are for laundry and nothing else?"

"Yes, I believe so, Sergeant." Norm nodded.

"Oh, you believe so, huh? Well, you damn better believe so, Morexo." There was some murmuring down the aisle and Diamond Jim's light blue eyes darted away from Norm as he shouted, "Keep your asses quiet, you idiots, or youse all are gonna end up digging six-by-sixes under the barracks with your intrenching shovels."

He turned back to Norm. "You heard what I said about using the laundry bags only for laundry, right?" Norm nodded. "Okay then, asshole, did you also hear what I said about not putting boots and shoes in the bags?" Norm nodded again. "And did you hear me say it was no skin off my ass if you put a damn elephant in your laundry bags as long as you didn't put no boots and shoes in there?"

Norm squinted, adjusted his eyeglasses, blinked rapidly, and said, "Perhaps you did say that, Sergeant."

"Perhaps your ass, Molinko! You know damn well I said that, you pisscologist mother-fucker. Now explain how come the elephant was in there if you ain't trying to make your first sergeant out to look like an asshole."

Norm sputtered, "Sergeant, I already ex . . . exp . . ."

"Spit it out, for Christ's sake!" shouted Diamond Jim, waving the stuffed elephant in Norm's face and propelling a spray of spit through the space between his two protruding upper front teeth. "Spit it out, you cruddy four-eyed pisscologist!"

"I already explained the matter. I have nothing further to say about the elephant, Sergeant."

"Well I got something further to say!" shouted Diamond Jim, throwing the elephant down so hard on top of Norm's foot locker that it split a seam in the toy, sending a cloud of stuffing around the area. "What I got to say is you can take this here elephant and shove it up your four-eyed pisscologist ass!"

Turning on his heel, Diamond Jim faced the men lined up on both sides of the aisle. "You assholes better believe your laundry bags are for laundry and nothing else." His eyes darted up and down the aisle as he stood in profile in front of my bunk. "Damn trash of the Army is what you assholes are. You're nothing but eight balls and misfits." He waved his right hand at us. "You hear me, huh? You're nothing but fuck-ups!"

After retrieving his clipboard from Norm's bunk, he shouted for emphasis, "You're nothing but assholes, all of you, and all's you're good for is shit details 'cause you're nothing but shit anyways. Heh-heh. That's pretty good." He burst into a manic laugh. Then he pulled himself together and pointed his finger at Norm. "I ain't gonna forget about this here matter, Mularko."

He pointed to his badge of rank. "When you screw with your first sergeant, you're screwing yourself, Mister Pisscologist. Don't think I ain't gonna ream your four-eyed ass first chance I get." He took his gig list and mumbled as he wrote. "Molumpko. Unauthorized object in laundry bag and litter on foot locker." The litter on the foot locker was the toy stuffing that the first sergeant had settled there in his burst of temper.

If I were Norm, I thought, I'd take that stuffed elephant and dip it in olive drab paint and tuck it up Diamond Jim's rectum and pound it home with an M-1 rifle butt. I bet Norm's attitude about bugging out is in for a drastic change.

At that moment, Diamond Jim announced to the whole floor, "You better believe your asses belong to your first sergeant. We're having a special formation in the Company Area in a minute, so get your asses out there when the whistle blows!"

A minute later, when we were standing in formation outside, he shouted, "This here gig list is gonna be posted in the barracks, and every asshole that was gigged is restricted to the Post this coming weekend." He handed the roster to Sgt. 1st Class Lemmond, who strode into the barracks to post it on the bulletin board. "Okay, you morons, fall out for chow. I'll be seeing you again at the reg'lar morning formation."

The men of the 402nd Military Government Company fell out of formation and drifted into the barracks where, to nobody's surprise, we learned that we had all been gigged and all of us would be restricted to Camp Gordon on the weekend.

At the latrine, as we washed our hands before breakfast, I asked Norm, "Were you putting Diamond Jim on with the elephant bit?"

"No, I was truthful with the psychotic, but his abuse irritated me, Tom. I'm very upset with him now. I feel as though I may vomit at any moment. Do you think perhaps he mispronounces my name on purpose, just to irritate me?"

"Maybe, but it's best to ignore it. Hey, I don't blame you for letting him get to you, but I thought you handled him very well."

"Thank you, Tom."

"You're welcome." I paused. "Well, to bug or not to bug, Norm, that is the question." I dried my hands and breathed a sigh. "I still think you should take a trip to the Pentagon and find some sympathetic alumni from either Columbia or Fordham . . . or both."

"What about you? Why haven't you gone to the Pentagon?" he asked.

"Boston College is a relatively small Catholic college and our alumni wouldn't have the kind of influence you need at the Pentagon. Trying to find a B.C. grad there in a high position would be like trying to find a touch of sanity in Diamond Jim's mind."

"His sanity is very questionable. But it's not his sanity I'm concerned about. It's my own sanity if I have to remain here any length of time. I've tried to adjust but I believe I'm failing." He blinked rapidly. "The idea of bugging out no longer seems alien to me, Tom. I'll consider taking that trip to the Pentagon. I must make every effort to get myself released from this distressing and depressing organization."

"God helps those who help themselves, my grandmother always says. I'm glad to see you're getting the message."

"If it weren't for Diamond Jim I might resign myself to staying here as surplus, but our first sergeant seems to be after my lower anatomy and I've no intention of relinquishing it to him without a struggle."

"He's after everyone's ass today, Norm. It's nothing personal. Hey, it's only my first day back and I'm already wondering if maybe I should have persisted when I made my try for the Section Eight. But I'm supposedly better adjusted now. In other words, I'm less maladjusted. The problem is that after those days at home, I'm seeing this place objectively again, and speaking objectively, this place shits. Speaking of shit, let's get the hell out of this latrine. I think I hear Wilson groaning, and when Wilson groans, pity the man who's around to sniff the aftermath."

Wilson's voice reverberated from one of the toilet cubicles. "I is gonna shit my brains out, you mens out there. We has all been shafted and I is now gonna shit my one-each brains out of my one-each head."

As we were about to step out of the latrine, I turned and shouted, "No Atlanta ass for you this weekend, huh, Wilson?"

"No Atlanta ass," he echoed back. "I has been shafted by The Diamond and that's what all's got me shitting my brains out of my ass. That old Diamond Jim confuses my ass somefin' awful."

"Hey, no sweat, Wilson," I replied. "You've got food, clothing and shelter."

"I has somefin' else," said Wilson.

"Like what?"

"Like I has chicken shit up to my ass."

I laughed, and Norm did too, and then we left for the Mess Hall, where we did our best to analyze our first sergeant's foul mood. We came to no specific conclusion. The Diamond's foul moods, by their very frequency, defied simple analysis. On our way back to the barracks after a breakfast of hard poached eggs and leathery bacon, I summed up our discussion. "I think I know what Diamond Jim's problem is, Norm. I think I know why he's a maladjusted, power crazy, abusive bastard."

"Why?"

I laughed. "It's because he thinks he's unloved . . . and he's right!"

Norm giggled, hitched up his trousers, and went into his step dance. "Unloved! Of course. He thinks he's unloved and he's right, and it's driving him insane." He giggled again, then he became serious. "And I, for one, am helping him to believe he's unloved, Tom, because I hate him!"

"Welcome to the club, Norm. But we shouldn't waste our hate on that bastard. He thrives on it. Guess what else I've learned about him."

"What?"

"I saw his personnel file and it confirmed what someone else said about him. He's got a duodenal ulcer. Maybe his whole life is getting on his nerves, so he takes it out on everyone around him."

Norm nodded. "Yes, I'm afraid he does. So I'll try not to hate him openly, but I definitely intend to bug out of here soon. I'll go to the Pentagon, as you suggested, and I'll pull strings to get myself transferred to the Disciplinary Barracks where I can serve my country more rationally as a clinical psychologist."

"Oh, do you still think of yourself as a psychologist?"

"Certainly. Why do you ask?"

"Because Diamond Jim has us all thinking you're a pisscologist!" We both laughed and strolled on, getting back to the barracks just as the whistle blew the signal for police call, which was followed by the usual morning formation.

"At ease!" shouted Sergeant First Class Lemmond. "Smoke if y'all's got 'em."

I all ain't got 'em, I thought, and I all ain't had a smoke for years, and even if I all had a butt and I smoked, I wouldn't smoke it, just to be ornery, Lemmond.

A moment later an "Atten-hut!" came from Lemmond's mouth, and then our master sergeant leader appeared, with his three stripes up and three down and the diamond in the middle, and stood before us with his clipboard. "Those asshole birds!" He shook his fist at the trees in the rear of the Company area. "Some day I'm gonna kill 'em all." He tried to concentrate on the roster on his clipboard but the birds, as if conspiring to distract him, chirped all the louder. "Fly north, damn you!" he shouted. "Get off my ass and fly north, you birdbrains!"

I stifled the urge to laugh because I and my fellow draftees were well aware that Diamond Jim did not consider himself a stand-up comedian, except on rare occasions when he saw humor in his own abusive behavior and went "Heh-heh."

The sparrows did not fly north. They remained totally unresponsive to the wishes of Diamond Jim as he made his morning announcements. "First off, the damn eight balls living in the barracks had a little inspection today and all their asses got gigged. You off-post guys better watch your asses too, or they'll be mine. Don't get the idea that you only work nine to five like civilians. Anytime I damn well please I can lift your passes and keep you on the post cleaning weapons or anything else I see fit for ya to do."

He rotated his head, scanning all the men in formation. Then he continued, "You guys answer to me and I only answer to two people. The major and the Post Commander." He pointed to his emblem of rank. "I got the damn diamond, see? You assholes better fucking-A not forget it."

We're not about to forget it, I thought. With your constant reminders about your status as our leader and our status as warm bodies, how could we ever forget it? You've got the repetitive instinct of a professional teacher, Diamond Jim. I have to admit one thing about you. You're amazingly good at getting a clear message across.

He was not finished yet. "All you assholes can end up cleaning weapons or sweeping floors if your first sergeant sees fit!" he shouted. "And it won't be punishment either. Heh-heh. It'll be extra training." He scratched his head as his shifty blue eyes roved the ranks. "How's them for fucking apples?"

I wonder if he actually wants an answer, I thought. He was pretty upset when I said "no comment" to the same question in the barracks. I wish we could all reply in unison that we love apples. But we won't reply because we prefer to keep our asses attached to our bodies. Wow, has Diamond Jim got a tight hair stretched across his ass today, and I have a feeling that hair is gonna stay there till the IG inspection is over and done with. In the meantime, if anyone steps out of line he'll find his own ass handed to him on a diamond-shaped platter.

The formation soon ended, and the Headquarters personnel went to the Headquarters Building while the remainder of the men were sorted into groups for work details. I walked slowly through the Military Government Team Area where nothing was being done. Then I made my way up the stairs to the second level and entered the Administrative Area where nothing was being done. It was just one of those frequent times when nothing was being done.

My superior officer, Captain Nelson Solomon, was seated at his desk, reading the Wall Street Journal and smoking his early morning cigar. I stood before his desk. "Good morning, Captain."

Looking up, he flicked the ashes from his cigar and said, "Oh, it's you, O'Connell. How was your leave?"

I told him about my trip home and Peggy's birth. Then I said, "I want to thank you again for putting in that plug for me at the last minute, sir. It really helped."

"Don't mention it, O'Connell. My pleasure. Glad things worked out for you. I imagine you're anxious to have your wife and child come down here so you can live off-post with them."

"That depends on how long I stay on here as permanent party, sir."

While I had been on leave, on 16 September 1954, Headquarters, The Provost Marshal General's Center had issued **Special Orders Number 182:**

*4. PVT-2 THOMAS F O'CONNELL, JR. US 51 305 178 (Cau) (Unasgd) (Term of Induction 2 yr) (ETS Mar 56) rel asg (PIPELINE) Co B, MPTC 8801-6 TU this sta rsg* [meaning "reassigned"] *402d Mil Govt Co this sta. No tvl involved. EDCSA: 25 Sept 54. Auth. TWX DA TAG 547638 from AGPA-*

*NR Wash 25, DC dated 13 Sep 54. PAC SR 615-25-25 EM awarded Pot Prim MOS 4405.*

The captain blinked his eyes a couple of times, fished into his "In" basket, and handed me the set of orders. "No sweat, O'Connell. You're on the roster and you'll be with us indefinitely. Your transfer from the MPs came through while you were gone." A wave of relief surged through me when I heard the word "indefinitely." Then I smiled as the thought of living off-post filled my mind.

"Hold on, O'Connell," said the captain. "There's something else written into the Special Order. You've been given a potential primary MOS of 4405, Clerk-typist. How does that strike you?"

"Fine, sir. It sure beats an MOS of combat infantryman or MP." I knew I could be honest with Captain Solomon. "Tell me, how does that word 'potential' affect the MOS?"

"After you finish the USAFI typing course, we'll give you the permanent MOS. Your course starts this afternoon down the street at thirteen-hundred hours." USAFI was the brief way of saying U.S. Armed Forces Institute. In the Army there were initials for just about everything, and if you didn't know them it was a form of illiteracy.

So many good things were happening at once, a mist came into my eyes and my throat choked up a little. What a bug-out opportunity the typing course was. It would give me a couple of hours of freedom away from MG every afternoon for eight weeks. "Thank you, sir."

As I turned to walk to the desk where I had been working, the Captain grinned and said, "You're going the wrong way, O'Connell. Don't you remember we said we might put you in Kattus' Message Center slot? Well, Kattus is a civilian now and you're our new Message Center Clerk. Do you think you can handle it?" Captain Solomon winked.

Recalling how easy Kattus' job had been, I smiled and said with a touch of irony in my voice, "I can try to handle it the same way Kattus did, sir."

"That's the spirit, O'Connell. Oh yes, you need to turn in your M-One and get yourself a .45 instead, and the cartridge belt you carry it with. It goes with the job." He waved for me to come closer and he whispered, "Hey, what's the matter with the first sergeant today? He's been doing a lot of shouting out there." He chuckled. "I can hardly concentrate on my newspaper."

"He's been reminding us that we're nothing but warm bodies, sir."

The captain laughed. "He gets quite upset sometimes, doesn't he?"

"That's the understatement of the year, sir." I nodded. "He wants us to know beyond any shadow of a doubt that our asses are his."

"Well, that's the Army game, O'Connell." He leaned back and took a deep drag on his cigar. "The major lets us officers know it and the first sergeant lets you fellas know it." He cleared his throat. "Well, I have to get back to my paper work here." He looked down at his newspaper and puffed on his cigar. "Go in and get the feel of the Message Center, why don't you?"

"Right, sir, and thanks again."

"No sweat, O'Connell. Anytime. Mm-hm. Anytime."

I went to my new post. It was a small office with a Dutch door separating it from the corridor. When the bottom half of the door was closed it gave the impression of being an important place. I took a look at the rows of Army Field Manuals on the wall shelves and poked through stacks of Army Orders and miscellaneous correspondence filed in the Message Center. Then S-1 Clerk Raftery, a corporal who had been activated in the Reserves, came in and familiarized me with my new duties as a time-stamper and router of the organization's correspondence. As Raftery left, he winked at me. "Do you think you can handle the job, O'Connell?"

"That's what Captain Solomon asked me. Yup. All I have to do is follow the example Kattus set for me." I put my feet up on my dusty oak desk and put my hands behind my head, and this brought a laugh from Raftery as he left. Then I began to act busy. I was not "a short-timer" almost finished with the Army, as Kattus had been. And if I openly goofed off it would be very self-destructive.

As I sat there congratulating myself on my new role and enjoying the privacy of my room the size of a large closet, I heard loud footsteps on the stairs leading up from down below, and then I heard the voice of Diamond Jim mumbling, "Eight balls! Fuck-ups and eight balls is what they are!"

I could see Diamond Jim entering the Orderly Room directly across the hall from the Message Center, and I thought, This job has one distinct drawback. I'm right under his psychotic nose. But that's life, I guess. You have to take the bad with the good. The only thing is, the Army is mostly bad and very little good. But I can't complain today. A few things are really going my way all of a sudden and . . .

My thoughts were interrupted by footsteps on the stairs and a knock on the Orderly Room door across the hall. "I is here wif the jeep." I smiled when I heard the good-natured voice of the major's chauffeur, Corporal Gore, who had the distinction of having been the brunt of Diamond Jim's insulting "Up your Gore" which eventually had led to the now rampant expression, "Up your diamond."

"For Christ's sake, Gore,"growled the first sergeant. "Where the fuck you been?"

"I got held up, Sarge," drawled Gore.

"Bullshit you got held up. If the major's pissed 'cause you're late, I'll have your black ass reamed and you'll be a damn private again."

"I's sorry if I's late."

"Sorry your black ass," shouted Diamond Jim. "Don't give me that shit, you slow-as-molasses black bastard. Get your ass out of here and go wait in the damn jeep."

"But I said I was sorry I was late. I's apologizing, Sarge."

"Apologize your ass!" shouted Diamond Jim. "Take off out of my sight, you damn black eight ball."

"I is going now, Sarge. I is going!"

I could hear Gore shuffling into the hall and trudging slowly down the stairs. Then I thought, There's one thing about Diamond Jim. He doesn't discriminate because of race, color, or creed. Everybody's treated equally rotten. Everybody gets his turn. Everybody gets the shaft.

# 16

**Letter, Saturday, 16 October 1954**
**10 p.m.**
**Army Service Club**

*Your voice is so beautiful, honey. I couldn't hang up after three minutes on the phone with you if twenty operators reminded me. I will be so happy when we won't have to worry about long distance phone calls because in about three weeks you'll be here with me and I'll just love you so much, sweetheart.*

*I bet I'll have our little apartment by next Saturday when I call. Don't worry, hon, everything will be ready and waiting. I'll have the apartment in plenty of time so that you can send the baggage beforehand.*

*Today I finished reading Hemingway's "A Farewell to Arms." It was a great novel. I like great literature so much. Boy, do I dislike the trash that fills the newsstands and takes up much of the space in bookstores. Maybe I can't fight it, but I won't go along with it. I'm no highbrow. I just appreciate great writing. There are so many worthwhile books, dusty on the shelves, unread.*

*There was a time when a book with small print and over 300 pages would never be read by me, at least not very often. Nowadays it seems I enjoy reading the long novels that really have what it takes.*

*There was no mail today because somebody goofed at the Main Post Office and didn't get the mail from Augusta, so I'll have to wait till Monday to read my honey's sweet handwriting.*

*Anyhow, I talked with you tonight, and I heard you sweetly say "I love you." I love you so very, very dearly, sweetheart.*

*I watched TV tonight till a while ago. Gleason was great. He's quite an actor! Imogene was okay too, I'd say. Also, Jimmy Durante was entertaining.*

*I told you on the phone about looking for an apartment. I hounded Roberts all week to take me to Augusta to look at the different places advertised. Now I am informed that someone took guard duty for him and he's gone home. Oh well, soon I'll hop a bus for sure and look at some places.*

*I am yours,*
*Tommy*

When Diamond Jim had a mind to, he would restrict us to the base or to the Company Area for a weekend or a full week, just to let us know that he had the power and we had none. In honor of one of those occasions I sat down and took a very old song titled "I'm Just a Prisoner of Love" and did a parody of it:

> *Alone from night to night you'll find me*
> *I goofed and now the barracks bind me*
> *I need no CQ to remind me*
> *I've been restricted a week*
>
> *For one command I stand and wait now*
> *From Sarge who's master of my fate now*
> *I can't escape for it's too late now*
> *I've been restricted a week*
>
> *What's the good of my griping*
> *I'll still go on wiping these windows clean*
> *Although I can see through them I still have to do them*
> *Till I am free*

*I scrub and rub awake or sleeping*
*Upon my knees I do my weeping*
*The gosh darn floor needs so much sweeping*
*I've been restricted a week*

On a Friday evening late in October, at a time when we were not restricted, I was sitting on my bunk examining the Apartments-for-Rent section of the *Augusta Chronicle*, which was described in its masthead as "The South's Oldest Newspaper."

"Did you come up with anything yet?" asked Norm, who was lying flat on his back on his bunk, staring up at a set of orders he held in the air about a foot above his face.

"I found a couple of places we can check out tomorrow." I saw how he was gazing at his mimeographed orders and smiling broadly. "What are you doing? Hypnotizing yourself with those transfer orders?"

With a giggle, he leaped from the bunk and onto the linoleum floor, waved the prized orders with his left hand, hitched up his right trouser leg with his right hand, and danced across the aisle near our bunks and shouted, "It's great! I'm bugging out of here next Monday to work in my MOS at the Disciplinary Barracks. It's great! I can think of nothing in the world so great!" His narrow brown eyes beamed at me through his pink-plastic Army-issue eyeglasses and he leaped in the air, clicked his heels together, and came down with a resounding thud. The gold fillings in his teeth sparkled as he once again shouted, "It's great!"

"Well, your persistence paid off, Norm. You went to the Pentagon and made your contacts and now things are looking up."

He stuck his hand out toward me. "I owe it all to you, Tom."

"Aw, come on, Norm, you owe it to yourself. All I did was give you a little nudge in the right direction. You did the work."

"Without your nudge, I wouldn't be about to work as a clinical psychologist." He giggled, closed his eyes, leaped into the air again, and came down with another crash. Despite the noise, not a head turned in the barracks. Not a head but one, that is.

Wilson's voice boomed out from the other end of the barracks. "Y'all look at the nut what thinks he's a pisscologist! He's done got it made in the shade now, man, 'cause he's cracked in the head, that's what he is. Look at him jump like one-each crazy man."

"Norm's crazy like an old fox," I retorted.

Wilson, who loved repartee, laughed. "He sure is foxing his ass out of this MG Company."

I laughed and said to Norm loud enough for Wilson to hear, "You're gonna miss Wilson's comments, right?"

A quick response came from Wilson. "I sure is gonna miss the pisscologist and the white socks bug-out."

"I'll miss you too," I said. "There's only one Wilson! When they made you they threw away the mold, and that's a good thing!"

Norm, sitting up on his bunk, said, "I'll miss you too, Wilson, but I won't miss Diamond Jim." He leaped up and clasped his arms around himself. "Am I really bugging out of here, Tom? Or is it just a wish-fulfillment fantasy?"

"It's a wish-fulfillment reality, Norm. No fantasy at all. It's as real as this heat that never eases off down here."

"Are you hot? It's only in the high eighties."

"For late October, isn't that hot? I'm a seventy degree man." I wiped my brow. "Life down here is one big cruddy sweat."

"I thought you believed things were looking up for you." Norm squinted his narrow brown eyes and adjusted his eyeglasses.

"It's relative, Norm. Things are definitely looking up since I became permanent party and got the Message Center racket. Also, now that I have hopes of getting Mary and Peg down here so we can live off-post in Augusta in a couple of weeks, I shouldn't complain. But I'm allergic to this kind of heat and this kind of arbitrary authority, so I'm still a little depressed. I've got seven months in and almost seventeen months to go and I can't picture putting up with all this bullshit for that long a time, Norm."

"I have almost the same period of time left, but I'm optimistic about it now."

"I was an optimist once. I was gung-ho to put in my time and get the GI Bill. I thought it was gonna be a breeze. But it's one endless round of horseshit and bullshit and chicken shit, Norm. How much of this shit can a guy take?"

"About two years worth, Tom." He put his hand on my shoulder and said, "You'll be able to take it till your time is up."

"I guess I can, if I can restrain my bug-out urges. I'm getting so that's all I think about. I'm such a compulsive bug-out it's ridiculous. Every day I bug out of a hundred things, just for drill. Even when I walk, I'm bugging out. I walk slower than I have to. I type slower than I have to. I even make mistakes in the Message Center on purpose so I'll have to do things over! I guess I think of each little bug-out act as one run for O'Connell versus zero for the Army. I'm pretty screwy, Norm."

He shrugged. "Think of it as your defense mechanism. I think of it as the Bug-out Syndrome, a newly discovered mental condition in the avoidance category. I wonder how you'd feel if you just did what you're supposed to do and accepted your fate."

"Once in a while I do, but it always backfires on me. Then I take a special oath to bug out every chance I get. Like I say, it's a compulsion with me now, or you can call it the Bug-out Syndrome if you want to. I'm always second-guessing what Diamond Jim might want me to do next and coming up with a way not to do it. Hell, I'm even doing the same thing with Captain Solomon and he's a nice guy."

"Do you feel guilty when you bug out?"

"Sometimes I do, just a tiny bit, but not guilty enough to give my warm body and soul to the U.S. Army. Look, do you feel guilty because you pulled some strings at the Pentagon and won yourself a transfer?"

"No." He shook his head. "I only feel exultation."

"That's the bug-out's reward. Now you feel like you're helping to shape your own destiny, don't you?"

Norm nodded and looked at his orders once again. "My destiny is here in my hands, Tom. I am destined to serve as a clinical psychologist at the Disciplinary Barracks." He smiled and exclaimed, "It's great!"

"I'm so glad you pulled it off, but I'm gonna miss you around here."

"I'll only be up the street, and besides, you'll be living off-post with your Mary shortly."

I put aside my copy of the *Augusta Chronicle*. "Say that again, Norm. Very slowly."

"You will be . . . living off-post . . . with your Mary shortly."

"Guess what, Norm? I heard music in the background when you said that. Do you know what the melody was? The March of the Bug-outs."

Norm did his customary routine, leaping in the air with the enthusiasm of a four-year-old, hitching up his trousers, and shouting, "The March of the Bug-outs. That's great, Tom!"

"Norm, it looks like you've pulled me out of my temporary depression. What say? Are we heading for the Service Club?" Norm nodded as I grabbed my writing pad and my half-read Thomas Costain novel. "Let's get out of here."

Norm squinted at the book title. "I thought you were reading *The Decameron*."

"I couldn't finish it. It was too dull."

"But it's a great book!"

I grinned. "Some so-called great books are very dull, and they're filled with words nobody gives a damn about reading. Watch this, Norm." I let the Costain novel fall onto the top of my foot locker and the noise resounded through the barracks, "Did you hear that noise?" Norm nodded. "Well, that's what I like to get from a book. A bang. Hey, I just noticed something. When I slammed the book down nobody looked up."

"They seldom do. Crowded living causes a turning inward for privacy."

"Is that the Molesko Theory of Crowded Living? Hey, between the Bug-out Syndrome that you developed while observing me, and your Crowded Living Theory, you may become renowned in the annals of psychology, Norm."

"Shall we test the Crowded Living Theory?" he asked with a giggle, waving his wooden shower clogs toward his metal wall locker.

I laughed. "Why not? We'll see how much noise these guys can tolerate."

First he banged on his metal locker with a shower clog. Then he leaped up and down on his wooden foot locker, while I pounded on my own wall locker with a wood-handled hairbrush. As a follow-up we both shouted meaningless phrases. The result? No result. The other men on the second floor of our barracks were unmoved by the din.

Griffin, a mulatto sergeant with wavy black hair, continued to brush his hair and examine his reflection in his wall locker mirror. Medina did not lift his eyes from the centerfold of his Esquire magazine. The poker players at the other end of the floor continued to concentrate on their game.

Klein, known as "the professor" because of his inhibited bookish nature and thick glasses, did not look up from his volume on Civil War History. Napoli, who was filing his nails, continued to file them. All of the other men on the second level, engaged in personal activities, remained unaffected.

As we strolled by Griffin's area, I said softly to Norm, "He's still basking in his own reflection."

Norm responded, "Without his mirror he would be psychologically denuded."

Passing the professor's bunk, I whispered, "He's still buried in his book."

Norm nodded. "He's more of a bookworm than I am. He thinks the Civil War is still being fought."

When I laughed, Klein looked up and asked, "What time is it?"

"In civilian time it's about six-forty-five," I replied.

"Thank you," he said, returning to his book.

I whispered to Norm, "That's the longest conversation I've ever had with Klein. He's very talkative today. He must have had the same training as Calvin Coolidge."

As we walked on past the poker players, I pointed to them. "Now that's a lesson in concentration."

"It's more than a game with them," observed Norm. "It's a way of life or perhaps a substitute for life."

We reached the end of the row of bunks and were about to descend the stairs when Wilson, whose bunk was at the top of the stairs, propped himself on his elbow and announced, "Here they goes. The nut that's shagging his crazy ass out of here and the damn buck slip wif his one-each white socks and his cruddy feet and his letters and his book. Both of them is crazy in the head. What was y'all doing making all that stomping and carrying on down the other end?"

I laughed. "You noticed the racket?"

"My dead Mammy in Alabama was woke up wif it! You like to wake the dead, you mens."

Norm fixed his narrow brown eyes on Wilson, blinked, and adjusted his eyeglasses. "You're an exception to the rule, Wilson. You are an extremely aware and exceptionally other-oriented person."

Wilson laughed. "And y'all's a one-each nutty pisscologist."

When we reached the foot of the stairs, I excused myself. "I have to make a visit, Norm. My back teeth are floating."

I went to the urinal and as I was relieving my overstocked bladder I heard Pfc. Jackson, a colored Georgia native, talking to Corporal Newhouse, a quiet moody mulatto. "I is gonna get me some snatch in Augusta and I is gonna shack up wif my queen at that big cathouse hotel downtown."

"They's gonna roll your ass sure as shit," replied Newhouse, a lean six-footer with a complexion the color of a deep tan. "Come

Monday, y'all's gonna have a nice case o' clap, man. I don't need clap, Jackson. I likes my womens clean like my girl Sarah. She's a one-man woman, she says, and I believes her. She don't shack up wif no other mother-fuckers wit' dirty peckers." Jackson and Newhouse both began to roar laughing.

"You're a disgrace to the Negro race," came the voice of Sergeant Tucker from one of the johns. "You men think of nothing but satisfying your lust."

Newhouse laughed. "Hey Jackson, that all sounds like ole Tucker talking. He goes to some university in Detroit a couple years and now he's like some professor thinking it's better filling his brain wif books than getting his pecker tired from snatch."

I was zipping up my fly when the door to Tucker's stall flew open and the handsome sergeant with the olive complexion and neat mustache stepped out and stood next to Jackson and Newhouse, glaring at them as he zipped up his fly and tightened his belt. "You're hopeless, you two men. You're uncivilized and uncouth. As far as I'm concerned, you're just one step from the jungle."

"Why's y'all upset?" Jackson laughed. "So what if a brother gets hisself some snatch wif his money? Wifout snatch it'd be no use to live, man."

Newhouse chimed in. "What we does off duty's our business, Tucker. If I feels like talking about ass or getting ass it's none of your no mind. You know somefin', Tucker, you been acting like some Negro Baptist preacher lately."

"That's what I says, too," agreed Jackson. "You're just like a preacher wif' his sermons and his hallelujah. If I wants to shack up wif my queen and I ends up wif the clap, it's no skin off your pecker, Tucker." This triggered a huge laugh from both of them.

As for me, I tried to hurry through my hand-washing because I had a strong feeling that although I was in the right place for my urinary mission I was there at the wrong time for a racial skirmish, and as the discourse continued I could feel myself beginning to blush.

Sergeant Tucker shook his head. "It disappoints me that you men don't have more self-respect. Without self-respect, we'll never gain the respect of the white man."

"Up the white man's ass," said Newhouse.

"Up the white man's ass wif a cactus," shouted Jackson, laughing. "Anyhow, Tucker, I has self-respect."

"Shacking up with a whore gives you self-respect?" retorted Tucker.

Jackson laughed. "It's the queen what don't have no self-respect. I pays for my snatch and I shacks up and I gets what I pays for, and I likes getting laid, Sarge. I likes it somefin' awful, and I has plenty of self-respect, Tucker. Pull-en-tee!"

Sergeant Tucker shook his head in exasperation. Then Newhouse shrugged and said, "Them's my feelings too, Tucker. I don't shack up wif no hotel whores, but if Jackson does, I says let him. That's his ole tough titty if he gets the clap." He laughed. "I couldn't get it up for no hotel whore. I needs a woman I loves, like my Sarah."

Sergeant Tucker now stood with his hands on his hips, as he continued the verbal combat. "Do you plan to marry your Sarah?"

"Shit, no. I don't plan to marry nobody less I has to." Newhouse smiled.

Tucker persisted. "That's what you call love? That's self-respect?"

"Shit, I loves my Sarah and I loves her ass and I has self-respect, man."

I was about to leave the latrine when Tucker called out to me. "O'Connell, what do you think of these men and their morals?"

I had no trouble coming up with a self-protective reply. "Hey, I don't think, Tucker. I'm a private, remember? We aren't supposed to think." Jackson and Newhouse laughed at my comeback.

"But you're a college man like me," said Tucker. "You must have some ideas on this subject. How about giving us your opinions?"

"Well, Tucker, I say each man to his own philosophy, as long as he doesn't screw up his fellow man. That's my opinion." I waved at Tucker, Jackson and Newhouse, headed for the exit, and said, "I have an appointment to keep at the Service Club, so stay loose, you guys. Loose as a three-fingered goose." I let out a huge laugh as I made my exit from the latrine and rejoined Norm.

As we began our walk across the warm red Georgia clay toward the Service Club, Norm said, "You took your time."

"I've got two speeds, like Wilson. Slow and stop. Let's go."

"I could hear the discussion the colored men were having," he said. "You did an excellent job staying out of it."

I nodded. "Where I grew up I had to learn to talk my way out of trouble. Look, Norm, I respect Tucker for his views, but I don't think he'll ever get through to Jackson and Newhouse. They like their lifestyle the way it is."

"Everything is relative," said Norm.

"Except for some absolute things."

"Like what, for instance?"

"Like God and truth and love. For you they may be relative, but for me they're absolute."

"What about Diamond Jim?" asked Norm with a giggle. "Is he relative?"

"Yuh, he's relatively insane."

Norm giggled and kicked up his heels and scattered a cloud of red dust around his feet. "Relatively insane! That's great! He's more than just mentally impaired."

"I think it's better if we try not to talk about him. I prefer to act as if he doesn't exist. I exist and you exist but that guy is nothing but a phantom, and the more we talk about him the more reality we give him. If I'm going to survive my future months in the 402nd Military Government Company I'll have to put the Diamond out of my mind as much as possible. Otherwise, I might push my bug-out philosophy too far and do something self-defeating just to get away from him. The one thing I have to preserve in this man's Army is myself."

"You'll preserve yourself."

"With the help of God."

Norm, who was basically agnostic, responded, "You need no universal spirit to help you. You need only your determination."

"If it weren't for that universal spirit, we wouldn't exist and there'd be no such quality as determination."

He asked, "Are we about to set off into another one of our theological discussions?"

"Not tonight. I don't have the energy. What's the point of it anyhow? We just go round and round and you end up with your original beliefs and I end up with mine."

"You don't think you're converting me?"

"I doubt it, and if you suddenly started agreeing with all my ideas, I'd probably think you were going soft."

Norm focused his small brown eyes on my face, blinked rapidly, and said, "You make an interesting psychological study."

"So do you."

"I suppose I have a few idiosyncrasies," he agreed. Then he giggled, and while his eyes were directed toward my face, his eyes involuntarily closed and remained that way for several seconds.

"Everybody does."

His eyes opened. "Speaking of idiosyncrasies, did you hear how Rawson tried to break out of the Disciplinary Barracks?"

"Uh-huh. Maybe you'll get to give him an ink blot test one of these days."

"Perhaps I might," agreed Norm, "but Rawson is quite obvious in his habits. He is strictly masochistic; whereas Diamond Jim is a sadist."

"So Rawson's a sucker for punishment, huh? Well, there's one thing about him I respect. He may be Regular Army but he's smart enough to get frustrated by the Army. So he's a fellow bug-out, and it's hard for me to find fault with any kind of bug-out."

"But his goals aren't positive like yours."

"I'm sure he thinks they're positive, Norm."

"Perhaps you're right."

"Once in a while everybody's right. Look, I can't help liking any guy that hates Diamond Jim's guts. Actually, if it weren't for Kattus and Rawson and Gore we wouldn't have our favorite expression: 'Up your diamond.'"

Norm said, "I have an irresistible urge to say it myself." He propelled himself into his customary routine of giggling. Then he shouted "Up your diamond" several times, went into his step dance, and laughed with gusto. When he calmed down, he said, "I feel relieved now. I've vented my spleen at Diamond Jim's expense."

"I wonder what he'd think about your spleen being vented on him."

Norm squinted at me. "Up his diamond!" Then he closed his eyes and said, "I can't wait to part company with that sadistic paranoid manic-depressive. Come Monday I will no longer be under his authority, and I still don't quite believe I've achieved a transfer."

"Well, there are two things I don't quite believe, but they're also true."

"What are the two things?"

I sent a wad of spit flying at a nearby tree and hit it. "Bull's eye!" Then I said, "The two things I don't quite believe are Diamond Jim and the U.S. Army. They are both very unreal to me."

Norm giggled and shuffled his feet in the red clay dust which went swirling around our feet just before we went into the Service Club. Then he looked at me with a straight face and said, "You're a living contradiction, Tom. You're both a believer and a non-believer at the same time."

I grinned. "That's no contradiction. That's just human."

# 17

Late in October the apartment search ended. I had found Apartment A, a first floor unit at 2242 Central Avenue, Augusta. It was a very old house in a good location, and had several fairly small apartments. The rent was $60, not including utilities, and was "furnished." The furnishings were pretty rundown, but at least they were furnishings. Although the apartment was not what you would call "aesthetic," and left much to be desired in its ancient decor, the rooms were large, with high ceilings. We had a roomy living room and bedroom, plus a small kitchen and a tiny bath, with tub.

The location was only about a three-minute walk to the Camp Gordon bus, and the bus to downtown Augusta stopped about 10 feet from the house. So it seemed like a good deal, especially since many landlords would not take babies. For $20 down, the landlord, Mrs. Brinkley, was holding it for us. This made it possible for Mary to ship our belongings whenever she wished.

When I communicated to Mary about the apartment I focused on the positive aspects of the location, the space, and how wonderful it would be for Mary and Peggy to be with me in a matter of days. Actually, I was a bit concerned about what she would think of the apartment, but I figured the main thing was that we would finally be together.

**Letter, November 4, 1954**
**Thursday night**

*Just five more days apart, honey. Then you'll be with me at 9:50 a.m. on Wednesday. I got the day off, and Thursday is a holiday, so we'll have time for plenty of hugging and relaxing besides getting things ready. Most likely it will take my honey a day at least to recover from the train ride.*

*Last night after I got back from the show I went to my back pocket to get your sweet letters that I got yesterday, and they were both gone. It almost broke my heart. I looked every place and finally remembered how I sprawl out in my seat in the movies. I must have lost them there.*

*But pretty soon I'll have you and you'll never slip out of my back pockets. You'll just always be with me, that's all. Your pictures that you sent me are so sweet. I just take out the folder and see you loving our Peggy and I feel older now.*

*My faith in God has increased so much. There were so many times when I thought I couldn't stand it any more, and yet God must have helped me to see things more clearly. Our love has pulled us through and in just a few days, we'll be a family again and we'll share so much Love.*

*I'm so grateful to God for bringing you to me and for bringing Peggy to me. I hardly know Peggy, and she's almost seven weeks old. I haven't seen her for about six weeks. I'll get to know her next week.*

*I just keep thinking about Wednesday, when I'll meet my darling and take you home and just love you and be happy with you. Just rest on the train and watch the way the scenery changes as you head South. Well, look at you, going South for the winter!*

*It's funny. We're supposed to be young. When we were married a year ago this month, I was 21 and you were nineteen. Now we're a family. I am 22, you are 20, and Peggy is 7 weeks. I don't feel young, do you? I feel happy in love with you. But these past months have seemed so long, and now we're quite a bit older. Who ever thought that eight months would pass like eight years.*

*Physically, we're only a few months older now, but mentally and even spiritually we've gained years. Yet in a few days we'll be a family again.*

*See you Wednesday, Honey. I'll call you Saturday night.*

*I am your own,*
*Your loving husband,*
*Tommy*

Now that it was November the wilting intensity of the Georgia heat and humidity had abated to a slight degree, so I could breathe some deeper breaths again. We were in the Day Room listening to the weekly Troop Information and Education (TI&E) lecture, delivered by Corporal Rafe Ezekiel whose six foot frame, olive complexion, and horn-rimmed glasses were right in my line of vision and clearly visible.

However, his image was hazy to me, and his voice was only coming into my mind in short periodic bursts. "Now that we have reviewed the bombardment of Quemoy by the Communist Chinese, and the ensuing groundwork laid by our State Department to help bring about a Southeast Asian mutual defense treaty, let us go on to consider . . . ."

Rafe talked on but my attention span had reached its terminus. I reverted to my own private reflections: My off-post papers have already been approved for Monday, but just for spite Diamond Jim is letting them sit there on his desk till the last minute. Well, if he thinks I'm gonna crawl for them, he can go fry his diamond-shaped ass. Well, maybe I'll crawl after all. Mary and Peg are on the train right now and they'll be here tomorrow morning, and I told her I'd meet her at the station.

Captain Solomon said there'd be no sweat about me leaving the barracks tonight as long as Diamond Jim didn't need me for anything on Saturday morning. I bet the Diamond will dream up something for me to do. Yuh, he wouldn't just give me the papers and let it go at that. He has to make me hang by my thumbs waiting, the sadist.

It's always something, right? If it isn't Diamond Jim trying to botch up our plans it's the Killorens. When we were getting married and wanted their cooperation they gave us nothing but hard times. Now when we start making plans to live off-post they keep filling Mary's ears with stories about how hard it's going to be living on private's pay in a strange place like Augusta, Georgia.

Augusta is a strange place, but what's stranger than living with the Killorens? Mary's been wanting to get out of there since the day when I was drafted and she went back to stay with them. The last thing we need is two self-appointed omniscient oracles telling us what to do. We've got our own lives to live and we're gonna live them our way, not theirs. To hell with the Killorens and their half-baked ideas.

Rafe Ezekiel's voice interrupted my thoughts. "On September eighth, in Manila, the SEATO pact was signed, it says here, to protect Laos, Cambodia and South Vietnam from Communist aggression. The signatories were the United States, Thailand . . ."

South Vietnam, I mused. To hell with South Vietnam. All I care about is Mary and Peggy and me, and maintaining some sanity in these insane surroundings. South Vietnam can take care of its own problems.

All I want is to keep my body and soul together and bug out of here so I can live off-post with my wife and daughter. South Vietnam? Who cares what's going on in South Vietnam? I do! It'd be tragic if they ignored my L3 buck slip and I got shipped overseas after Mary and Peggy came down here. It would be . . . .

Someone shouted at Rafe, "Hey, Rafe!" It was Corporal Eads of the Legal Team. "Tell us your off-the-record opinion of the SEATO treaty."

Rafe shook his head. "I'm not standing up here to think and give opinions. I'm here to tell you what it says on this sheet that came from Washington."

"Aw, come on, Rafe. Give it to us straight," insisted Eads. "Suspend the lecture and give us a short rest break and tell us unofficially what you think."

Rafe tossed his head nervously. "Okay then, the lecture's suspended. Take a break. And those who wish to have a little chat with me, stick around."

Several of the men applauded, and they all happened to be draftees. The Regular Army personnel were not fans of Rafe Ezekiel, who was inclined to interpret Pentagon edicts and opinions in a less than favorable way when Diamond Jim was not present.

"Sergeant Faber?" Rafe directed his attention to Sgt. 1st Class Faber of the Public Information Team, who was editor of the Company's bi-weekly publication. "Faber, I respectfully ask only one thing of you. Please don't quote me in *Behind the Eight Ball*, or you'll be putting an eight ball up my rectum." The Day Room filled with laughter.

"You have my pledge," replied Faber. "I mean my word. I have no intention of taking the pledge." The men laughed because Faber's love for his bottle was no secret.

Rafe began. "In my opinion there's no such place as Vietnam. I know I've often said the same thing about this Military Government Company. In jest, of course. We know we're here, don't we? We know we're not simulated. Am I right?" The draftees laughed heartily and some of the Regular Army men laughed moderately and a few of the RA's did not laugh at all. To them the Army's philosophy was a fundamentalist religion that permitted no attack, humorous or otherwise.

"I'll say it again. There is no such place as South Vietnam. The seventeenth parallel is only a demarcation line, not a national boundary, but our SEATO pact implies a political character south of the line, or should I say south of the border?" Rafe chuckled. "According to the SEATO pact . . ."

I went off into my own world again, mentally checking off preparations for living off-post. I had been accepted as a passenger in Arthur Goldstein's car pool. I had bought the necessary articles for little Peggy's care and feeding. I had lined up an apartment and had paid the first month's rent in advance. Also, I had saved enough money from my recent pay to buy most of the groceries for the month ahead. The last vestiges of our savings account had been used to pay Mary's train fare to Georgia and to ship Peggy's crib and other belongings by Railway Express.

The apartment I had found was near the top of Central Avenue which ran up a long, large hill in the outskirts of Augusta. The section was very appropriately called The Hill, and there were many fine older homes there that had been converted into apartments. It was also on the bus line. The rent, at the upper limit of our economic capability, was sixty dollars a month. I knew it was overpriced but apartments were scarce and I had taken it reluctantly.

The brown double-decker had peeling green trim paint. The so-called "furnishings" included a bed propped up on red bricks instead of the legs that had once been attached to it. The tiny kitchen had a gas stove that was held over from the first years of the Twentieth Century and the bathroom had such wide cracks in the floor that the earth in the crawl space below could be seen through them. This did not bode well for any pest control.

"It's not fabulous," I had said to Norm when we had looked at it together, "but it's better than nothing."

Norm had agreed. "It's definitely not fabulous, but at least you'll be living off-post with your wife and daughter, and you can look for a better place later on."

"Mm. I just hope my best laid plans don't get loused up by Diamond Jim."

As I was reflecting on my visit with Norm to the Central Avenue apartment, Rafe's voice interrupted my reverie. He had said something about a person named Ho Chi Minh, and then I heard the loud raspy voice of Sgt. Fulghum who hailed from Kentucky. "That Ho Chee feller's a commie, ain't he?"

Rafe frowned. "The experts see him as more of a nationalist."

Fulghum persisted. "He's still some kind of damn commie, ain't he?"

"It's his own particular brand of communism," replied Rafe.

"A commie's a damn commie!" shouted Fulghum. "There ain't no such of a thing as a good commie except maybe a dead one!"

"Them's my sentiments, too," chimed in Sgt. Lemmond.

A round of applause came from the Regular Army personnel. Then Rafe announced nervously, "I want to remind everyone that we're on a break and my observations are strictly personal."

"Come on, Rafe!" called out Corporal Eads, a short-timer. "You're a Far East expert. Give us some more of your ideas and we can argue about them later."

"Well, I don't know . . ."

"Go ahead," urged Fulghum. "It don't make no difference to us fellers that don't think like y'all do."

"Thank you for your generosity," said Rafe the corporal to the sergeant first class, with a straight face. "Why don't we go back to 1946 and review a little Vietnamese history, starting with the French bombardment of Haiphong. Six thousand civilians were killed on that occasion, gentlemen, and I'm convinced that this action strengthened Ho Chi Minh's leadership position and . . ."

Who cares about Ho Chi Minh, I thought. Right now I'm only interested in Ho Chi O'Connell and Ho Chi Mary and Ho Chi Peggy. Ho Chi Minh can solve his own problems. All I want is my off-post papers in my hand. Then I'll be all set to take off tonight and get things set at the apartment and be at the train station in the morning when Mary arrives with the baby. It's unreal to think I'll be actually seeing Mary tomorrow. She's bigger than life in my mind now. She's the angel of my salvation. And when she gets here I'll have my whole soul back again.

Living off-post will make my warm body less the Army's and more my own. It's a wonder the Army even lets our warm bodies live off-post. Damn the Army. It's one massive anxiety trip for me and my independent psyche. I need to stop thinking about it so much. My head's beginning to ache.

I should restrain my anxiety about those off-post papers in The Diamond's custody. I know they've been approved and that's the most important thing. But I won't be able to rest my mind until I have them in my hand. I promised Mary I'd meet her at the train and when I promise her something, I mean business. So Diamond Jim better not screw me up by giving us some kind of hair brained restriction! If he does, then I'll just have to . . . I'd better get my mind off this and maybe actually listen to Rafe for a while.

"I think we can be grateful that President Eisenhower decided not to send help and allowed the French to lose their own battle at Dien Bien Phu last spring, but our ambiguous stand at Geneva this past summer really puzzled me. I believe the Vietnam situation is fraught with peril for our leaders. It seems strange that we haven't absorbed the lessons learned at such great cost by the French. I can't understand why we refuse to allow the Vietnamese to map their own destiny. All this business of us sending military advisers over there seems to me to be . . ."

The Day Room door swung open, and in strutted Diamond Jim. "Uh . . . hello there, Sergeant," said Rafe. "We were just having a little break. Now we'll return to our official TI&E lecture. It says here, gentlemen, that the seventeenth parallel divides Vietnam into two nations, one in the north controlled by the communists and one in the south controlled by forces interested in democracy. The two nations, it says here, are called the Democratic Republic of . . ."

To hell with the Democratic Republic of Vietnam, I thought. What I'm concerned with is the Democratic Republic of Tom O'Connell, and now Diamond Jim, the tyrannical sealer of my fate, is on the scene with his buck teeth and manic depressive psyche. Did he stroke those off-post papers with his pen? That's all that separates me from Mary tomorrow. Captain Solomon made his pen strokes and now it's your turn, Diamond Jim! Are you playing sadistic games with my head? You and your pen strokes. If only . . .

My outrageously resentful thoughts were interrupted by Diamond Jim. "You almost through with that bullshit TI&E lecture, Ezekiel?" I watched our first sergeant standing at the rear of the Day Room, with his hands on his hips, waiting for a reply.

"Yes, Sergeant, we're through as of right now." Rafe folded up his propaganda tent and stood off to one side.

"I got one announcement to make before you off-posters take the hell off out of here for the weekend. I got some rifles for you to clean in the ordnance shed. The ones you didn't do last Saturday. You got a choice. Heh-heh. Youse can do 'em now or tomorrow morning."

His remark was greeted by moaning. "Youse guys think you got some eight-to-five job, for Christ's sake? This is the U.S. Army and it ain't no damn picnic."

That's true, I agreed. It ain't no picnic, Diamond Jim. Thanks to idiots like you, and the cadre in basic, and those assholes at the MP Training Center, it ain't no picnic. And you all have one thing in common. You're sadistic. Sure, I know you need to train us in the art of war, but do you have to be so inhuman about it?

Diamond Jim ordered the men to leave the Day Room, so I rose and followed the others. When I was about to pass our leader at the doorway, he shouted into my ear, "O'Connell, I wanna talk to you."

My heart leaped. "Uh . . . yes, Sergeant."

He paused and darted his shifty blue eyes from my face to the last of the departing enlisted men, then back to me. Suddenly he asked, "What the hell do you want, O'Connell?"

"You said you wanted to talk to me."

"Oh, let's see. What the hell did I wanna talk to you about? Oh yuh, it's about these here off-post papers you wanted by tonight." He shoved a folded set of papers at me. "Here's your papers, O'Connell."

"Thanks, Sergeant." I grinned as I examined the long-awaited papers.

He ordered, "Check your stuff in at Supply before you take off, and don't forget to put your name in the sign-out book in the Orderly Room."

"Uh . . . what was that, Sergeant?" I had been distracted by my own thoughts.

"For Kee-rist sake, O'Connell, didn't you hear what I just said to ya? Before you go, check your gear in at the Supply Room and sign out at the Orderly Room. Now did ya hear what I said, Private?"

My face reddened as I nodded and said, "I heard what you said, Sergeant."

Diamond Jim shook his head in exasperation and stepped out of the Day Room mumbling, "Damn college boy eight balls. They don't hear nothing and they don't understand nothing about nothing."

I understand one thing, I thought as I left the Day Room to head for the ordnance shed where the rifles were waiting for us to clean. Yes, Diamond Jim, I understand that you've been misinformed about your existence. There's no such person as you!

After cleaning my share of rifles, I went to the barracks, organized my gear, and then took the stuff to the Supply Room to check it in before closing time. After that, I went to the Mess Hall, gulped down my evening chow, and returned without delay to pack the rest of my belongings in bags for taking off-post. I was in the middle of my preparations when Norm came to help me move.

Norm's arrival was accompanied by a greeting from Wilson at the other end of the barracks. "Look who's here!" he shouted. "It's that nut from the DB wif his pisscology book. He's gotta be touched in the head, man. He gets his transfer out of here and he comes shagging his ass back here every night wif his book and off he goes wif buck slip white socks to the Service Club or night school or some such. Nutty as hell, the two of 'em. Never seen nothing like it."

Norm was grinning his gold-filled grin as he approached. "Tom, it's great! You're actually going to live off-post."

He extended his hand, which I shook with enthusiasm. "Yuh, it's really great, Norm. But how am I gonna live without Wilson's running commentary on life in the barracks?"

Wilson was still talking loudly. "Them's what I calls soldiers. The buck slip wif his cruddy feet and his white bug-out socks and the nut what keeps thinking he's some kind of pisscologist. If I was locked up in the DB you bet your ass I wouldn't open up my head for that nutty pisscologist, no sirree, y'all better believe it, man."

I yelled, "I'm really gonna miss you, Wilson. You're something else!"

"I sure is somefin' else, buck slip." He laughed. "But y'all say you're gonna miss Wilson? Y'all's gonna be off-post cuddling wif the little woman and you are not gonna be missing nobody in this here barracks no time, O'Connell. You is bugging out of here wif your gear and your books and your white bug-out socks flying like two bug-out flags, man. Your name ain't O'Connell, your name is one-each bug-out!"

"It takes one to know one, Wilson. I could take lessons from you."

"And I could take lessons from you, O'Connell. I could . . ." His voice trailed off as he suddenly decided to take a catnap.

I continued with my packing, sometimes assisted but more often hindered by Norm's attempts to help. At one point, Norm blinked rapidly and squinted at me and asked, "Just how do you feel at this exact moment, Tom?"

I laughed at his psychological approach to an ordinary situation. "Here's what I think, Norm. Every dog has his day, they say, and every eight-ball like me has his corner pocket. I've sunk myself into the corner pocket and I feel pretty good for a change."

"There must be something wrong with you, Boston." It was Napoli's voice from across the aisle. "When a guy starts feeling good around here, he's got problems."

"Hey, with my wife on her way down here and me about to live off-post with her, you think I've got problems? Not me, Philly."

"But you're still in this outfit, aren't ya?" he asked. And I nodded. "Then you got problems, buddy. Hey, was that you I saw beautifying the damn area this morning?"

"They wanted some parallel rake marks out there on the dry red dust, so I made a few. But after five minutes I said to hell with it and showed Lemmond my buck slip."

"So he let ya bug out of it?"

"What could he do? It says no prolonged standing, and five minutes is prolonged, isn't it?" I grinned. "So I bugged out of it, Philly. That old buck slip of mine is a bug-out's best friend. I'd feel depressed, devastated, and disillusioned without it."

"You're a hot shit, Boston. Hey, don't get too much ass this weekend, know what I mean?"

I was about to reply when Norm said, "You're totally unromantic, Napoli."

Napoli laughed. "Look, Molesko, where there's life there's ass. It's that simple. I don't need romance, I need ass. What's your story, Molesko? Are you still cherry?"

"My sexual status is my own business."

"You got a girl back in the big city?" Napoli wouldn't stop.

"I have a girl I see once in a while . . . when I'm not studying." Norm adjusted his classes. "I have no intention of getting serious with a female until I've earned my Ph.D."

Napoli threw his hands in the air and roared, "You mean a damn piece of paper's a substitute for a broad? You're a hot shit, Molesko. I hope the hell you get a big charge out of shacking up with your diploma."

"I choose to pursue one goal at a time, Napoli."

"Listen," I said to Napoli, "if Norm wants to pursue one goal at a time, it's his business, right? Everybody can't be a one-man stud service like you." I laughed.

Napoli laughed too, then crossed the aisle and the three of us sat on my bunk, continuing our conversation. Napoli said, "Boston's right. Hey, it's no skin off my ass what you do with your love life. You can go steady with Mary Palm, or you can tuck it to a book." He chuckled. "Or maybe you can tuck to to a simulated broad. Everything else is simulated around here, why not a broad?" He turned to me. "Boston, I think this weekend I'm gonna go up with the shade. The broad's in between periods and hot to trot, know what I mean?"

"I know what you mean about going up with the shade, pal. The original story was about a sexually obsessed Frenchman who found the ideal mistress and gave up everything for her, including food. They had sex day after day, and night after night. Then one morning he went over to the window to put up the shade and he had lost so much weight that when he tugged on the shade he went up with it." We all laughed.

For a while, Napoli did a sex-oriented monologue, telling us about enough recent exploits to make Don Juan seem lazy. First he told us about his sexual encounters in Augusta, then in Atlanta. Then he displayed snapshots of his latest conquest. And when he had exhausted his repertoire of sex stories we found the conversation shifting to the Vietnam situation. Finally, we got into the favorite subject of all enlisted men who had ever been connected with the 402nd Military Government Company: Diamond Jim.

"I've got a nice racket in the Message Center now," I said, "but there's one big drawback. I'm right across the hall from The Diamond, and it's a bitch keeping myself from getting affected by his moods. One minute he's almost half decent, then the next minute he's yelling, 'Hey, O'Connell, shag your skinny ass in here with that damn manual and make it snappy or I'm gonna ream your ass!'"

Napoli laughed and Norm giggled as I went on. "Did you guys notice the new pet phrase Diamond Jim's using to replace 'How's them for fucking apples?'"

"I know it," said Napoli. "The new one's 'If you got a fucking complaint go see the major.' Just what have they got you doing up there in the Message Center?"

"The same thing Kattus used to do."

"What's that?"

"I sit there with my arms folded and my feet up on the desk, what else? Seriously, I do things like practice for my USAFI typing course so I can get my permanent clerk-typist MOS, and I write letters to Mary, and if I get bored I always have a paperback tucked in my desk drawer so I can sneak looks at it."

"And that's it?" asked Napoli.

"Yup. Just about. But I've got another project I'm working on right now. It's a time chart that's going to be set up so that on any given day I can know exactly how many days I have left in this man's simulated Army. Captain Solomon came in while I was working on it this morning and when he realized what I was concentrating on, he laughed so hard I thought he was gonna wet his pants."

Napoli asked, "He wasn't pissed off?"

"Nope. He understands us draftees. Back in the big war, he was a draftee himself. I guess he got a battlefield commission and then got out of the Army, but Korea came along and they took him in as a captain and so he's resigned himself to an Army career. He's a great guy to work for. He doesn't take things too seriously."

"But he's allowed himself to become institutionalized," said Norm.

Napoli rose from the bunk. "What the hell, he's an officer and a gentleman. They've got slobs like us cleaning up their damn quarters. They've got it made in the shade, like you're gonna have it made off-post, Boston." He put out his hand and shook mine. "Good luck downtown with your bride and the kid."

"Thanks, Philly. I'll be seeing you around the area."

"I hope you won't be seeing me around here too long," he said. "If I have to put in for FECOM or go Airborne I'm gonna get the hell out of this shit hole." FECOM meant the Far East, and many troops in Georgia preferred the worst assignment overseas to the heat, humidity, and monotony of Georgia.

"It's a funny world, Philly," I said. "You're doing all you can to get out of here and I want to stay here till my time's up so I can have my own little family with me."

"That'd be me too, if I had a wife and kid, but all's I got is some local quail, and if I don't get my ass out of here soon this latest one's gonna try waltzing me down the aisle."

"You're not interested in marriage?" asked Norm.

Napoli's face reddened. "Being stuck with one broad would drive me ape-shit. Speaking of broads, I better get going 'cause I got a rare piece waiting for me downtown. Take care, O'Connell."

"Keep loose, Philly."

I soon finished packing and then Norm and I made our way down the aisle with my bags. As we passed Klein, better known as "the professor," he looked up from his book on Civil War history and asked, as always, "What time is it?" As always, I checked my watch and responded with the current time. "It's seven o'clock civilian time. To hell with Army time." The professor returned his attention to his book without reacting to my comment.

As we passed Chandler, who was scratching his psychosomatic rash as usual, he stopped scratching for a moment to wish me good luck off-post.

Then we walked by Sergeant Griffin, a handsome mulatto, who was at his mirror combing his wavy black hair. "Hey, O'Connell." As he spoke those words he did not turn from his own image in the mirror. "Enjoy yourself off-post, pal."

"Thanks, Sarge. I'll try."

As we passed the poker players, Fulghum looked up. "Hey, y'all bugging your ass out of the barracks, O'Connell? Shoot, y'all's gonna miss the three hots and a flop."

I winked. "Yup, it's gonna be tough adjusting to sleeping in Augusta and bringing my lunch here to MG every day."

Pearse, who had reacted so violently two months earlier to my wisecracks about re-enlisting, got up and came toward me. "Hey, O'Connell."

I laughed. "If I've said something out of turn, I apologize, Pearse! Or if I'm about to say something that rubs you the wrong way I apologize in advance."

The hand that had once had a strong grip on my neck came out at me for a handshake, so I put down my barracks bag to complete the gesture. "I think the heat got to me that night, O'Connell, and I was losing at poker, and I guess I was a little pissed off at not getting transferred the hell out of this half-assed outfit. No hard feelings?"

"No hard feelings."

"See you around the area, O'Connell."

"Yup. I'll be around."

I picked up my bag and as Norm and I reached the head of the stairs which was "guarded" by Wilson's bunk, there he was in his usual position, flat on his back with his long legs dangling out over the bottom of his bunk. Raising himself up on his elbows, he drawled, "There he goes, the damn one-each cruddy foot buck slip wif his white socks and his book under his arm and the nutty pisscologist going off wif him."

"Wilson, I'm gonna really miss you." As I grinned at him, his broad gleaming white smile came back at me from his coal black, friendly face.

He wasn't finished. "Hey, pisscologist, you gonna live off the post wif one-each bug-out and his woman?" He laughed hard and Norm shrugged and giggled.

Then Wilson slowly got up and came toward me with his hand out, and again I put my bag down to shake his hand. He said, "I gets my kicks pulling legs, O'Connell. Don't mean no harm. It's just my way. Wif the pisscologist gone over to the DB and you going downtown now, this here place won't be no home sweet home no more!"

I replied, "Be it ever so humble, this barracks sure is no place like home anyway, Wilson. No home no more nohow!"

"No home no more nohow," he repeated after me, nodding his head as he released my hand and returned to his prone position. "I guess I'll have to get off my butt pretty soon and shag ass to Atlanta and see my pretty woman there."

"Stay loose, Wilson," I said as I picked up my bag and began to descend the stairs with Norm. "Enjoy your weekend, and I'll see you around the area Monday."

He laughed. "All y'all's gonna see Monday is my ass going off to the Dispensary wif one of my big headaches!"

Norm and I both chuckled as we went down the stairs, but Wilson was still not finished with his monologue. "There they goes, the one-each bug-out wif his white socks and his cruddy feet and his low quarter shoes, and that nutty pisscologist that looks into soldiers' heads to see what they is thinking about. They is two soldiers, they is. They is two mens born and bred for the soldiering life. They is born and bred bug-out soldiers like I is, that's what they is. They is going off to Augusta and they is . . ."

I had always been one of his best audiences, but Wilson's very best audience was himself, so he kept amusing himself after I was out of his line of vision. This was his pattern. He would lie there very quietly daydreaming until someone captured his interest. Then he would start, and once he started he was unstoppable. Even after we had exited from the barracks I could still hear Wilson upstairs doing his commentary.

# 18

A while later, after a short bus ride to the Main Gate, we were on the bus to Augusta. As we rolled toward town, I told Norm about recent days at the MG Company, and Norm filled me in on life at the Disciplinary Barracks. Then we began philosophizing. I said, "The real question, Norm, is whether or not the MG Company and the Army exist."

"For some they exist, for others they don't."

"You're right," I said. "The Army definitely exists for Diamond Jim."

"I'm not too sure of that." He blinked rapidly and adjusted his eyeglasses. "He may act as if he and the Army exist, but I believe he doubts his own existence, and if he doubts his own existence, why should he think the Army is real?"

I chuckled. "For a guy who doubts he exists, he sure makes a helluva lot of noise."

Norm nodded. "Doubters usually do make a great deal of noise!"

"Good point, Norm."

Three quarters of an hour later, after much philosophical reflection, we were at the apartment in Augusta where Norm helped me put away my things. I double-checked the supply of baby bottles and formula, and the other items Mary had asked me to get. Then I lined everything up neatly on top of the bedroom dresser with its peeling imitation mahogany veneer.

We sat in the small kitchen, sipped coffee, and speculated on our future months at Camp Gordon. Then it was time for Norm to go back to the Camp, and as we stepped out onto the ramshackle front porch with its loose floorboards, I said, "I really appreciate your help, Norm."

"Don't mention it."

"We'll have you out here for Sunday dinner some weekend soon, Norm. We'll have a spread of hominy grits for y'all, and hush puppies, and maybe some black-eyed peas if y'all are lucky."

He focused his small brown eyes on me and blinked rapidly, then he closed his eyes completely and leaped in the air in his customary fashion and shouted, "It's great!" As he came down on the porch with a loud thud, I was afraid he might fall through it. Then he hitched up his trousers and went into his unique step dance. When he was done he shouted once more, "It's great! I'm at the DB working in my clinical psych MOS and now you're living off-post with your wife!"

"Yup, Norm, it's great!" I grinned. "Things are looking up for both of us."

With a wave, Norm left and I was alone in the apartment. It was an odd feeling for me to be completely alone. During my childhood years at the group foster home the house had always been bustling with people. In my teens at Granny's house it had been quiet on our side of the duplex, but Uncle Bill's family on the other side stirred up plenty of background activity. After getting married to Mary we had never spent a day apart until the Army separated us. And since then I had lived in a very busy Army barracks.

Now I was more alone than I had ever remembered being, but I knew that on the following day after Mary joined me I would no longer be alone. What a difference it would make to have my wife and baby girl in Augusta with me. The very thought of it filled me with good feelings. I hadn't had such a set of good feelings during my time in the Army, except on those short weekend visits home during basic training and during my times home on leave.

I locked up, checked to see that all was in order for the next morning, turned off all the lights except the one in the bathroom, left the bathroom door open a crack, and slipped into bed.

This bed isn't too fancy, I thought, but it's better than an Army cot. It's hard to imagine that tomorrow night she'll share this bed with me. It seems like forever since we've been together.

I stretched out flat on my back, as usual, and when I closed my eyes my first eight months in the Army passed in a series of images within my mind's eye, with me on the reviewing stand, and the thoughts did not necessarily come in a logical sequence. They just arrived on their own, with no concern for logic.

Intermixed with thoughts of Mary's pre-natal difficulties I recalled the Army outfits I had been affiliated with, and a parade of faces and events marched across the pavement of my mind. They were faces and events that were indelibly impressed into my memory bank.

The most vivid face belonged to Charlie Olivera. My bug-out mentor. My escapist consultant. My avoidance guru. What an impact he had made on my life during basic training. Without him I would never have gotten home on so many weekends. And those weekends were medicine for my spirit. His humor was like medicine too. I'll never forget the look on his face when we were out in the field and I leaped up in my sleep and took the whole pup tent with me, in the pouring rain.

There were other basic training faces too. Mario, the incorrigible Italian, running through the Company Area in the nude except for his helmet liner. The rigid first sergeant. The company commander who could have posed for Army recruiting posters. Charlie's pal, the corporal, whose high speed weekend rides through New Jersey, New York, Connecticut, and Massachusetts had been such a welcome relief from the endurance test known as basic training.

Then came the memories of my health problems. Aches. Pains. Strains. Dangerously infected feet. It had been quite an ongoing physical and mental challenge to get through basic without being recycled and having to start again from scratch or being discharged. I had no interest in being discharged then. After all, an important motivation for volunteering for the draft was to get the GI Bill later so I could finish college.

I recalled the marching, marching, marching, with full field packs that I could hardly lift. "Jody was there when you left . . . you're right . . . Jody was there when you left . . . you're right . . . Sound off . . . one two . . . sound off . . . three four . . ."

The feet. Oh boy, what a problem they were for me during basic. Sick Call. Clinic. Post Hospital. But I had played down the problem, concealed it, and by the time I was treated for it basic was almost over and I had received the most important training. Combat ready, that was me.

I grinned as I recalled the bug-out marching band. Percussionist? Me? Very funny. The triangle and cymbals virtuoso! And another guy had to carry my rifle. But the troops loved our music. We took "When the Saints Come Marching In" to new heights, or maybe it was to new depths. And every time they had the troops doing dirty work in the barracks we could go to the Day Room for "practice" and relaxation. What a bug-out brainstorm Charlie had when he created that band.

I remember getting the news that I would not have to go on for more Infantry training but would be an MP instead. Hey, no big deal. I could handle that. What a fantasy I created in my mind about me in my MP uniform with my .45 on my hip, acting as an authority figure. That would suit me, right? God, what a rude awakening I was in for. It was worse than the Infantry.

Then my feet got infected all over again, so there I was in the hospital with my foot problem, hoping the doc would get me discharged. But no such luck. God, how that depressed me. Next I got the strange idea of going on a hunger strike. Then when that didn't work I started bucking for a Section Eight medical discharge. I pretended I was losing my marbles. But wasn't that actually the most sane thing I could have done? Pretending to be insane seemed to be the only way to escape the Army's insanity.

Well, I didn't succeed in convincing the doctors. And it became a turning point for me when I realized that trying to get out of the Army might hurt me more than help me. This brought me to a new level of awareness about adapting and bugging out. I will never forget the burst of renewed energy I got when I slammed the door on that psychiatrist and told him to shove it!

Then there was my on-the-job training in Military Government, with the demented Diamond Jim and the rest of the cast of characters in one of the Army's most unusual outfits. Thank God for Norm Molesko. He helped me keep my mind off my own emotional turmoil. And so did Wilson's running commentary on everything we did at the other end of the floor and as we passed by him on our way to the Service Club.

And the heat. What an endurance test this assignment has been for me. Oh my God, the heat and humidity. This body of mine was not made for a tropical clime. It's a Temperate Zone body and for me to be in Georgia or any place south of the Mason-Dixon line is a contradiction of the first order.

What an eight months this has been. It's as if I've lived a lifetime since last March. I've been dipped in shit and rolled in mud. I've had a peek at Purgatory and a hot hiatus in hell. I feel like I'm a human towel that got lost in an Army laundry. I've been soaked and washed, wrung out, and hung up to dry in an endless series of cycles.

Emotionally, I feel like an old man right now. Rip Van Winkle O'Connell. But tomorrow I'll wake up and I'll meet the train, and we'll hug and kiss and she'll be here with me and I'll feel young again. Tomorrow the Army's horseshit, bullshit, and chicken shit will be wiped out temporarily and we'll be with each other so we can celebrate our first wedding anniversary in a couple of weeks.

Out of a whole year, we've only lived together the first few months, from November to March, and that time seems so very long ago. Now I hope we can spend the next sixteen months together. I don't really think I could endure another lengthy separation from Mary.

Well, tomorrow I'll be back in one piece again. I'll have the other half of my soul back. It's not gonna be easy supporting the three of us on private's pay, but we'll make out okay, with a little help from God.

I breathed a sigh and turned over onto my right side and thought of the psychological changes that had taken place in me during my Army months. I wondered, Will I always be a bug-out? It's such a habit with me now. I never knew what a bug-out was before the Army. I had never even heard the word. Now I'm a confirmed bug-out. If it's a psychological syndrome the way Norm thinks it is, then I'm the prototype. Bugging out has certainly become a way of life with me!

Is bugging out a form of mental disorder? Or is it a way to retain sanity in the face of horrendous stress? Have I simply discovered another way to cope with extreme challenges? I wonder if there's a bit of the bug-out in everybody. And I wonder what God thinks of bug-outs.

Does it offend God if I defend myself against intolerable abuse by bugging out? Isn't self-preservation a top priority in this life? If God made us in his image and likeness, like our Catholic catechism says, then I'm a reflection of some part of God's psyche. Does this mean that there's a bug-out aspect in God too? Who knows? Only God knows, I guess. I certainly don't. It's all a great mystery, isn't it? But I know one thing for sure. I've bugged out of that barracks at Camp Gordon and I don't have the tiniest iota of guilt about it. Touchdown! And the point after too. O'Connell seven. Army nothing!

Turning onto my back again, trying to find a comfortable position on the mattress which had springs pushing through the stuffing, I crossed myself. Then I said an Our Father, a Hail Mary, and a Glory Be To The Father. This was followed by a request that my future life with Mary and Peggy could be lived without interruption. At the close of my prayer, I whispered, "Just one more thing, God. Don't bug out on me, okay?"

My eyes became heavy and soon the U.S. Army was out of my mind. Instead, my soul was comforted by the memory of Mary's face smiling at me with sparkling tear-filled eyes as the train had pulled away from South Station in Boston two months before. With the memory of her face in my soul, and a trace of a smile on my lips, I allowed my body to drift into sleep.

As I drifted off toward a very deep sleep, I sincerely believed that my most difficult endurance tests in the Army were coming to a happy ending. It would be so different from now on, having Mary to come home to each evening and on weekends. Yet I was realistic enough to know that my time in the Army would not suddenly become a picnic. The main thing was that I was sure I would have no problem meeting any challenges that would face me in the months ahead.

Yes, I was sure. Quite sure, that is.

## The End

# Epilogue

The arrival of my wife Mary and my daughter Peggy in Augusta marked the beginning of a very different part of my Army service. You might call the first part of my two years as the "solitary" part and the rest as the "off-post" part.

Although my deep-seated resistance to arbitrary authority would remain with me during each weekday as a clerk-typist in the 402nd Military Government Company, and later as a writer in the Public Information Office of The Provost Marshal General's School, the off-post part of my life gave me the solace of family life on weekends and at the beginning and end of each day.

This doesn't mean I suddenly began to love the military life. The Army still fit slogans such as "The right way . . . and the Army way" and "SNAFU . . . Situation normal, all fouled up." Also, the title of my column in *The Eight Ball,* our own little newspaper, reflected my own view of the Army: "Ours is not to reason why."

In all candor, although I have deep love for my country, I must confess that no matter how good a deal I had in the Army it never became easy for me to adjust to being a soldier. And it was an ongoing challenge to my own sanity to live under the authority of Diamond Jim and his various forms of madness.

My close proximity to The Diamond in the Message Center right across from the Orderly Room didn't help my attitude about him, yet it was a very good job for me to have. So I look back on that part of my Army life as a mixed blessing.

Operating the Message Center gave me a measure of freedom, and you might say it was a bug-out's paradise. At almost any time of day, without asking permission, I could take one of our large manila message envelopes, pretend to be bringing it somewhere, and treat myself to a nice walk to break the monotony and say hello to friends around the area.

Also, I have to admit that during certain military events it was actually fun to walk around with my .45 on my hip instead of carrying a heavy rifle. Despite my difficulties with authority, there were times when I could get into the role and actually feel the exhilarating excitement of being a citizen soldier.

Yet the dark aura cast by Diamond Jim's erratic mood swings kept all of us enlisted men off balance most of the time. This was especially true for those of us who happened to be "college boys" because it seemed there was no class of people he hated to a greater degree.

I have learned more than once during my life that insanity is contagious, and anyone exposed to it every day suffers from traumatic stress. Life with Diamond Jim surely triggered such effects in those who were around him. The stress of functioning under him led to many requests to be transferred elsewhere, and most of them continued to be denied with a rubber stamp stating "Essential personnel."

There was also a steady stream of people who found traditional Army ways to deal with their stress. Some escaped for a few hours a day by going on Sick Call. Others went AWOL right after payday. Naturally, there were men who drank much more than they might have under other conditions. And there were people who ended up in the neuropsychiatric unit at the Post Hospital.

Also, there were men who would make the mistake of openly bucking The Diamond. So they found themselves exposed to very harsh and abusive treatment, company punishment, or a court martial.

It was in my best interest to keep most of my distaste for Diamond Jim to myself. Nevertheless, as long as I was in the Military Government Company, I experienced a deep irritation that such a person existed and had power over me and many other people. But I was powerless to change his behavior and had to do the best I could to deal with my chronic frustration and anxiety.

Sometimes my anger at him erupted in my dreams, and I would have a terrible rage and call Diamond Jim enough insulting names to get me thrown into the Disciplinary Barracks pending court martial. When I woke up in a sweat I would be grateful that it had only been a nightmare, and I was relieved that I was not in the DB. Yet my behavior in my nightmares was a vivid reflection of how deeply I despised Diamond Jim.

As I reflect on my Army years, I have to say that it was a serious emotional struggle on a daily basis. But for my sake, and the sake of my little family, it was necessary for me to avoid extreme reactions.

Bugging out continued to be a critical coping skill for me; however, when I bugged out of something I tried to do it judiciously. It didn't take a genius to realize that the less obvious I could make myself in the Army, short of actually becoming invisible, the more likely it was that I could stay out of trouble.

I should also note that it was not easy living off-post on private's pay, but we managed to carry it off, and it was well worth the sacrifice. But that was another adventure that doesn't seem appropriate to add to the story I've been telling here.

In brief, Mary and I had no training program for marriage and parenthood, had no ideal parents to turn to as role models for marital bliss, and had to learn as we went along. So at times our life was joyful and at times it was very confusing and emotionally painful.

When my tour of duty ended, in March 1956, after two years of service in the "peacetime Army" during the period when the Korean Conflict was officially over and the Vietnam Era was an embryo, I was given an Honorable Discharge. On leaving the

Army as a specialist third class, I was recommended for the Good Conduct Medal, awarded the National Defense Service Medal, and got a special commendation for my exemplary service to the Army and my country.

Considering the confession I have been making in this book, these honors make me chuckle a little, because I still look back on my military service as one of the extremely low points of my life. I was very far from the image of "a good soldier." And I wonder how I managed to avoid a court martial.

It's no exaggeration to state that the stress of Army life threatened my physical endurance in the early months, and later threatened my mental stability. I was not in combat, but there was always an inner battle raging within me. It was a clash between my extreme need to be my own boss and my desire to complete my two years of military service the way countless thousands of others had done, regardless of my discomfort with the whole process.

How deeply I was affected by the Army was reflected in the periodic nightmares I experienced for many years after my discharge. There I was again, in the 402nd Military Government Company, serving under the cyclical madness of Diamond Jim. He would be acting even crazier than usual, and I would be there in a self-defeating rage setting myself up for his wrath. Then I would wake up trembling at first, but soon would have a wonderful burst of gratitude at the realization that it had only been a nightmare and I was no longer under Diamond Jim's control.

Looking back now, after 50 years have gone by, I believe I can see myself at that early stage of my existence fairly objectively. Essentially, I was unsuited for military life because of my independent "lone wolf" disposition, my hypersensitive nervous system, some neurotic tendencies, and my inherent resentment of any kind of arbitrary authority. Obviously, when I was in the Army there could be no such thing as "lone wolf" independence, and all of the Army's authority was arbitrary!

As the years passed, I came up with a very short commentary on my Army service. It's an exaggeration that I still use in conversations sometimes, and it goes like this: "The day before I went into the Army I was a patriot, and the next day I became a pacifist!" No, I didn't become a conscientious objector; I just became an objector to dehumanizing treatment. And my way of coping with that treatment was "bugging out."

Actually, I still get tears in my eyes when they play "The Star Spangled Banner," when I'm watching presidential State of the Union messages, or when I read early U.S. history. I do love this country and the freedom of self-realization we have here.

However, my Army experience taught me that I have an allergic reaction to rigid institutional and corporate life, no matter how noble its purpose may be. The Army years also made it clear to me that personal freedom and autonomy mean more to me than most other values. And my civilian life choices since that time prove my point.

Based on my Army experience as a volunteer for the Draft, and my own observations on the state of the world since those days in the 1950s, I have come to believe that international problems should not be solved by wars. Instead, when diplomacy falls short, problems should be solved by games of ping-pong, tennis or golf!

I believe a sports contest would make more sense than killing and maiming each other just because we're unable or unwilling to resolve differences in a civilized way.

Obviously, if this became the accepted solution for international quarrels, there would be no need for armies that would draft and try to make soldiers out of hypersensitive "lone wolves" who would need to preserve their integrity by "bugging out." And the world would be a better place.

NOTE: Agents and editors interested in reprint or film/video rights may contact publisher at info@sanctuary777.com

## Books by Tom O'Connell
## Published by Sanctuary Unlimited

___Bugging Out: An Army Memoir (1954)
This memoir tells how the author dropped out of Boston College to marry, then volunteered for the Army draft to qualify for the GI Bill of Rights on his return to college. Demoralized by cruel superiors during infantry basic training, and lonely for his pregnant wife, he is caught between duty and self-preservation. Reluctantly, he turns to "bugging out." With wit and irony, O'Connell uses candid dialogue and vivid descriptions to relate how he dealt with the military assaults on his independent personality. The author's "battle of wits" shows one young man coping with the Army's challenges to his sanity, and offers scenes reflecting outrage, despair, and hilarity.

**"Bug out: 1. To leave or quit, usually in a hurry 2. To avoid a responsibility or duty."**

*"Tom O'Connell's years as an arrested free spirit in Mrs. White's group foster home prepared him to be a 'volunteer draftee' in the U.S. Army. He survived both periods of emotional torture to write another fascinating and gripping memoir."*

*—Dr. Finbarr Corr, author, educator, therapist*

___The O'Connell Boy: Educating "The Wolf Child"
~An Irish-American Memoir (1932-1950)

This memoir provides lively impressions of the author's early "wolf child" life in two homes run by Irish immigrants. First he is in a **Catholic Charities group foster home** in Norwood, where the perfectionist widow exerts her **"reign of terror."** Later he is in **Granny O'Connell's unkempt place "on the other side of the tracks"** in blighted East Dedham. He has a **"battle of wits"** with her while pursuing his goal of freedom from restraint.

*"a page-turner . . . heart wrenching . . . mind boggling . . . stunning view into life in the '30s and '40s"—Cape Cod Magazine ~~ "a fascinating memoir . . . a charming and honest writing voice"—The Cape Codder ~~ "O'Connell writes compellingly . . ."—Cape Cod Times ~~ "compelling and inspiring"—The Barnstable Patriot ~~ "a stroll down Memory Lane . . . a very serious book but there's a lot of humor"—Mindy Todd, Cape & Islands National Public Radio Stations ~~ "O'Connell connects with readers soul to soul . . . inspires"—Jordan Rich, WBZ News Radio 1030, Boston.*
*(published by Sanctuary Unlimited with Xlibris.com)*

___Improving Intimacy: 10 Powerful Strategies
~*A Spiritual Approach.*

A look at spiritually based intimacy, addictive relating, control, listening, communication, conflict.

*"Positive . . . powerful . . . very readable style."—Cape Cod Times ~~ "It's the finest example of anyone writing on this subject."—Don LaTulippe, WPLM, Plymouth.*

___The Odd Duck: A Story for Odd People of All ages

A cheerful, inspiring fable for all "adult children." A lost duck raised in a chicken coop feels odd. After an identity crisis, she begins a quest for self-worth and healthy, lasting love.

*"A cheerful, punning little allegory mostly for grownups."—Bostonia Magazine ~~ "a parable for spiritual reawakening . . ."—Seniors Cape Cod Forum.*

____**Danny The Prophet: A Fantastic Adventure**
An unforgettable novel about a man reluctant to be God's last prophet. A trip into another dimension with a politician, a sage, an angel, perilous adventures, and divine revelations.
*Readers' comments: "Wow!" "Astounding!" "Funny!" "A wonderful book!" "A pleasure to read!" "Imaginative!"*

____**The Monadnock Revelations: A Spiritual Memoir**
The true story of Tom's mystical journey. He reports on his own highly unusual experiences of other dimensions of reality, including what is called Cosmic Consciousness.
*Readers' comments: "Encourages, energizes and inspires . . ." "It warmed my heart and inspired my soul." "A treasury of inspiration." "Extremely visionary, well written, inspiring . . . a great book." "I loved it!"*

____**Addicted? A Guide to Understanding Addiction**
This is a useful, practical, educational guide that explains addiction's causes, effects, recovery process, relapse, prevention.
*"provides a wealth of information . . . highly readable . . . You have done the job remarkably well. Congratulations!"— Blaise Gambino, Ph.D., Gambling Program, Center for Addiction Studies, Harvard Medical School, The Cambridge Hospital.*

____**Up In Smoke: The Nicotine Challenge in Recovery**
Nearly 20,000 of these motivational booklets have been used to help people kick the life-threatening nicotine habit!
*"It makes little or no sense to ask people to cut out other drugs, even caffeine, and permit smoking."—Richard Hurt, M.D., Mayo Clinic, Rochester, Minn.*

(To read excerpts from these books visit www.sanctuary777.com)